PROBLEM SOLVING: TOOLS AND TECHNIQUES FOR THE PARK AND RECREATION ADMINISTRATOR

Fourth Edition

Margaret L. Arnold
Linda A. Heyne
James A. Busser

Sagamore Publishing, L.L.C.
Champaign, Illinois

Book design: Janet Wahlfeldt
Cover design: Michael Morgan

Library of Congress Catalog Card Number: 2004098690
ISBN: 1-57167-504-3

Printed in the United States

10 9 8 7 6 5 4 3 2 1

http://www.sagamorepub.com

Dedication

We dedicate this book to the ones who have mentored us in administrative problem solving:

Joseph J. Bannon, Cheryl Beeler, Frances Cannon, Sue France, Helen Giles-Gee,

John Bonaguro, Dori Denelle, Burt Garr, Stuart J. Schleien, Steven Siconolfi,

Joseph J. Bannon, Jerry Burnham, Stuart Mann, Carol Peterson, and J. Robert Rossman.

CONTENTS

ACKNOWLEDGMENTS

We wish to acknowledge the efforts of several individuals who contributed to the development of this textbook. Without their support, insight, and professional competence, this updated edition would not have been possible.

- The leisure services practitioners and recreation and park board members who participated in focus groups to help us gather examples of current issues and practices: Jeff Boles, Beth Brunelle, Steven Colt, Andrea Dutcher, Jennifer Glaab, William Hurley, Janice Johnson, Joanie Groome, Leslie Leonard, John McNearney, Patrick Mercer, Todd Miner, Tom Murray, Frank Towner, and Nancy Zahler.

- The many practitioners and students who provided ideas and scenarios for the case studies. We particularly thank Krystal Kauffman, our student worker, who assisted in editing the case studies.

- Jean Greenwood, who wrote Chapter 8 on Conflict Resolution and Mediation Techniques. Her expertise in social justice, conflict mediation, and community building adds a new dimension to this textbook not previously included.

- Betty Powell and Nancy Zahler who reviewed drafts of portions of the manuscript and provided us with invaluable feedback.

- Steven Siconolfi, Dean of the School of Health Sciences and Human Performance at Ithaca College, who provided grant support to sponsor the focus groups and hire consultants to review or contribute to the manuscript.

- Lana Morse and Courtney Theriault for their administrative assistance in preparing the manuscript.

- Joseph J. Bannon, Sr., M. Douglas Sanders, Janet Wahlfeldt, and the staff at Sagamore Publishing for their expertise in preparing this textbook.

- New York State Recreation and Park Society for their assistance in securing copyright permissions.

- And to our families for their endless support and encouragement: Sue, Tom, Anna, Cynny, and Katie.

FOREWORD

In 1972 I completed the first edition of *Problem Solving in Recreation and Parks*. The motivation for writing this book was a result of my association with Charles K. Brightbill as a student and my experiences as a practitioner in the field of parks and recreation. Charles Brightbill felt that all students studying to become practitioners in our field should be exposed to situations that they would one day confront. The idea of developing "real-life" case studies and a process to solve everyday problems was born. In the last 33 years there have been three editions printed and over 40,000 books used by students and practitioners throughout the U.S. and abroad. For the past two years, a number of professors urged me to update and revise the text. After giving this much thought I decided that it was time that new ideas and fresh thought be brought to the problem-solving process. The new authors who will now carry on the writing of the text are Dr. Margaret Arnold and Dr. Linda Heyne of Ithaca College, and Dr. James Busser of the University of Nevada, Las Vegas. Each one of these individuals brings a unique background to the task. They all possess practical experience in the field and have the intellectual training and capacity to continue this important work. I am personally delighted they have agreed to do it.

The Fourth edition has been derived from the authors' diverse experiences in dealing wisely with a wide variety of problems in the field. As stated by the authors, this book's purpose is to provide guidelines to park and recreation personnel in developing a systematic and creative approach to problems and vital issues facing our profession. In this fourth edition, the authors bridge a serious gap by providing a basic process through which individuals can learn specific knowledge and functional skills of human relations. The authors' process of problem solving is an innovative approach; it helps people to deal effectively with conflicting social value systems and decision preferences by recreation personnel involved in all types of recreation and park systems. The book should be useful to recreation educators in carrying out their responsibilities for preparing the next generation for effective service in recreation and parks. The need for this book is apparent, because few recreation curricula include courses in problem solving. It is true that many texts dealing with recreation describe policies and procedures that have proved successful and effective, but they do not deal with obstacles that have been met or the manner in which they have been overcome. Clarification and discussion of these matters seem the appropriate responsibility of the professor and the instructor, both in colleges and universities and in the service training programs. In this forth edition, the authors have made a unique contribution to park and recreation administrative theory and practice. Its content provides many insights and will provoke reactions and discussion. Most important, it presents a practical approach to meeting the functional needs of students, teachers, and park and recreation practitioners. It is hoped that this edition will prove more useful and relevant for students both in the classroom and in the field.

Joseph J. Bannon
Professor Emeritus
Department of Recreation, Sport,
  and Tourism
University of Illinois

PREFACE

The fourth edition of *Problem Solving: Tools and Techniques for the Park and Recreation Administrator* retains one author from the previous edition, James Busser, and introduces two new authors, Margaret L. Arnold and Linda A. Heyne. In this edition, we attempt to integrate practical with academic approaches to problem solving, offering both the theoretical and pragmatic viewpoints, combining these wherever possible. As a result, this book should be useful not only for teaching students in leisure studies how to handle hypothetical problems systematically, but also as an update and refresher for practitioners and board members who are involved with actual problems in agencies and organizations. Thus, the concepts and ideas presented in this book should increase one's problem solving ability and offer a systematic multi-idea approach to problem solving.

A problem cannot be solved by the same consciousness that created it.

Albert Einstein

In this edition, greater attention is given to organizational culture and problem solving approaches and techniques than in previous editions. Additionally, the problem solving model has been expanded. Not only have all chapters been substantially revised, the majority of the case studies are new and reorganized into five themes: Human Relations, Marketing and Publicity, Planning and Policy Development, Liability and Risk Management, and Financial Management. These case studies represent a wide array of more current problems, since the issues facing leisure, recreation, and park professionals change as rapidly as the times. All cases are drawn from actual situations collected from students and practitioners in the field, as well as news stories that have appeared in newspapers and on the world wide web. The case studies are related to leisure, recreation, and park services, however, it is important to note that they can easily be modified for use by other human service organizations. Finally, each of the five themes concludes with a list of helpful websites for further inquiry.

As mentioned in earlier editions of this text book, there is no need for this book to be confined to classroom use only. It can be readily used in staff development programs for in-service trainings, by recreation and park boards, or by a wide variety of social and educational institutions. We are grateful that several leisure, recreation, and park professionals, as well as recreation and park board members, participated in focus groups to help us strengthen the content of this textbook. We trust you will find this edition to be more useful and relevant as we continue to solve problems in leisure, recreation, and park services.

CHAPTER ONE

PROBLEM SOLVING: A PROFESSIONAL NEED

During the winter of 2003, several professionals who are involved with leisure, recreation, and park services participated in lengthy focus groups to discuss issues and trends surrounding the profession. While many issues were discussed at great length, the most common issues confronting our profession (in no particular order) were identified as follows:

- Funding constraints (e.g., expected to do more with less)
- Managing personnel and staffing concerns (e.g., low wages, high turnover)
- Educating the public about the value of leisure, recreation, and park services
- Volunteerism (e.g., lack of training, overburdened by job expectations)
- Civil Service employees (e.g., political climate)
- Working with boards
- Connecting with legislators and politicians
- Monitoring and documenting programs and services
- Programming for youth, merging youth services
- Technology issues (e.g., computer training, updating technology)

Never doubt that a small group of thoughtful, committed citizens can change the world; indeed, it is the only thing that ever has.

Margaret Mead

The participants in the focus groups then were asked to identify trends they had observed during the past 10 years in leisure, recreation, and park services. The following trends were identified (again, in no particular order):

- Increased accessibility (e.g., Americans with Disabilities Act, greater public awareness of people with disabilities, increase in inclusion)
- Increased mental health concerns of participants (e.g., particularly among children and youth)
- Increase in incidence of attention deficit disorder and individuals requiring medication
- Increased diversity (e.g., customers, employees, programming)
- Increased violence and the need for security
- Technological advances
- Emphasis on outcome assessments (i.e., increased by the need for greater accountability to the public)
- Increased sense of entitlement to leisure and recreation (i.e., expectations and standards are now higher for agencies)
- More human resource issues (e.g., job sharing, childcare issues, domestic partnership benefits)

- Online networks (e.g., advocacy, sharing best practices)
- Increased risk management and liability concerns, and rising insurance costs
- Increased entrepreneurialism (e.g., emphasis on marketing and public relations)
- Increased outsourcing (e.g., paying outside contractors to provide programs and services, collaboration with other organizations)
- Increased life expectancy of baby boomers (e.g., are we planning adequately for this segment of the population?)
- More reliance on volunteers

Leaders are visionaries with a poorly developed sense of fear and no concept of the odds against them. They make the impossible happen.

Robert Jarvik

Based upon these findings, overlapping issues and trends include accountability, technology, and volunteers. This is no surprise. As professionals we are being held more accountable than ever before, primarily due to budget constraints and the society's increased sense of entitlement to leisure services. Technology is constantly changing the way we do things (e.g., registering participants, the provision of online courses) and keeping current with new software programs requires time, money, and a great deal of patience. Finally, the use of volunteers in recreation, leisure, and park services is very instrumental in the survival of recreation programs and departments. Particularly as we are required to "do more with less" in these financially troubling times, the need for trained and competent volunteers is paramount to the success of our field.

Interestingly, the National Recreation and Park Association (NRPA) recently announced the "Vision 2010" plan—a strategic plan for the future of the profession. NRPA's mission statement is "to advance parks, recreation, and environmental conservation efforts that enhance the quality of life for all people" (Mission Statement, 2001). To carry out this mission, NRPA affirms the following goals:

1. To promote public awareness and support of park and recreation services and environmental and natural resource management;
2. To develop and promote public policy for parks and recreation;
3. To enhance citizen and professional development; and
4. To promote the development and dissemination of the body of knowledge.

Vision 2010 sets forth a clear course of action for NRPA and its members over the next decade. The six strategies appear below:

1. Develop the public's awareness of the importance of parks and recreation programs to the enrichment of America's human and natural resources;
2. Create a membership of citizen/board members and professionals prepared to articulate NRPA's mission, advocate on behalf of the Association and its mission and promote quality programs and services;
3. Build partnerships to advance NRPA's mission;

4. Create a citizen and professional membership reflective of America's diverse population;
5. Assure NRPA's financial ability to carry out its mission, vision and goals; and
6. Maintain an organizational structure sensitive to changing membership needs.

Based upon NRPA's strategic plan and vision and the feedback from the focus groups, the trends, issues, and strategies confronting the field of leisure, recreation, and park services are vast. Nevertheless, it is important to remember that the future is not some unknown entity over which we have little control, but a prospect we can do much to create, envision, or attempt to accomplish, as individuals or as part of a group. Even though the world may seem out of control in these troubled times, we should not forget that each of us helps to create the future through our awareness or ignorance, convictions or apathy, passivity or actions.

In the aftermath of September 11, 2001, many recreation professionals began to question our role in the world. According to Williams, Dustin, and McKenny (2004), "Many of us wondered if there could be any real meaning in the work we do in the wake of a terror that ripped apart the security we once felt" (p. 12). But for those of us in the profession, we know we have a vital role in society. Leisure helps us define who we are and makes life livable. Zuefle (2004) stated, "And when we're honest with ourselves as a society, and we should be every once in a while, we must admit that we desperately need what it has to offer: recreation, play, rest, contemplation and the possibility of wholeness" (p. 14). In order to positively influence our society of leisure, recreation, and park services, we must plan strategies that adhere to "Vision 2010" so we can respond as a profession.

New and creative ideas will be necessary to solve the issues facing us in the 2000s. If leisure, recreation, and park services professionals do not begin to work at systematically addressing the problems confronting the field, when we review our progress in the year 2010, for example, we may still face many of the same problems.

A Look Toward Problem Solving

As the exterior world becomes more complex, and at times bewildering, it is crucial that our imagination becomes richer, more flexible, and courageous. Remember, the future is not a fearsome unknown toward which we are hopelessly heading. It will be a composite of much that we decide to do now. A strong sense of curiosity, coupled with a well-developed ability to question, is vital to creativity (Pollack, 1999).

Many people can think more creatively if shown how to draw more effectively on their imaginations and trust their abilities to do so. Most adults were naturally quite imaginative as children, but as people grow older, they tend to grow inhibited as well. Because of various cultural pressures, including compulsory and formal education, they are too often taught to distrust the products of their own minds. Creative people tend to ask a lot of questions, and the simple question, "Suppose we did this...?," lies behind many great achievements (Pollack, 1999).

Problem solving is the ability to formulate new answers. Bransford and Stein (1993) use the acronym IDEAL to describe the process of problem solving:

I—Identify the problem
D—Define and represent the problem visually
E—Explore possible strategies to solve the problem
A—Act on the chosen strategy
L—Look back and evaluate the outcomes

An idealist is one who, on noticing that a rose smells better than a cabbage, concludes that it will also make better soup.

H.L. Mencken

There is much we can do to wean people from the habit of thinking as others do, to encourage creativity, and to support the outcome of such efforts. It is through departure from more traditional methods of teaching and learning that people's imaginations can be freed. Only when students, for example, truly feel that their ideas will be valued, will they become more creative thinkers. New ideas are limited only by the boundaries of individual skill, imagination, and the ability to grasp the complexity of information.

There is a real need for problem solving to address the issues confronting the profession as well as the concerns facing the leisure, recreation, and park professional. The beginning of this chapter identified issues, trends, and strategies of concerns to our field. The next chapter will introduce the use of the case study method in problem solving. The dilemma for leisure, recreation, and park professionals is to analyze and resolve problem situations. Therefore, the concepts and ideas in this textbook are designed to meet the following ends:

1. Increase problem solving ability;
2. Offer a systematic, multi-idea approach to problem solving; and
3. Improve individual, group, and organizational performance through more effective problem solving skills.

Bibliography

Bransford, J., & Stein, B. S. (1993). *The ideal problem solver: A guide for improving thinking, learning, and creativity* (2nd ed.). New York: W. H. Freeman and Company.

National Recreation and Park Association, *Vision 2010 Plan*, Retrieved January 15, 2004, from http://www.nrpa.org/content/default.aspx?documentId = 490

Pollack, T. (1999). To solve a problem, ask the right questions. *Supervision, 60*(5), 18-21.

Williams, R., Dustin, D., & McKenney, A. (2004). Staking our claim. *Parks & Recreation, 39*(5), 12-14.

Zuefle, D. M. (2004, April). Do folks in the recreation field get the last laugh? *Parks & Recreation, 39*(4), 14-16.

CHAPTER TWO

THE USE OF THE CASE STUDY METHOD IN PROBLEM SOLVING

The Case Study

The case-study method has been practiced in the United States for many decades. It was first introduced by Harvard University's Business School and, later, by Harvard University's John. F. Kennedy School of Government. Now cases are widely available from these two schools as well as on the world wide web. The primary use of the case study method continues to be in professional education and training in the areas of planning, business, and public administration, yet the case method is potentially appropriate for just about any teaching and learning situation at the undergraduate, graduate, and professional level (Lynn, 1999).

Based on the long-term practice of using actual court cases in legal training, the case study approach was one of the first teaching methods in the social sciences to depart from more traditional lectures in which information was transmitted to, rather than elicited from, students. However, most teachers are not adequately trained to use case studies and therefore prefer to use the more traditional approach (i.e., lecturing). It is also true that too much is expected from using the case method approach. As an aid to teaching, it is not meant to replace other methods of learning and obtaining information. To the contrary, case studies can successfully complement other teaching methods when used appropriately. Nevertheless, those educators and trainers who have made the effort to learn about and apply the case study method in their teaching and training come to feel, most with great enthusiasm, that they have become better teachers for having made the effort.

The case study method emphasizes individualism, the power of reason, the value of argument, and the importance of self-expression (Foundation for Advanced Studies on International Development, 1996). Using the case study method is appropriate whenever a teacher or trainer wants to place an emphasis on creative thinking, stimulating new ideas, assuming leadership roles, and independent thinking. If these skills are not to be encouraged, perhaps the use of a case study method is not appropriate for the situation, and a more traditional approach should be used. Lynn (1999) cites other objectives for using the case study approach:

- To give practice in making decisions
- To apply knowledge to a "real world" situation
- To develop the skills required in order to use others as resources
- To learn to think analytically and objectively
- To develop initiative
- To gain skill in projecting outcomes

New ideas come into this world somewhat like falling meteors, with a flash and an explosion.

Henry David Thoreau

What is a Case?

A case is a story, describing or based on actual events, that justifies careful study and analysis by students. For example, the case studies in this textbook are based upon actual events that have taken place in leisure, recreation, and park services. Using the case-method approach enables the student to read about a "real-world" situation and to practice on an actual scenario. By using case studies, students can practice their problem solving skills, under the guidance of an instructor, in anticipation of solving problems when they become leisure service professionals.

According to Lynn (1999), a good teaching case contains "no right answer" to the problem and no "correct" way of thinking about or analyzing the situation. Rather, a teaching case provides the student with issues, problems, choices, and information and expects the student to come up with solutions and to propose actions using the information in the case.

A teacher uses different case studies for different audiences. Undergraduates, new to the use of case studies, new even to the practice of problem solving, require simpler cases than do graduate students or professionals. Case studies used with experienced leisure services managers require even more complex cases. Regardless of the audience, case studies should not be merely "filler" in a course of instruction, or a form of entertainment. Such abuses only negate the material's possible advantages. Time is wasted, and everyone will feel cheated. There must be a reason for using case studies, and it should not be a trivial one. Key questions to be considered are

- What do I want to achieve in this session?
- Which case, if any, will best aid me in this session?
- How can I best present this case?

Preparing to Use the Case-Study Method

Planning and organizing the discussion are essential to the effectiveness of using the case study method. The following helpful hints (Cascade Centre for Public Service, 1999) are provided to assist you with preparing for the best possible outcomes:

For the teacher or facilitator, preparing for the case discussion means

- Mastering the facts, issues, calculations, and other material in the case;
- Anticipating questions that might arise, issues that are raised by the case, and the kinds of arguments that might take place; and
- Visualizing how you want the discussion to progress and where you want it to end.

For the case method to be effective, the instructor must know his or her students fairly well, be a skilled and enthusiastic discussion leader (not just a lecturer!), and be well versed in the subjects of the case studies. The instructor must be able to anticipate the responses of students, ask the proper questions at strategic times, and maintain a relaxed atmosphere during discussions. Obviously, these qualities are not acquired quickly. An instructor who uses this teaching aid must be prepared for a great deal of study and practice; above all, he or she must have patience. Teaching with case studies is difficult, but it can be extremely rewarding for both students and instructors.

It is important for the instructor to carefully select the students who will participate in the problem solving sessions. It would not be advisable, for example, to include students who have much experience in leisure, recreation, and park services with those who have relatively little practical experience. This is not to say that inexperienced students should never be mixed with experienced students; this caution serves only to alert the instructor to potential difficulties in unintentionally mixing groups.

For the student or participant, preparing for the case discussion means answering the following general questions:

- Who is the decision maker in this case? What decision needs to be made?
- What are the decision maker's objectives?
- Are there other important actors? What are their objectives?
- What are the key issues at stake? What must be resolved?
- What would I do? Why?

Students are important to the success or failure of using case studies. Those who come to the session unprepared, not having done their background homework, will not be good presenters or receivers of ideas. Students also must be prepared to discuss the case intelligently. For example, if a case deals with the development of a therapeutic recreation program, students must at least be aware of the planning principles, budgetary requirements, and administrative practices of operating such programs.

With case studies, students must develop their own rationale for decisions, accept responsibility for these decisions, and be prepared to defend them. This will make them more rigorous in problem analysis. Realizing that they may be judged by classmates, they will more thoughtfully arrive at their final decisions.

Case studies not only encourage students to think independently, they are encouraged to work cooperatively in teams. Many decisions are the result of group discussions. For example, it is essential that a recreation and park board cooperate in formulating sound policies. A sound policy can be reached only by independent thinkers who recognize the importance of listening to other viewpoints. A recreation professional must work closely with boards, commissions, executive committees, advisory groups, and other community organizations. The recreation workers' success depends on the ability to think rationally, first as an individual, and then within a group.

Discovery is the ability to be puzzled by simple things.

Noam Chomsky

Listed below are seven procedures to assist instructors and stu-. dents in making case studies a productive teaching aid:

1. In presenting a case, it is recommended that the instructor ask students if there is anything about a particular case that is not clear. In each case certain assumptions are made; it is important that every discussant's analysis of a case be based on similar assumptions. For example, for a case on planning a comprehensive community recreation program, the problem solver makes certain assumptions about the amount of funds available for the program. If one discussant approaches the problem with the perspective that limited funds are available, and another that funds are no problem, the group discussion will be confusing, if not a waste of time.
2. The instructor must create an informal atmosphere for discussions; all ideas should be heard. No student should worry about the group's reactions to "inappropriate" ideas.
3. The instructor should not monopolize the discussion; otherwise, the students will quickly lose interest. The instructor's main responsibility is to help students build problem solving abilities and effectiveness through processes, not to demonstrate that he or she has all the answers.
4. The instructor should keep the discussion focused on case details, relationships, and implications.
5. The instructor should not anticipate the direction of the discussion or lead participants along predetermined lines of thought. To violate this rule denies students the responsibility they will need to gain if they are to become independent problem solvers.
6. The instructor should be alert to students who alter case facts. If overlooked, the discussion will drift from the principal aspects of a problem.
7. If the instructor knows the outcome of a case study, he or she should not reveal it until students have had an opportunity to explore the case thoroughly. To do so will bias the discussion.

Evaluating the Case Discussion

How do you know if using the case was appropriate or beneficial to the participants? According to Lynn (1999), there are several "vital signs" of a good case discussion:

- How much talking did the instructor do versus how much talking the students did?
- How many students were voluntarily active in the discussion?
- How many questions did the instructor ask? How many follow-up or challenging questions were asked?
- How energetic was the instructor? Did the instructor "travel" around the room?
- What was the level of energy in the discussion?
- How many "ah-hah" moments were there, i.e., moments when everyone was engaged, interested, and focused on an issue?
- How many times did students laugh?

- Did the discussion make sense? Was it coherent?
- Did the discussion conclude on an upbeat note?

Case studies require that students become problem solvers. When students use a case study, they are required to (a) determine what the problem is, (b) analyze the problem in relation to all presented facts, (c) produce ideas for possible solutions, (d) select alternatives, (e) make decisions, and (f) develop actions for implementation. Obviously, this is demanding. Students are required to think, not as their instructor might wish, but as would the employees confronted with an actual problem. Creating such independence in students is one of the most constructive outcomes of case studies. It brings reality into the classroom by insisting that the students reach a decision and be responsible for its consequences. It also requires that they become deeply involved in problem solving, and therefore more successful decision makers.

HELPFUL INTERNET RESOURCES FOR CASE STUDIES

How the Case Method Works—Harvard Business School
http://www.hbs.edu/mba/experience/learn/thelearningmodel/
 howthecasemethodworks.html

How to Teach with Cases by John Foran, Department of Sociology,
 University of California, Santa Barbara
http://www.soc.ucsb.edu/projects/casemethod/teaching.html

Teaching and Writing Case Studies: A Practical Guide by John Heath
http://www.ecch.cranfield.ac.uk/america/pages/obtain/casemats.html

---

Bibliography

Cascade Center for Public Service: Public Service Curriculum Exchange. (1999). *Welcome to case method!* Retrieved on February 12, 2004, from http://www.hallway.org

Colbert, J., Trimble, K., & Desberg, P. (1996). *The case for education: Contemporary approaches for using case methods.* Needham Heights, MA: Allyn & Bacon.

Foundation for Advanced Studies on International Development (1996). *What is a case method? A guide and casebook.* Retrieved on February, 10, 2004, from http://www.hallway.org

Gilmore, T. N., & Schall, E. (1996). Staying alive to learning: Integrating enactments with case teaching to develop leaders. *Journal of Policy Analysis and Management, 15*(3), 444-456.

Lundeberg, M., Levin, B., & Harrington, H. (1999). *Who learns what from cases and how? The research base for teaching with cases.* Mahwah, NJ: Lawrence Erlbaum.

Lynn, L. E. (1999). *Teaching and learning with cases: A guidebook.* New York: Chatham House Publishers.

CHAPTER THREE

THE PROBLEM SOLVING PROCESS

Leisure, recreation, and park services have entered a new era. Leisure services have been identified as one of the largest growth industries of the coming decade. This growth has been spurred by increased investment in leisure pursuits such as health, fitness and wellness activities, cultural arts, sports and outdoor recreational pursuits, vacation destination travel, and home entertainment. This increase in investment in leisure pursuits has resulted in the development and expansion of recreational facilities, activity programs, and leisure-related services and products. Leisure services can provide customers with both the opportunity to engage directly in activities or facilitate the customers' leisure involvement through skill development and the provision of equipment. Ultimately, leisure services seek to address the needs and desires of customers and provide the means for them to pursue satisfying leisure involvements.

The new era has also witnessed a more sophisticated and knowledgeable customer. Because of this, today's customer is more discriminating when it comes to leisure participation and related purchase decisions. Customers seek quality and value in their leisure involvements and these demands have been recognized by every organization and business in the field. As a result, there have been numerous quality improvements in the development and provision of leisure services.

The leisure services profession has also become more sophisticated. The body of knowledge regarding the delivery of leisure services continues to grow. One of the key ingredients in the success of a leisure service organization is the manager. What distinguishes one organization from another is often the quality of its management. Management is the process of working with and through people to accomplish the goals of a department and ultimately the organization. Today's leisure services manager requires a broad and complex understanding of management, as well as the necessary skills to deal effectively with stakeholders. Leisure services management is a people business that is exciting, dynamic, challenging, and offers rich career opportunities.

Due to the growth in the field and its increased complexity and competitiveness, today's manager may also face continuous challenges in the form of problems. A leisure service manager's ability to solve organizational problems is a highly valued skill. Problem solving is consistently rated as one of the most greatly sought after skills in employees at all levels of an organization (Sioukas, 2003). Employees' performance and organizational success can be directly attributable to managers' ability to navigate the difficult problems they face. Problem solving is an ongoing process that actively seeks a preferred future for an organization, its employees, and customers.

Problem solving is consistently rated as one of the most greatly sought after skills in employees at all levels of an organization.

Tasos Sioukas

This chapter introduces a problem solving model and a set of processes that will aid individuals and groups in identifying problems, developing solutions, and creating the change necessary to alleviate problems. This model, presented in Figure 3.1, is useful for simple as well as complex problems. The problem solving process draws on content from other chapters in the text as well as the provision of new material.

Before we introduce the problem solving model it is important to understand the cultural aspects of an organization. The culture of an organization permeates all aspects of employee behavior and has emerged as one of the key aspects of management (Alvesson, 2002). "Culture refers to the set of underlying values, beliefs and principles that serve as a foundation for an organization's management system as well as the set of management practices and behaviors that both exemplify and reinforce that system" (Dennison, 1990, p. 2). In other words, how employees think, feel, value, and work is guided by the ideas, meanings, and beliefs embedded in the organizational culture (Alvesson, 2002). A strong culture has been linked positively to several indicators of organizational performance, including profitability, market share, service quality, innovation, and employee satisfaction (Dennison, Haaland, & Goelzer, 2004).

Figure 3.1
Problem Solving Model

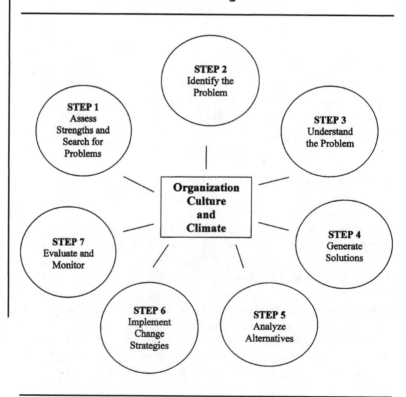

Dennison's (2004) model of organizational culture consists of four major elements, including mission, adaptability, involvement, and consistency. All of the elements have been found to significantly impact performance. The *mission* provides a clear purpose, meaning and direction for the organization. *Adaptability* consists of the organization's ability to change in response to both internal and external pressures. Employees in organizational cultures that foster high *involvement* have a sense of ownership, are empowered to identify problems, and, when appropriate, play a key role in resolving problems. *Consistency* means that an organization has a system of shared beliefs, values, and symbols that are understood and that govern behavior. The value system provides employees with a guide for approaching situations and offers useful parameters within which to exercise their decision-making power and resultant actions. For example, a recreation organization may value the full inclusion of all community members in its programs. Consequently, staff would make every effort to accommodate participants with disabilities.

In effect, the mission, adaptability, involvement, and consistency elements of the organization's culture impact each stage of the problem solving model. The culture may greatly facilitate constructive and enlightened problem solving or significantly impede and detract from the quality of solutions. Clearly, creating a positive and strong organizational culture will enhance the performance of employees and foster a proactive approach to addressing problems.

Concepts related to the impact of organizational culture and climate on problem solving are explored in greater depth in Chapter 4, Organizational Culture and Climate: Setting the Stage for Problem Solving. Similarly, concepts related to change, adaptability, resistance to change, and managerial responses to resistance are discussed more fully in Chapter 5, Change and Problem Solving.

The Problem Solving Model

The following sections refer to a seven-step process of problem solving that appears in Figure 3.1.

STEP 1: *Assess Strengths and Search for Problems*

Problems can prevent an organization from actualizing its vision and reaching its full potential. It is true with both people and organizations that coping actively with problems is much more effective than being unaware of them or avoiding them. An organization that desires a preferred future proactively builds upon its strengths and searches for potential problems or opportunities for improvement rather than waiting for important concerns, and ultimately crises, to appear.

Proactive managers are dependent on information to be effective in the search for problems that undermine organizational effectiveness. Management scholars have suggested that the most important ingredient in the manager's job is information. Key information related to potential problems can be obtained from a number of stakeholders including employees, customers, and governing authority officials. In order to facilitate the receipt of information from stakeholders, good interpersonal relationships are necessary to foster effective two-way communication.

Customers are a vital source of information, and information can be sought from them in a multitude of ways. Advisory board members are customers and an excellent source of information for managers. For the purpose of problem solving and decision making, these individuals serve the function of providing input regarding service delivery, including problems. They can be utilized as a sounding board to discuss issues, offer suggestions, and assist in supporting the role of the leisure service agency. They also provide an additional vehicle to communicate with customers.

Managers also rely on key informants who have the knowledge and ability to report on issues affecting the organization or its customers. Key informants may be opinion leaders in the community, such as leaders in government, business, education, and health and human services, who are aware of the problems and issues that are perceived as important by other stakeholders. Key informants are selected on the basis of (a) their stakeholder status, (b) their level of knowledge regarding the leisure service agency and surrounding community, and (c) their ability and willingness to share information (Gilchrist & Williams, 1999). Information obtained from key informants may cover a broad range of general and specific issues. Key informants may be invaluable in providing information necessary for a thorough understanding of problems within an organization that are impacting a community.

In addition to information developed through relationships, effective problem solvers seek a wide variety of data to develop an optimal understanding of the organization and its environment. These data allow them to acquire sufficient knowledge by which to detect problems, opportunities, and strengths. There are several structured approaches that can directly aid the problem search. Two prominently used organizational methods are SWOT analysis and benchmarking, which are described below.

SWOT Analysis

A SWOT analysis is a simple, yet comprehensive, examination of both the internal and external factors in the environment that have a direct influence on an organization's performance (Fleisher & Bensoussan, 2003). The internal analysis identifies the strengths and weaknesses within the organization. The external analysis identifies the opportunities and threats to the organization that lie outside of the organization.

S = **Strengths** are those resources or capabilities that the organization holds that can be used effectively to achieve its performance objectives. Appreciative inquiry (Hammond, 1996), discussed in Chapter 4, is a method that emphasizes what is working well within an organization and seeks to build from those strengths and assets. Strengths, for example, may include well-trained and responsive staff, services that meet customer needs, and first-rate facilities.

W = **Weaknesses** are limitations or inabilities within the organization that prevent the organization from achieving its objectives. For example, limited physical space may be identified as a weakness.

O = **Opportunities** are favorable current or potential situations in the environment. For example, a potential partnership with a community school may be an unrealized opportunity.

T = **Threats** are unfavorable situations that have a current or future negative impact on the organization. For example, a political action group may be working to defeat a bond referendum to support a public recreation initiative.

Strengths and weaknesses of the internal environment address the functioning of the organization in such areas as organization (e.g., structure, governing authority), management (e.g. level of cooperation and teamwork, staffing levels and expertise), programming (e.g., market size, program quality), and financing (e.g., stability of funding sources, debt). External situations may arise from the competitive, demographic, social, cultural, political, and legal environments. The organization has a greater opportunity to impact the internal environment, but must be fully aware of external opportunities. Some external threats, if not known or addressed, can seriously undermine an organization's forward movement.

Benchmarking

Another important method of uncovering strengths as well as potential problems that undermine superior performance is benchmarking. Benchmarking is a process of identifying the best practices in the field. Best practices represent superior performance or the benchmark that is desirable to achieve. The organization's actual performance is compared against the benchmark. The gap between desired performance and actual performance represents a problem to be solved. This method offers the opportunity to meet or exceed the benchmark of outstanding leaders in the field (Ammons, 2001).

Benchmarking can guide management's vision to develop the resources and the capabilities necessary to provide efficient, high quality, innovative, and responsive facilities and programs (Hill & Jones, 2001). Benchmarking, additionally, is a management process with which to address accountability, planning/budgeting, operational improvement, program evaluation, reallocation of resources, and contract monitoring (Ammons, 2001). Sometimes organizations establish benchmarks based on their own historical records or data. They use past performance as a point of comparison and attempt to either maintain or exceed this performance.

Benchmarking in leisure, recreation, and park services has mainly been used as an internal gauge to monitor year-to-year performance. This performance has been measured relative to workload, efficiency, and effectiveness. Some performance indicators have fo-

The best way to escape from a problem is to solve it.

Alan Sapora

cused on workload, which is the amount of work performed, or amount of service received. An example of workload would be the number of participants who took recreation classes or played a round of golf. Workload measures are limited in value because they only portray the amount of work done or service provided rather than the efficiency or effectiveness. Efficiency measures examine the relationship between the work performed and the resources expended to accomplish the work. For example, the number of acres maintained per employee would be specified. Effectiveness benchmarks address the degree to which organizational goals have been accomplished and customer needs have been satisfied. The ongoing measurement of organizational effectiveness is essential to the identification of problems. If an organization is not accomplishing its goals, it must understand and address the problems that may be undermining their attainment.

Internal benchmarking is important but does not allow a comparison with superior organizations in the field. External benchmarking, however, presents challenges also. It is often difficult to obtain relevant information from outside sources in order to make comparisons. A number of leisure service organizations have begun to share performance information allowing for external comparisons (Ammons, 2002). Accreditation standards, described in the following section, provide one source of external benchmarks.

Accreditation. An opportunity to conduct external benchmarking in public sector recreation exists through accreditation. Accreditation is a voluntary process that entails a rigorous self-study and external review based on national standards. Accreditation is available to local park and recreation agencies, including municipalities, townships, counties, states, schools, special districts, councils of government, and regional authorities through the Commission on Accreditation for Park and Recreation Agencies (CAPRA).

CAPRA is sponsored by the National Recreation and Park Association and the American Academy for Park and Recreation Administration with the support of the International City/County Management Association and the National Association of Counties. CAPRA uses prescribed national standards to evaluate all aspects of a park and recreation agency's operations. Accreditation is awarded to park and recreation agencies that meet the standards and therefore are judged to be providing quality professional services.

The standards address areas such as the agency authority, role and responsibility, planning, organization and administration, human resources, finance, program and services management, safety and security, risk management, and evaluation and research. The accreditation of an agency can result in positive publicity and the recognition that it is providing high-quality management and operations. Accreditation provides assurance to an organization's customers that the agency meets professional standards of quality. A second benefit of accreditation is that it can enhance the image and standing of the organization with other government units. Third, and most importantly, accreditation identifies the strengths and weaknesses of an agency for managerial and employee action.

STEP 2: *Identify the Problem*

The creation of a systematic flow of data by which to identify strengths, weaknesses, opportunities, and threats is essential to effective problem solving. *Webster's Dictionary* defines a problem as a difficult, perplexing question or issue; troublesome or vexatious; and a question proposed for consideration or solution. These definitions will likely ring true for managers who have faced challenging organizational situations. In more simplistic terms, a problem is a departure from some preferred or desired state that results in a need for change by management. If there is a deviation from some preferred state that is not a concern to anyone, then one can argue that a problem does not actually exist. A situation must be recognized and articulated as detrimental before it becomes a problem. As soon as someone notes the deviation, the problem definition can begin, no matter how intangible it might seem at first.

Problem identification is not as easy as it might appear. What seems an obvious deviation from a preferred state may not be the central problem at all, but symptomatic of a more critical problem. For example, employees may not be performing effectively, and it may be ascribed to a lack of employee motivation. Further investigation may illuminate that the real problem is insufficient staff training. One of the major reasons for failure in problem solving is making an incorrect diagnosis of the real problem and settling on addressing a symptom of the real problem (Robson, 2002). It is often the case that the visible problem is in reality the symptom. While symptoms may be significant concerns and need to be addressed, they are not the actual cause of the problem (Anderson & Fagerhaug, 2000). The separation of the symptoms of a problem from the problem itself is an important skill of a talented problem solver, as is the determination of the level at which to concentrate efforts.

Anderson and Fagerhaug (2000) assist in illuminating this issue of symptoms by thinking of problems within a hierarchy of levels. At the surface level are the symptoms that are observable and garner the attention of managers through routine detection or are brought forward through an episode or change in status. (The first-level cause leads directly to a broader problem). For example, a youth leader loses her temper and yells at a child for being disruptive. A higher-level cause is connected to the first-level cause and forms the links in the chain of cause and effect. For example, there is little behavioral or programmatic structure provided in the children's program. Moving to the final level in the hierarchy is situated the root cause. For example, the staff lacks the basic programming and behavioral management skills necessary for effective youth development programming. The root cause is ultimately the source of many problems that may affect the organization. For example, improperly trained youth leaders may become frustrated, which can contribute to high staff and participant turnover. Solving problems without addressing the root cause will only temporarily ease the situation. The real or root problem will eventually emerge in the form of other symptoms. This creates a vicious cycle in which only symptoms of the problem are dealt with rather than the real problem itself.

A problem solver must use self-restraint, for many problems are related to other and larger issues. Problem solvers must be able to determine the level at which to concentrate efforts or they will be exhausted by the enormity of a situation and will accomplish little. Thus, the manager must establish which problems are more critical than others, and which can realistically be solved. Otherwise, an administrator is lost, gathering more and more facts, expanding his or her viewpoint to encompass larger and grander issues while the dike leaks. Managers must decide at which level of awareness to begin defining and solving a problem and at what cut-off point to cease defining solvable problems as symptoms.

> *I have not failed, I've just found 10,000 ways that won't work.*
>
> Thomas Edison

Because analysis of the problem situation is the first step in the problem solving process or model, it is also the most critical in determining how effectively a problem will be handled. Although individuals are usually impatient to get on with the problem solving method once it has been determined that a problem does exist, sufficient time must be spent defining the problem situation. A rapid, generalized definition of a problem in the haste to find a solution should be avoided.

Multiple Viewpoints

The personal and professional viewpoints of those involved in problem solving or those likely to be affected by its outcome must be anticipated and examined during the problem identification and analysis stage. The viewpoints of everyone involved or implicated must be judiciously considered when analyzing problems and solutions. No one concerned about a problem or likely to be affected by its solution should be excluded from problem analysis, no matter how encompassing the approach to problem solving appears. If one seeks to solve a problem based exclusively on one viewpoint, without consideration given to all those involved, solutions will be ineffectual.

Priorities

After listing all of the problems, some of which may be symptoms of broader problems, the problems need to be ranked. One problem will surface as more important than the others as the process unfolds. Answering three questions can help determine which problem is most important (Kepner & Tregoe, 1981):

1. How urgent is the departure from the standard?
2. How serious is it?
3. What is the potential for improvement?

That is, which of these symptoms, if alleviated, would improve the situation, and which of these symptoms is potentially the root cause that, if alleviated, would have a positive effect on all the other symptoms?

Ideally, problem specification must be free of problem speculation, biases, and assumptions. Managers need to draw on as many relevant facts as they can. This is a somewhat systematic, mechanical action that requires discrimination on the part of managers as they decide what is to be taken into account and what is to be discarded. To do so, specific questions must be asked (Kepner & Tregoe, 1981):

1. What is the deviation?
2. Where is it occurring?
3. When does it appear?
4. How large is the deviation?
5. Whom does the deviation involve or affect?

The question "why" is not asked at this stage, since a manager is seeking a definition of the problem, not the cause. "Why" will come once the problem has been isolated and stated clearly. To seek the cause of a problem before it has been properly stated is a dead end, no matter how good one's hunches.

Once the problem solvers consider the various facets of problem definition—objectives, priorities, symptoms, and viewpoints—they are ready to state a tentative problem statement and to begin gathering facts and information that appear relevant to that problem. The problem statement should be made in the most concise form possible. Since this statement will be conveyed to others, it is best to compose as precise a statement as possible before showing it to individuals who are external to the problem solving process. It is important to actually write the problem statement. Putting a problem statement into writing gives others a better opportunity to assist in finding a solution. It keeps the problem solvers focused on the actual problem and not on peripheral issues that may continually arise.

A legitimate problem statement is one that reflects the viewpoints of those who should be represented in any solutions considered. It is legitimate not only because it is equitable but also because it is realistic, due to the input of all concerned. Furthermore, a problem statement is legitimate if it reduces biases or assumptions that result from one viewpoint dominating all others. A biased approach to problem definition limits the possibility of obtaining an accurate problem statement.

External Viewpoints

It is often necessary to obtain additional external information in order to understand an identified problem more fully. Typically, the solicitation of outside information occurs after the problem has been narrowed down and the statement of the problem has been written. There are a number of methods available that can be utilized to obtain data from sources outside the organization that will aid in understanding problems. Methods for the acquisition of external data include reviewing secondary data, focus groups, interviews, and surveys.

Secondary data. Secondary data is an excellent approach to acquiring problem information, because it is relatively quick and inexpensive to gather. Secondary data is information that has already been gathered and published. Sudman and Blair (1998) note that the following secondary information and data sources may be obtained through most libraries:

- Industry statistics are accessible from government documents through the American Statistics Index and through private sources by using the Statistical Reference Index.
- Background information on companies can be found through Predicasts F & S Index.
- Financial data on companies can be obtained though Standard & Poor's publications.
- Computerized databases may be found in the *Directory of Online Databases*.
- Trade associations provide statistical information that can be found in the *Encyclopedia of Associations*.

There are a variety of additional data collection methods that leisure services managers can employ to gather information about problems. Three of these methods—focus groups, interviews, and surveys—are featured in the following section.

STEP 3: *Understand the Problem*

While several methods of data collection are appropriate for gathering information, three techniques are highlighted that may be easily incorporated by leisure service organizations: focus groups, interviews, and surveys. Focus groups are particularly useful in providing insights into issues and problems identified by a leisure service organization. These insights may be investigated further through more in-depth types of data collection, such as interviews and surveys. The use of research methods to support a problem analysis requires specific knowledge and skills in order to ensure that the data collected are valid and reliable. A trained researcher may need to be contracted to carry out these approaches.

Focus groups. The use of focus groups is designed to provide general insights into the beliefs, attitudes, experiences, and feelings of customers (Litosseliti, 2003). In focus groups, it is through group interaction on specific topics, led by a moderator, that individuals' views are shared. The dynamics of the group interaction create a natural environment in which group members influence each other and provide multiple viewpoints (Litosseliti, 2003). Focus groups have been used to understand a variety of organizational issues, including customer satisfaction and service quality (Krueger & Casey, 2000). See Chapter 7 for a complete discussion of the focus group method.

Interviews. The personal interview is a face-to-face interpersonal situation in which an interviewer asks individual customers questions relevant to the issue or problem. A scheduled interview with structured questions has the most advantages for gaining useable information. "Structured" refers to questions that are the same in wording and sequence for each interviewee. Questions are written prior to the interviews and remain identical for every individual.

To the man who only has a hammer in the toolkit, every problem looks like a nail.

Abraham Maslow

The structured interview has several advantages over other methods of collecting data. Great flexibility can be used in the questioning process to probe areas of concern to the leisure service agency or constituents. In addition, the response rate is generally high with this method, as opposed to the mail or telephone survey. The disadvantage of an interview is the higher cost and time involved in collecting the information. Interviewers also have to be trained in the techniques of effective interviewing. One final obstacle to this method is its lack of anonymity for the respondents. That is, individuals who participate in the interview recognize that the interviewer knows their identities. Therefore, if the information to be collected is sensitive in nature, a more anonymous method of gathering information, such as a survey, may be preferred.

Surveys. Surveys provide the greatest opportunity to solicit customer input and to generalize the findings from a smaller group of individuals to the entire clientele. Successful survey implementation requires expertise from knowledgeable individuals. The use of marketing departments could be extremely beneficial to most leisure service organizations conducting surveys. There are five steps in the survey process (Punch, 2003) and these include

1. a clear statement of the objectives of the survey;
2. design and pretesting of data collection instruments (i.e., the questionnaire or the interview guide);
3. selection of a sample;
4. data collection; and
5. analysis of data.

The design of the questionnaire includes both the development of the specific questions to be answered by individuals, and decisions concerning their form (e.g., multiple choice, fill in the blank). In addition, the directions for completing the survey, the procedures for carrying out the survey, and the method of returning completed questionnaires are determined. Pretesting the data collection instrument is essential in order to uncover or eliminate any difficulties that may exist in the data collection procedure. Pretests can be considered mini-surveys and are conducted with a small group of respondents. The questionnaire is administered and respondents identify any difficulties in understanding directions, questions, or the type of information solicited. Further, the survey process is actually tested to determine if there are any difficulties that require changes.

Sampling is the use of particular procedures that allow the generalization of findings from a representative small group of individuals to the whole clientele. By selecting individuals through a random process (e.g., selecting every 10th person from a random listing of constituents), the results of the assessment are likely to be representative of the needs of all individuals, even though all constituents were not surveyed.

In collecting the data from individuals, it is important that the cover letter of the questionnaire explains the purpose of the survey and indicates that this information is confidential. It is the ethical responsibility of those individuals conducting the survey to ensure anonymity for respondents. After the questionnaire has been sent to constituents, it is important to follow up with phone calls, postcards, or other methods to continue to solicit the return of surveys. To be considered sufficiently representative, at least 35 percent of the surveys must be completed and returned. Inducements are often used to increase the return rate. For example, the leisure services agency could offer respondents a discount on programs for completing and returning the survey.

Once the data has been collected and tabulated, the data can be analyzed. The frequencies and percentages of responses to particular questions may reveal significantly desirable information. The data should be carefully analyzed to answer the questions and purpose of the survey. In this case, the purpose is to solicit customer input on pre-identified problems.

The quality and quantity of facts gathered will depend partly on the money and time available, as well as the assumptions for their evaluation. Collecting facts can be tedious and time consuming. Therefore, it is essential that the problem solvers not spend time collecting irrelevant facts. Gathering facts can be frustrating also because many are simply not available. The problem solvers must make every effort to secure all possible facts but should not become discouraged if these are not as precise as desired.

STEP 4: Generate Solutions

New ideas are central to fostering the development of an organization and its ability to create effective methods of solving problems and ultimately serve its constituents. Creative ideas are a sought after, but unfortunately scarce, commodity. We have all heard the recently coined phrase, "think outside the box." Thinking outside the box has become a metaphor for breaking loose of traditional thinking and developing more creative ideas. It is easy to become trapped in traditional approaches to problems that rely on what has worked in the past. Traditional thinking can box individuals in through an over-reliance on norms, rules, and habitual practices, thereby limiting new ideas. "Outside the box" thinking requires different approaches, moving beyond what has worked in the past, and taking an optimistic look toward the future.

Each problem that I solved became a rule, which served afterwards to solve other problems.

René Descartes

Creativity is at the heart of new ideas and an essential element in the problem solving process, especially in the generation of optimal solutions. Creativity has been described as the process of developing and expressing novel ideas that are likely to be useful (Leonard & Swapp, 1999). This definition suggests that the ideas resulting from creative efforts have a utilitarian outcome. That is, they will be ideas that are pragmatic and can be implemented. In organizations, creativity is the "production of novel and useful ideas by an individual or small group of individuals working together" (Amabile, 1998, p. 126). Organizational creativity has also been viewed as the generation of ideas that results in the improvement of the efficiency and effectiveness of the workplace (Matherly & Goldsmith, 1985). Viewing creativity in this fashion enables us to incorporate creativity in the overall problem solving model. Chapter 6 provides a full discussion of the role creativity plays in finding innovative solutions to problems. Chapter 7 presents specific techniques, such as brainstorming and Nominal Group Technique, which can facilitate the problem solving process.

STEP 5: Analyze Alternatives

The generation of a variety of creative solutions to the identified problems sets the stage wonderfully for the next phase of problem solving—analyzing the alternatives and making the decision that will be implemented. Once again, effective management will foster intrinsic motivation throughout this process by promoting self-determination, competence, and relatedness among the employees involved in analyzing the alternatives.

Highly involved organizational cultures empower employees throughout the organization. At the heart of empowerment is the ability of employees to make and implement decisions. Participation in decision making is a significant role for all members of the organization. In order for shared decision making to be effective, there are important fundamental factors that must be present for both employees and managers.

Competence is identified in Chapter 6 as an important requisite to creativity. Similarly, employees must have competence, i.e., the knowledge, skills and abilities necessary to deal with the simple and complex issues requiring decisions. To be competent, decision makers will require managers to share information freely and completely. This may be difficult for managers especially with regard to sensitive information.

In addition to being competent, employees must be motivated to take responsibility for participation in decisions. Again, managers have a role in employee motivation. Empowerment means that managers must freely give up some of their power to subordinates. Employees must find the tasks worthwhile and engaging and have real power to enact decisions in order to be intrinsically motivated. Managers who also recognize and validate the contributions of employees will contribute to their level of motivation.

The underlying issue in creating an effective culture of empowerment is trust. Trust encourages the free exchange of ideas and information. The crucial elements in trust are openness and sharing of information, along with acceptance, support, and cooperative behaviors (Johnson & Johnson, 2001). If group members trust each other, they will be willing to share their beliefs and feelings about the problem under consideration and the issues surrounding a potential decision (Levi, 2001). Trust is a reciprocal concept. Managers tend to delegate decision making to individuals they trust. Employees will only fully engage in problem solving and decision making if they in turn trust management. A lack of trust will undermine empowerment and sabotage decision making, while successful empowerment will contribute to effective and efficient organizational functioning.

Nothing in this world can take the place of persistence. Talent will not; nothing is more common than unsuccessful people with talent. Genius will not; unrewarded genius is almost a proverb. Education will not; the world is full of educated derelicts. Persistence and determination alone are omnipotent. The slogan 'press on' has solved and always will solve the problems of the human race.

Calvin Coolidge

Trust permeates all levels of management but can be greatly affected by the organization's leadership (Lawler, 1986). A leader who co-creates a vision for the organization, communicates that vision clearly to employees, and stays open to feedback and the sharing of progress will have a significant impact on creating and sustaining trust. Empowering leaders moves decision making to the level of expertise most appropriate. They give people throughout the organization a sense of competence.

Consensus Building

With empowered groups, an effective decision-making procedure is consensus. The consensus approach to decision making fosters group discussion of the problem and alternative solutions until there is widespread acceptance of the best course of action. Acceptance by group members means that individuals are willing to get behind and support a decision even if it is not their favorite choice (Levi, 2001). Consensus seeking clearly takes time to facilitate. It does require a thorough discussion of issues and a great deal of trust to accept a course of action. Johnson and Johnson (2001) have developed several guidelines for consensual decision making:

- Steer clear of over arguing in support of your own position. Present a position clearly and logically while listening to feedback and reactions to others before continuing to make your case.
- Refrain from changing your mind to avoid conflict and reach a solution. Some conflict is unavoidable but only support solutions that you can accept and that are objective, logical, and sound.
- Avoid conflict reducing procedures. Processes such as majority voting, tossing a coin, or letting others decide detract from consensus and ultimately acceptance.
- Seek out differences in opinion. The pooling of knowledge is a key ingredient in consensus groups, and considering different view points is critical.
- Don't take a win-lose approach. In consensus decision making there are no winners or losers; everyone looks for the best solution for all.
- Discuss the underlying assumptions. Listening carefully and encouraging participation will flesh out the various bases from which individuals approach the solution.

PMI Decision Making Technique

In addition to utilizing techniques that have an inherent decision-making component to them such as the Nominal Group Technique (see Chapter 7), a PMI analysis may be useful. Developed by de Bono (1992), PMI stands for "plus, minus, and interesting" and is a basic decision-making tool. The process of creating a PMI is simply to write out the solution alternatives and, for each alternative, generate a list of the pluses or positive points, minuses or negative points, and interesting aspects that would result from the solution regardless of whether it is positive or negative. It is possible to select a decision at this stage of the PMI. However, a further step is to assign scores to each PMI statement ranging from positive to negative. For example, one solution to a lackluster volunteer program may be to establish a strong service learning partnership with the recreation program at the local university. The relationship may result in agency volunteers that really have an interest in the field, so it receives a score of + 3. Because the service learning relationship will require staff time to cultivate, it also receives a score of -1. This solution may open up some other interesting options with the university, such as internships, and new student members of the state professional association, so it receives a score of + 2. The statement scores are then added for each column. A final score is calculated of P + M + I. If the score is a positive number, then the decision is supported, while a negative score would indicate lack of support for the decision.

STEP 6: *Implement Change Strategies*

The ultimate aim of problem solving is to address deviations in performance through change. Change may take a minor role in the organization and affect few employees, or change may play a significant role in the entire delivery system that impacts all stakeholders. An adaptable culture is one that embraces change and moves forward with deliberate action.

As will be discussed in Chapter 4, Organizational Culture and Climate, not everyone is likely to be receptive to change. Change upsets the status quo, which may be very uncomfortable for individuals. Doing things the way they have always been done does not require the acquisition of new skills, procedures, communication, and a host of performance related issues. There is a great deal of anxiety that also goes along with change that causes resistance, especially among people who were not intimately involved in the decision-making process. Fear of the unknown is powerful and can cause individuals to dig in their heels to prevent change from occurring. So, change, while difficult for employees and other stakeholders, is inevitable.

Fortunately, there are some approaches to assist in lessening the impact of change and facilitate successful implementation of creative solutions. For example, Kotter (1999) has conducted research on change in organizations and developed a series of strategies. These strategies have been found to positively and systematically effect change. The inviting feature of his eight-step approach to managing change is the action orientation for its implementation. Managers can establish specific targets of change, processes for change, and employee involvement mechanisms for creating and managing change. The eight changes strategies are listed below:

I cannot say whether things will get better if we change; what I can say is they must change if they are to get better.

G. C. Lichtenberg

1. *Establish a sense of urgency.* Identify and discuss the problems and issues confronting the organization.
2. *Form the guiding coalition.* Bring together a team with the power to lead change.
3. *Create the vision.* Visioning directs the change effort and strategies to foster the achievement of that vision.
4. *Communicate the vision.* Develop a variety of communication approaches to convey the vision and the strategies.

5. *Empower employees to act on the vision*. Remove barriers that underlie the vision. Encourage new and creative ideas, processes, and actions.
6. *Target short-terms wins*. Plan for performance improvements that will be observed quickly, and reward those employees who contribute to the win.
7. *Produce more change*. Use the credibility of short-term wins to continue change to fit the vision. Facilitate broader involvement of employees who can implement the vision and take on new projects.
8. *Embed new approaches in the culture*. Highlight the connection between behavior and organizational success. Develop leaders for promotion.

Ultimately, change is best viewed as a plan that has several stages, steps within each stage, and objectives that facilitate each change strategy implemented. In the development of a change plan, it is important to consider the factors that will help facilitate the change and those that will inhibit change. A force-field analysis is a technique that can aid in understanding the factors that face change.

Force-Field Analysis

In force-field analysis, the problem solution is presented. Group members generate a list of the forces that will help drive change and the forces that will restrain change. The two sets of forces create an equilibrium that keeps the change from occurring (Johnson & Johnson, 2001). A force-field diagram can provide a visual look that will facilitate the discussion, and an example is provided in the following paragraph. In addition, ranking each driving and restraining force assists in understanding the ones that are most important to consider.

There are three strategies that can be undertaken to address the forces at work. It is possible to (a) increase the number and strength of the driving forces for change, (b) decrease the number and strength of resistance forces, or (c) change the problem solution. The most desirable approach is to decrease the restraining forces (Johnson & Johnson, 2001). This is more effective than increasing the driving forces for change, which may have the adverse effect of creating more resistance to change. Group members should take each restraining factor separately and generate approaches to minimize its strength or eliminate it completely. In practice you would want to address both if possible. Changing the problem solution would be considered if the equilibrium could not be impacted.

We cannot change anything until we accept it. Condemnation does not liberate, it oppresses.

C. G. Jung

Step 7: Evaluate and Monitor

Effective managers will want to verify that their problem solving has been effective. The final stage in the problem-solving process is to determine whether the planned change is having the desired effect to resolve the performance problems and move the organization toward the desired future. Management will develop an evaluation plan to monitor the process and outcome of the changes instituted. An evaluation plan should be developed concurrently with the implementation plan. As noted in the previous section, it is imperative to plan changes that can be realized in the short term. Short-term wins should be shared with stakeholders, which will in turn create more support for change.

As the change process unfolds, evaluation will also determine whether the implementation strategy is effective in creating the needed change. If the change objectives are not being realized, then evaluation provides the basis for adjusting the plan to get back on track. Process evaluation data is conducted while the implementation plan is being carried out. Process evaluation can be used to determine if the incremental action steps that were delineated in the implementation plan are being accomplished as planned. If the process evaluation uncovers that the plan is not being enacted as planned, the manager can identify the reasons and, if appropriate, correct it. The manager may find that the implementation plan itself is inappropriate and adjust the plan.

Process evaluation data must be collected at meaningful intervals. This information allows for a description of the change efforts over time. It is important to recognize that process evaluation data simply describes what is happening relative to the implementation plan. Process evaluation does not determine if the intended strategy has been successful or the problem actually solved. Process evaluation questions might include:

- Was the specified action taken as planned?
- Were the appropriate staff involved?
- Were the necessary resources available?

The manager may also want to investigate any unexpected positive or negative consequences associated with the change.

The outcome evaluation will be conducted at the conclusion of the implementation of the change process. With outcome evaluation, managers are attempting to answer the million-dollar question, "After all of this problem solving, are we providing the quality of services and programs that we hoped would result from the elimination of the problem or impediments?" In order to be able to answer this question, managers must have first delineated the problem and their objectives very clearly. Otherwise it is extremely difficult to know if the problem has been eliminated and the desired objectives accomplished.

The outcomes address effectiveness and might be benchmarks, accreditation standards, or internal, well-specified organizational objectives. After an established specified period of time, a determination would be made whether you had met that benchmark or internal objectives. Even though the outcome data may be analyzed at the conclusion of the change process, the collection of data to be analyzed may have to be collected throughout the change process. Finally, efficiency may be the needed change. Efficiency determines whether the organization's resources are being utilized well. In other words, the provision of programs, facilities, and services should be considered in terms of their cost.

There is a logic and progression to evaluation (Posavac & Carey, 2002). It starts with a clearly defined problem statement indicating a need for a change, leading to effective implementation of the change (process evaluation), the determination of meaningful change resulting from planned actions (outcome evaluation), and finally a determination of the cost effectiveness of the change (efficiency evaluation). Evaluation is a complex and time-consuming process, that many organizations do not adequately prepare for and consequently implement. Each stage of problem solving is critical to the overall success of the process. Stopping short without thorough evaluation will greatly limit management's accountability.

As the change process is evaluated and monitored, the problem-solving cycle will loop back to the beginning stage of assessing the organization's strengths and searching for problems that need correcting. The organization will then move again through the model presented in Figure 3.1 to identify and understand the problem, generate and select solutions, implement change strategies, and ultimately evaluate the effectiveness of the agency's corrective actions.

Bibliography

Alvesson, M. (2002). *Understanding organizational culture.* London: Sage.

Amabile, T. M. (1998). How to kill creativity. *Harvard Business Review, 76*(5), 76-89.

Ammons, D. N. (2001). *Municipal benchmarks: Assessing local performance and establishing community standards* (2nd ed.). London: Sage.

Anderson, B., & Fagerhaug, T. (2000). *Root analysis: Simplified tools and techniques.* Milwaukee, WI: ASQ Quality.

de Bono, E. (1992). *Serious creativity: Using the power of lateral thinking to create new ideas.* New York: Harper Business.

Dennison, D. R., Haaland, S., & Goelzer, P. (2004). Corporate culture and organizational effectiveness: Is Asia different from the rest of the world? *Organizational Dynamics 33*(1), 98-109.

Dennison, D. R. (1990). *Corporate culture and organizational effectiveness.* New York: Wiley.

Fleisher, C. S., & Bensoussan, B. E. (2003). *Strategic and competitive analysis: Methods and techniques for analyzing business competition.* Upper Saddle River, NJ: Prentice Hall.

Gilchrist, V. J., & Williams, R. L. (1999). Key informant interviews. In B. F. Crabtree & W. L. Miller (Eds.), *Doing Qualitative Research* (pp. 71-88). Thousand Oaks, CA: Sage.

Hammond, S. A. (1996). *The thin book of appreciative inquiry.* Plano, TX: Thin Book Publishing.

Hill, C. W. L., & Jones, G. R. (2001). *Strategic management theory: An integrated approach* (5th ed.). Boston: Houghton Mifflin.

Johnson, D. W., & Johnson, F. P. (2001). *Joining together: Group theory and group skills* (7th ed.). Boston: Allyn and Bacon.

Kepner, C. A., & Tregoe, B. B. (1981). *The new rational manager.* New York: McGraw-Hill.

Kotter, J. P. (1999). *What leaders really do*. Boston: Harvard College.

Kreitner R., & Kinicki, A. (2001). *Organizational behavior* (5th ed.). Boston: Irwin McGraw-Hill

Krueger, R. A., & Casey, M. A. (2000). *Focus groups* (3rd ed.). London: Sage.

Lawler, E. E. (1986). *High-involvement management*. San Francisco: Jossey-Bass.

Leonard, D. A., & Swapp, W. C. (1999). *When sparks fly*. Boston: Harvard Business School Press.

Levi, D. (2001). *Group dynamics for teams*. London: Sage.

Litosseliti, L. (2003). *Using focus groups in research*. New York: Continuum.

Matherly, T. A., & Goldsmith, R. E. (1985). The two faces of creativity. *Business Horizons, 28*(5), 8-11.

Posavac, E. J., & Carey, R. G. (2002). *Program evaluation: Methods and case studies* (6th ed.). Englewood Cliffs, NJ: Prentice Hall.

Punch, K. F. (2003). *Survey research: The basics*. London: Sage.

Robson, C. (2002). *Real world research* (2nd ed.). Blackwell: Oxford.

Sioukas, T. (2003). *The solution path: A step-by-step guide to turning your workplace problems into opportunities*. San Francisco: Jossey-Bass.

Steiss, A. W. (2003). *Strategic management for public and nonprofit organizations*. New York: Marcel Dekker.

Sudman, S., & Blair, E. (1998). *Marketing research: A problem-solving approach*. Boston: McGraw-Hill.

Zeithaml, V. A., & Bitner, M. J. (2003). *Services marketing: Integrating customer focus across the firm* (3rd ed.). Boston: McGraw-Hill.

CHAPTER FOUR

ORGANIZATIONAL CULTURE AND CLIMATE: SETTING THE STAGE FOR PROBLEM SOLVING

The culture and climate of a leisure, recreation, and park agency set the tone for every interaction that occurs within the organization—from assessing participant needs, delivering services, and evaluating outcomes, to addressing the mishaps and obstacles that may arise along the way. If the people who work in the organization lack direction and focus, have poor morale and commitment, or communicate ineffectively, realistic solutions to complicated problems are difficult, if not impossible, to accomplish. If, on the other hand, the culture and climate of an organization encourage self-assessment, open communication, flexibility, quality improvement, and a sense of community, creative solutions to complex issues may not only be found more readily, they may serve their purposes longer.

Problem solving approaches and techniques, such as the model presented in Chapter 3 and the strategies presented in Chapters 7 and 8, are only as effective as an organization is healthy, vibrant, and open to the problem solving process. Tools and techniques for addressing problems rarely work in isolation. Rather, these approaches depend upon a positive organizational culture and climate to support solutions, changes, and actions over time.

Culture and Climate

What do we mean by the *culture* and *climate* of an organization? In popular usage, these terms are often confused or used interchangeably. People may refer to the "feel" of a place, or the degree of competition or teamwork among employees, as the culture of an agency when, in fact, these aspects reflect an agency's climate.

In his foreword to a text that contains numerous essays on organizational culture, Shein (2000) views *culture* as the "hard stuff" (p. xxiii) of an organization, that is, the agency's structures, systems, and strategies. The agency's structure is steeped in cultural assumptions, which may or may not be known to the members of the organization. For example, a cultural assumption may be that administration does, or does not, reward teamwork among employees. Another assumption may be that input from participants is, or is not, encouraged and valued. Cultural assumptions and the organization's structure are directly tied to the organization's history of successes or failures, which either confirm the underlying assumptions or disconfirm and eventually alter them. While the culture of an organization may appear fixed or frozen in time, it is in fact continually evolving as people respond to important historical events and influences over time.

If culture is the broad canvas, or structural context, of an organization, *climate* reflects the colors, shapes, lines, and overall vibrations displayed upon the canvas. Shein (2000) defines climate as "a cultural artifact resulting from espoused values and assumptions" (p. xxiv). Artifacts are those sentient features of an organization that can be seen, heard, and felt. The climate of an organization is often obvious upon entering the physical space of an agency. How does the environment look? How do people interact? Are people friendly or distant? What is the degree of openness and teamwork? What amount of emotionality is expressed? How are questions handled? The answers to these kinds of questions reflect how people perceive an organization's climate.

Visitors and new employees are often keenly aware of the climatic aspects of an organization, if not the underlying culture. For example, how might visitors perceive the lobby of a rigid, hierarchical organization compared to the lobby of an inclusive, participatory organization? Consider the examples below (N. Zahler, personal communication, June 21, 2004):

> *Hierarchical Organization Lobby:* The lobby of the hierarchical organization might have uncomfortable, straight-backed chairs. An aloof receptionist might be busy with paperwork and unavailable to answer your questions. Signs might be posted with rules of what NOT to do and instructions to stand in line or take a number.

> *Inclusive Organization Lobby:* In the lobby of an inclusive organization, on the other hand, newcomers might find comfortable chairs with side tables offering interesting reading materials. Colorful posters might offer helpful guidance. Friendly, helpful people would take the time to answer your questions. Pictures on the walls might reflect the constituents who are served. A suggestion box or survey, in plain view, might invite feedback about the agency's programs, services, and policies.

While these examples border on hyperbole, they illustrate how the visible, physical features of an agency communicate a great deal about the prevailing climate.

How does one create a culture and climate that is conducive to solving problems effectively and collaboratively within an organization? The remainder of this chapter will address this question by first discussing the importance of establishing the underlying values, vision, and mission that guide an organization and inform strategic planning. Central to the chapter are seven guiding principles for cultivating an organizational culture and climate receptive to addressing administrative issues—principles gleaned from a collection of current resources in the disciplines of organizational culture and management. Closing thoughts are then offered on the role of leadership in creating a positive organizational culture and climate.

Where Is Your Organization Going?

The underlying values, vision, and mission of an organization are the building blocks that create a solid foundation for organizational problem solving. To create a culture and climate that responds well to community concerns, group members must first reflect upon what they value and where they are going. When these discussions have taken place, group members can then engage in long-range strategic planning. While a full explanation of the processes for developing this organizational groundwork is beyond the scope of this book, we offer the following thoughts, guidelines, and examples to show how these aspects are fundamentally linked to the organization's culture and climate as well as to the organization's capacity to solve problems.

As examples of organizational groundwork, we include the actual values, vision, and mission of an organization that has dealt successfully with fiscal and geographical constraints by forging a partnership. The Inter-Municipal Recreation Partnership of Tompkins County in upstate New York is a consortium of eight towns, one village, one city, and the county government organized in 1995 to share the costs of a diverse set of programs serving over 4,000 youth that no single entity could afford to offer (N. Zahler, personal communication, June 23, 2004).

A reorganization of the Recreation Partnership occurred in 2000 to develop a new, mutually acceptable cost-sharing formula and governing structure without explicitly defining the consortium's values, vision, or mission. When it became necessary to decide which of the 40 programs would need to be cut, however, the committee charged with rating and ranking programs asked themselves, "By what yardstick will we evaluate programs, allocate our resources, and measure our accomplishments?" This question led to fuller discussions and the eventual design of the consortium's vision, mission, and values statements.

In 2003, the Recreation Partnership Board again found itself faced with severe budget cuts, a situation that challenges many public and private recreation agencies throughout the country today. Because the values, vision, and mission were in place, however, the Board could begin to plan ahead to adjust for the cuts that were anticipated in 2005. The consortium's guiding values, vision, and mission appear as examples in the following three sections.

VALUES: *What do people in your organization value?*

The values we bring to our work in leisure, recreation, and park services give our profession a sense of meaning and purpose. Our values inspire us to design and deliver quality services and programs. Our values encourage us to persevere to find solutions to the problems we face because we care about the people we serve and the services we provide. Translating personal conviction into organizational values shapes the very fabric of the culture and climate of our agencies, in a holistic and systemic way.

Each organization will need to clarify its own values in accordance with the composition, strengths, assets, challenges, and needs of its community. To identify organizational values, group members may ask themselves the following question:

What are the core values related to the future we envision for our organization?

The *process* of clarifying organizational values is every bit as important as the set of values that are created, if not more so. As people share their beliefs, tell stories that reflect their commitment to their profession, and voice the ideals that matter to them, group members encourage and uphold each other, potentially bridging other differences that might exist.

To begin the values clarification process, group members can brainstorm the personal values that each of them brings to his or her role or position (see Chapter 7 for guidelines on brainstorming). Once a list of values is developed, group members can then work together to cluster the values into overarching themes. The group may need to work through several drafts of a values statement, involving much discussion, editing, and wordsmithing. In due course, the group should arrive at a set of shared values that expresses their collective commitment to the community the agency serves.

When several groups come together in a partnership, such as in the case of the Tompkins County Inter-Municipal Recreation Partnership, formulating shared values is especially critical to construct a positive organizational culture and climate. The programmatic and organizational values established by this partnership appear in Table 4.1.

Table 4.1
Sample Values Statements
The Inter-Municipal Recreation Partnership
Tompkins County, New York

Program Values

Safety and Fun: All programs sponsored by the Recreation Partnership will enable participants to have fun in ways and settings that protect their health, safety, and emotional well-being.

High Quality: All participants and their families will be treated with courtesy and respect and program services will be provided by capable and caring staff and volunteers who are well trained and supervised.

Equity and Inclusiveness: Children of all abilities and backgrounds will be welcomed, actively included, and supported by caring and respectful staff and volunteers. A wide diversity of programs will be maintained to accommodate the varying needs, interests, requirements, and skills for all interested youth.

Diversity: Programs will be designed to actively foster interaction across differences and to engender greater understanding of and appreciation and respect for children from all of the diverse backgrounds and communities that comprise our multi-cultural county.

Affordability: All children and youth, regardless of income, will be able to participate affordably in a wide range of leisure time, educational, social, and cultural activities. As a publicly supported partnership, municipal subsidies will be used to lower the cost of selected programs to assure universal affordable access. Lower cost or specialty programs that can pay for themselves should break even. Scholarships will be available to assure no interested youth will be excluded based solely on inability to pay.

Continued

Table 4.1 (continued)
Sample Values Statements
The Inter-Municipal Recreation Partnership
Tompkins County, New York

Accessibility: Programs will be offered at times and locations that are convenient for working families. The mix of service will need to balance the economies of scale offered by centralized programs with the convenience of decentralized programs offered in partnering facilities.

Organizational Values

Advocacy: Members of the partnership recognize the importance of well-founded recreation programs to the quality of life in our community. The partnership intends to advocate for the value of introducing, supporting, and engaging youth in lifelong recreational opportunities. We would like to offer all youth the opportunity to try out new programs that provide fun, educational, and growth opportunities without the pressure of high-level competition or the expense of specialized equipment.

Good Investment: Members of the partnership recognize the value of the subsidies that they are investing in youth programs. Programs that support the physical and mental health of youth translate into a much larger savings down the road from avoided costs. Children who are kept active in programs that promote not only physical fitness but also good character pose less risk to society in the future. The cost of keeping children healthy and out of trouble is much less expensive than the alternative, and is therefore a good investment.

Inter-Municipal Cooperation: The partnership's success depends on having well-informed representatives who trust each other and can work together to find creative, collaborative ways of addressing shared interests and concerns.

Creative Use of Resources: All partners have information and experience with local programs, access to community facilities, informational networks to help with recruitment as well as varying levels of financial resources to contribute to the partnership. Sharing of information, training, and facility resources will be actively pursued across municipalities and agencies. Recreation partnership programs will be developed in concert with existing local programs. We will define decentralized program opportunities and reciprocity of common programs across participating communities.

Contracting with Qualified and Responsive Providers: The partnership was designed to offer supplemental services by contracting with well-qualified, creative, and responsive providers.

Accountability: The partnership board needs to be responsible stewards of public funds used to offer community recreation. It will routinely review the costs and benefits of each sponsored program and periodically assess the performance of the board itself, the contracted providers, and the staff support provided by the Tompkins County Youth Services Department.

Flexibility: Community needs and local governmental circumstances change continually and the partnership board needs to be able to respond flexibly to changes in ways that create opportunities out of potential crises.

Organizations that take the time to develop an integrated set of values are immeasurably more successful than organizations without them (Napier, Sidle, & Sanaghan, 1998). When people align themselves with core values, and *live* by them, the diverse elements of an organization can work as a whole to deliver services that reflect those values. Core organizational values create opportunities to build trust and commonality, to provide consistency, to guide decision making, and to reinforce a sense of community. Shared values also set the stage for creating an agency's vision and mission.

VISION: *What is your organization's vision for the future?*

If you can dream it, you can do it. Always remember that this whole thing was started by a mouse.

Walt Disney

An organizational vision is a shared picture of hope for the future that group members seek to create (Barry, 2001). A vision inspires us and gives us a clear image of a brighter future (Napier, Sidle, & Sanaghan, 1998). A good vision statement also challenges us to work for a future that we may not yet know how to create (Cummings & Worley, 2001; Greenleaf, 1977).

The vision of an organization acknowledges the agency's historical roots and underlying cultural assumptions as it serves to guide the organization into a desired new future. Cummings and Worley (2001) identify two basic elements of vision statements:

1. *Bold and Valued Outcomes:* The specific human and performance outcomes that the organization wishes to achieve

2. *Desired Future State:* What the organization will look like, written in language designed to engage people and compel them toward the organization's future

The vision statement of the Tompkins County Inter-Municipal Recreation Partnership, which contains both these elements, appears in Table 4.2.

Table 4.2
Sample Vision Statement
The Inter-Municipal Recreation Partnership
Tompkins County, New York

Any Tompkins County youth who wants to participate in a recreational program to meet new friends, learn new skills, or have positive new experiences will be able to find a well-supervised, appropriate activity at an affordable price at convenient times and locations.

Envisioning an organization's future is an intuitive process that involves visualizing how the organization should look and function. Just as all group members develop an agency's core values, individuals at all levels and in all roles of the agency contribute to creating the vision. Napier, Sidle, and Sanaghan (1998) recommend building a group vision around the group members' personal visions by asking questions suggested by Marjorie Parker (1990):

- What is meaningful about your work?
- What is meaningful about your contribution at work?
- What is meaningful about your contribution to society?
- What difference should we make?
- What are we good at?
- What makes us distinctive or unique?
- What are customers asking from us?

If we don't change the direction we're going, we're likely to end up where we're headed.

Ancient Chinese Proverb

When group members have formulated a unifying vision, they can then work together to articulate a collective statement of mission.

MISSION: *What is your organization's mission?*

A mission statement clarifies the purpose of an organization, indicates what it does, and provides a rationale for what it does. Similar to the process of developing the organizational values and vision, designing a mission statement is a collaborative effort that optimally involves all members of the organization. Input is gathered from key stakeholders, for example, program participants, board members, staff, and similar service providers in neighboring areas. While such collaboration requires extensive time and energy, it is critical to create the buy-in necessary for later teamwork. Planning and delivering services, making decisions, and solving problems will go more smoothly if everyone has contributed to formulating the underlying unified approach and frame of reference.

To develop a draft mission statement, Napier, Sidle, and Sanaghan (1998) recommend posing the following kinds of questions to group members:

Nothing happens unless first a dream.

Carl Sandburg

1. Who are we?
2. What is our purpose?
3. What basic social and political needs do we exist to fill?
4. What do we want to do to recognize, anticipate, and respond to these social and political needs or problems?
5. How should we respond to our key stakeholders?
6. What is our philosophy, and what are our core values?
7. What makes us distinct or unique?
8. What is our organization's current mission?
9. Is our current mission dated and, if so, how?
10. What changes in the mission would I propose?

As these questions reveal, the mission builds upon the values and vision previously established by the organization. Based on an analysis of the answers to the above questions, individual members of the organization, or a strategic planning committee, can draft a mission statement that would be shared with and reworked by the larger group. Ultimately, the mission statement will identify the key goals of the organization, as exemplified in the sample mission statement presented in Table 4.3 developed by the Tompkins County Inter-Municipal Recreation Partnership.

Table 4.3
Sample Mission Statement
The Inter-Municipal Recreation Partnership
Tompkins County, New York

To jointly plan, finance, provide, and coordinate shared, recreational services for youth of all ages and skill levels that supplement and complement those offered by localities and the private sector. By collaborating and pooling resources, the inter-municipal recreation partnership offers a wider and more affordable array of recreational programming than any single local government could offer on its own.

STRATEGIC PLANNING: What will your organization accomplish, and how will it be accomplished?

When the members of an organization have engaged in conversation to clarify their values, vision, and mission, they are well positioned for strategic planning that will continue to intentionally shape the organization's culture and climate. Strategic planning is used to direct the long-term focus and goals of the organization. Typically, strategic planning covers a period of three to five years, in contrast to short-range, yearly operational work plans or budget plans.

Barry (2001) suggests that strategic planning answers two fundamental organizational concerns: (a) what the organization intends to accomplish over a given time period, and (b) how the organization and its resources will be directed to accomplish its goals. Barry identifies several benefits of strategic planning:

- Increased organizational momentum and focus
- Enhanced teamwork and communication
- Increased learning and commitment
- A coordinated and systemic approach to problem solving
- Improved results

We cannot discover new oceans unless we have the courage to lose sight of the shore.

Anonymous

Barry also offers a five-step process to guide strategic planning, which is presented in an abbreviated form below:

STEP 1: *Get Organized*
- Identify your reasons for strategic planning and any concerns.
- Select a leader or group to keep planning on track.
- Determine who will be involved in the planning process, including outside consultants or resources.
- Outline planning steps that suit your organization.
- Secure approval to proceed with planning.

STEP 2: *Take Stock (Situational Analysis)*
- Review the organization's history.
- Assess the current situation.
- Identify future possibilities and choices.
- Identify the critical issues or choices facing the organization.

STEP 3: *Set Direction*
- Develop a vision of your organization's future.
- Identify goals and objectives.
- Identify strategies to achieve goals and objectives, possibly including resources needed, responsible parties, performance measures, and a timeline.

STEP 4: *Refine and Adopt the Plan*
- Review and refine the plan.
- Adopt the plan.

STEP 5: *Implement the Plan*
- Implement the plan.
- Monitor progress and make adjustments as needed.
- Periodically update the plan.

In summary, organizations that consciously and collectively formulate their values, establish clear vision and mission statements, and develop plans to realize their goals and objectives lay the groundwork for an organizational culture and climate that is open, inclusive, responsive, and forward thinking. Guiding principles to encourage these positive aspects of organizational culture and climate are offered in the section that follows.

Seven Guiding Principles for Organizations
The following seven principles, summarized in Table 4.4, have been gathered from a collection of resources in the disciplines of organizational management and leadership, as well as related sources (Bolman & Deal, 1997; Bruno, 1995; Cooperridge & Kretzman, 1993; Dinkmeyer & Eckstein, 1996; Gilbertson & Ramchandani, 1999; Lumsden & Lumsden, 2000; Ray & Anderson, 2000; Topping, 2002). Together, they represent much of the current thinking about cultivating organizations that are participatory, inclusive, and coopera-

Table 4.4
Seven Principles for Developing a Positive Organizational Culture and Climate

Principle 1: Encourage openness, flexibility, and teamwork
Principle 2: Commit to diversity throughout the organization
Principle 3: Keep a customer service orientation
Principle 4: Focus on quality improvement
Principle 5: Build on strengths, capacities, and assets
Principle 6: Build a sense of community
Principle 7: Recognize change as opportunity

tive and that involve people at many levels in organizational visioning, governance, decision making, and problem solving.

Inclusive organizations of this nature might be best represented by the figure of an "inverted pyramid" (see Figure 4.1). Most of us are familiar with the traditional hierarchical pyramid in which the executive director and/or board of directors, at the "top" levels, hand down decisions to staff and participants, at the "bottom" levels. In the inverted pyramid model, however, the roles are reversed. The individuals who are most directly involved in the delivery of services—front-line staff, receptionists, maintenance staff, program participants, and recipients of services—play a vital role in providing input that results in catching problems while they are still small, making the necessary adjustments to correct them, and ultimately improving the quality of services. The primary role of administrators is to listen to feedback, facilitate interpersonal communication, involve people in decisions, watch for what is going well, and support and encourage the members of the group. Essentially, the top administrators serve the common good of everyone in the organization.

Every member of the "inverted pyramid" organization is equal in worth and dignity. All are treated respectfully as equivalent participants and contributors (Dinkmeyer & Eckstein, 1996). People are connected through fluid communication and, regardless of the roles they perform, they are invested in the organization and committed to improving customer service.

While no organized human endeavor is "perfect," nor can we expect it to be, the following principles are offered as guideposts for leisure, recreation, and park administrators as they seek to create a positive culture and climate that allows for satisfying solutions to the problems they may encounter.

PRINCIPLE 1: Encourage openness, flexibility, and teamwork

How does an organization that is open, flexible, and team-oriented look? Topping (2002) offers us a portrait of such an organization from a business management perspective, a vision that also holds true for leisure, recreation, and park services.

Figure 4.1
Traditional Versus "Inverted" Organizational Pyramid

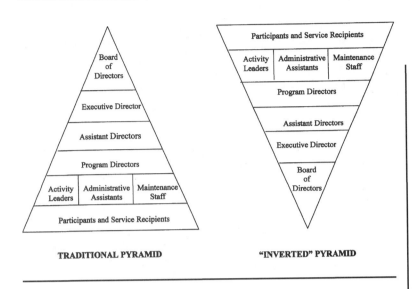

An "open" organization, as described by Topping, has clear communication channels that distribute information across all parts of an organization in a timely fashion. Accurate information is distributed to the right person at the right time and handled according to proper policies and procedures. Information travels uncensored and unfiltered, and bad news can be delivered to supervisors without fear of reprisal.

Topping sees a "flexible" organization as one that thrives even in times of turbulent change and transition. Resources are shifted to respond to varying environmental influences. Bureaucracy is minimal. No matter how large the organization, it operates as a small business.

In the ideal "team-oriented" organization, according to Topping, everyone is values-driven and works together to achieve the organization's mission and objectives. All employees are focused on the quality of the organization's performance, and people hold each other accountable for meeting goals and providing services. Because everyone is directed toward fulfilling the greater purposes of the organization, no self-serving associates exist in the organization.

Organizations that are open, flexible, and team-oriented do not, of course, develop overnight. As noted earlier in this chapter, they are founded on the philosophies imbedded in the agency's values, mission, and vision. They are also founded on trust, an issue that is discussed in the following section.

Trustworthiness. Trust is essential for all human relationships, including relationships within organizations. In leisure, recreation, and park agencies, where people work closely together and depend on each other to get the job done, trust must be present among all employees, starting with administrators.

You can only govern men by serving them.
Victor Cousin

Lumsden and Lumsden (2000) acknowledge that, to be trusted, one must first be trustworthy. They note that trust is a very fragile entity and may be violated easily. Because of this, they recommend that leaders take a look at their own communication styles and degree of trustworthiness by asking themselves the following questions (pp. 45-46):

- *Commitment:* Do you live up to what you say? Can you be trusted to follow through on a promise or commitment?

- *Confidentiality:* Do you protect another person's confidentiality? Do you stop rumors or pass them on? If someone shares personal information, do you keep it to yourself or share it with the rest of the world?

- *Ethics:* When ethical choices need to be made, do you speak up for the ethical action or remain silent and take the easy way out?
- *Truthfulness:* Do you consistently give the most truthful information? Do you choose to tell the truth, even when telling a small lie would be easier?

- *Communication:* Is your communication straightforward and open? Do you avoid manipulating others? Do you deal with issues in a straightforward manner?

Answering questions of this nature can enhance an administrator's personal awareness of the issue of trust and enlarge her or his capacity to develop trustworthiness in relating to others. The answers to these questions can also help administrators detect the "gray areas" in which trust might potentially be broken.

Trust is a very personal matter, individual to individual. Trust also needs to be nurtured within a group, if people are expected to work together as a team. The following section offers a method for creating an organizational climate that encourages openness and trust among group members.

Create ground rules to develop openness and trust in teams. People generally need to feel a certain degree of emotional safety in order to speak their opinions freely, consider options with an open mind, and work effectively as team members. To cultivate these positive interactions, issues related to trust are best discussed openly in the group.

Gilbertson and Ramchandani (1999) point out that group members may differ widely in their need for recognition, achievement, power, and inclusion in the group. People may also possess differing values, experience levels, personalities, cultural backgrounds, and interaction styles. These authors suggest that ground rules may address a range of dynamics related to group interaction, such as those that follow:

- Participation and involvement on the team
- Workplace conflicts and disagreements
- Personal conflicts, needs, and issues
- How decisions are made (e.g., consensus, majority vote)
- Confidentiality
- Leadership roles and responsibilities
- Communication
- Feedback and criticism
- Rewards and recognition

Establishing group norms, or ground rules, can help create a sense of safety so team members build trust and feel comfortable participating within the group. According to Gilbertson and Ramchandani (1999), establishing ground rules is advantageous because they

- Allow team members to express their values, needs, and desires
- Clarify expectations for team members
- Reflect the culture and climate of the organization or agency

Table 4.5
Establishing Team Ground Rules
(adapted from Gilbertsen & Ramchandani, 1999)

STEP 1: Individual group members write down potential ground rules.
Each group member takes a few moments to consider the following questions: What expectations do I have to work effectively as a valued member of this team? What are some ground rules on which our team could agree? Each group member writes down one to three norms.

STEP 2: Individual group members share their ground rules.
As each group member shares a ground rule, a facilitator or group member writes the rule on a flip chart, blackboard, or piece of paper that everyone can see. Rules should be recorded exactly as people say them.

STEP 3: As a team, discuss the entire list.
When everyone finishes contributing to the list, the entire team discusses it. Items on the list may be combined, eliminated, or modified as the group wishes.

STEP 4: Finalize the list and distribute it.
The team decides, either by consensus or by voting, which ground rules it will adopt. When the list is finalized, distribute it to all group members. Refer to the guidelines as needed to conduct effective meetings and work together respectfully as a team.

- Assist in monitoring and evaluating group members' performance and interactions
- Orient new members to the way "things are done around here"

A worksheet for developing ground rules, adapted from Gilbertson and Ramchandani (1999), is presented in Table 4.5. Using this format, group members have an opportunity to work individually to generate potential ground rules, share suggestions with the group, and then develop a composite list of group norms. Sample team ground rules are presented below:

1. We come to meetings on time and prepared to work.
2. We listen respectfully to each other's ideas.
3. We stay on the topic during meetings.
4. We all do our fair share of the work, as we are able.
5. We keep matters of confidentiality strictly confidential.
6. Other than confidential matters, we discuss all issues openly. No deals will be "cut" behind closed doors.
7. We affirm everyone's contributions.
8. We end meetings on time.

Nothing happens unless first a dream.

Carl Sandburg

PRINCIPLE 2: Commit to diversity throughout the organization

Problems, like crystals, have many faces, many angles. Viewing a crystal from a single perspective reveals only one aspect of the whole. To see the entire picture, diverse input is needed from diverse people. Involving input from various perspectives has the potential to yield numerous benefits. For example, diverse input can

- Help identify root causes to problems
- Reveal aspects that had not been considered previously
- Assist in understanding all aspects of a situation
- Generate solutions that take into account the impact on everyone who may be affected by a decision

Every attempt at problem solving is a cross-cultural experience. Differences related to race, culture, ethnicity, age, gender, ability, socioeconomic status, and sexual orientation add to the complexity of problem solving, but also enliven the dynamics and enhance the potential for learning and insight (J. Greenwood, personal communication, March 27, 2004). See Table 4.6 for a list of factors that may vary among cultures related to how they handle communication, problems, and conflict.

Cultural diversity self-assessment. How might an administrator prepare herself or himself for cross-cultural communication and exchanges? We offer the following Cross-Cultural Self-Assessment (J. Greenwood, personal communication, March 27, 2004) as a means to recognize personal biases and to guide the process of cross-cultural communication and problem solving. A self-assessment of this nature can help an administrator work through cultural biases and misconceptions in preparation for assuming the important leadership role of modeling an appreciation and acceptance of diversity.

Table 4.6
Communication, Culture, and Problem Solving
(J. Greenwood, personal communication, March 27, 2004)

Different cultures may handle problems in different ways. Here are some of the factors that can vary:

- *Preferred Communication:* Is the preferred communication verbal or nonverbal?
- *Eye Contact:* Is eye contact used or avoided?
- *Proximity:* How close do you stand when speaking to another person?
- *Body Language and Posture:* Do you lean toward or lean away from another person during conversation?
- *Hand Gestures:* Is the use of hand gestures acceptable or unacceptable?
- *Quality of Voice:* How does the voice quality vary in volume (loud or soft), pitch (high, low, or variable), or tone (smooth, raspy, sharp, or soft)?
- *Comfort with Silence:* Is the person comfortable with silence or does he or she fill all silences with speech?
- *Pace of Speech:* Is speech rapid or slow?
- *Style of Communication:* Is the communication style relaxed or intense, formal or informal, thorough or brief?
- *Interruptions:* Is the person comfortable with interruptions or annoyed by them?
- *Content:* Is the content rational, emotional, or a combination; objective or subjective; personal or impersonal; related to the past or to the future?
- *Decision Making:* How are decisions made? By the individual or family? By an elder or clan? Does the person seek advice or shun advice?
- *Confrontation:* Is confrontation valued or not valued?
- *Attitude Toward Conflict:* Is conflict accepted as a part of life, or avoided at all costs?
- *Self-Disclosure:* Is there a high level or low level of self-disclosure?
- *Mode of Conflict Resolution:* Are conflicts resolved directly (face to face) or indirectly (through another person or in writing)?
- *Comfort with Anger:* Is anger expressed or avoided?

Cross-Cultural Self-Assessment

In a real sense, all life is interrelated. All persons are caught in an inescapable network of mutuality, tied in a single garment of destiny. Whatever affects one directly affects all indirectly. I can never be what I ought to be until you are what you ought to be, and you can never be what you ought to be until I am what I ought to be. This is the interrelated structure of reality.

Martin Luther King, Jr.

STEP 1: Know thyself.
- Ask: What is my comfort zone? What biases do I bring?
- If you can't be neutral and non-judgmental, delegate the problem solving situation to an unbiased co-worker.

STEP 2: Know the other.
- Listen deeply, and ask questions thoughtfully.
- Check for understanding (yours and theirs)

STEP 3: Learn about differences.
- What differing factors might influence communication and problem solving? (See Table 4.6.)

STEP 4: Learn how to honor, respect, and appreciate diversity.
- How can diversity enhance and enrich your own life and the well-being of the organization?

STEP 5: Take your cues from the individuals.
- Avoid assumptions. The parties are the experts on who they are, what is important to them, and what they need.

STEP 6: Prepare the parties.
- Work with the parties to develop ground rules for problem solving.
- Inform the parties of the process of problem solving. (If the situation is highly controversial and potentially involves conflict, consult the conflict resolution and mediation approaches presented in Chapter 8.)

STEP 7: Guard the process.
- It is the administrator's responsibility to assure a space for safe dialogue.
- Maximize choice and power for all participants.
- Intervene, or terminate the discussion, if needed.

Practical actions that demonstrate a commitment to diversity. What specific actions might leisure, recreation, and park service providers take to show their commitment to diversity? Aguilar (2000) suggests that logistical difficulties, language barriers, bias and prejudice, and policies and procedures that are culturally insensitive can potentially stand in the way of serving a culturally diverse clientele. She recommends that leisure, recreation, and park agencies focus on removing "the stresses and inconveniences of operating in an unfamiliar culture" (p. 202) that particular members of a community might experience. She also offers several practical suggestions for providing customer service in a culturally diverse world, which appear below:

1. Observe the difficulties your customers encounter, and take pro-active steps to eliminate these barriers for future guests. Share your ideas for removing barriers at staff meetings.
2. Use international or multilingual signage.
3. Reduce language barriers by offering translated guidebooks, registration forms, public announcements, tours, or shows.
4. Develop a multicultural customer service resource list and post it in a visible place. For example, include information about community resources that have bilingual employees, language banks, foreign currency offices, religious services, restaurants or grocery stores that accommodate particular dietary needs, or emergency telephone numbers that respond in multiple languages.
5. Employ people from culturally diverse backgrounds.
6. Provide resources to support staff training related to cultural differences, and discuss these differences during staff meetings.
7. Learn about the common cultural taboos of your customers so you can avoid offending or embarrassing them.
8. Utilize interpreters during meetings. Provide key information in writing in the person's preferred language.
9. Listen to the needs and requests of your culturally diverse customers. Use a variety of methods to collect input. Consider that some customers may prefer to give suggestions or complaints directly (i.e., face to face), while others may prefer more indirect means (e.g., surveys, suggestion box).
10. Look for "cultural interpreters" who can assist in explaining cultural differences to staff.
11. Develop services and programs designed to meet the specific needs and tastes of a particular cultural group. For instance, offer food options and programming times that suit the group, or provide for holiday programming.
12. Reflect the diversity of your customers and staff in your marketing and publicity materials.

> *Though I am different from you, We were born involved in one another.*
>
> T'ao Chi'ien

Leisure, recreation, and park service providers are in a unique position to demonstrate their commitment to diversity through actions such as those identified by Aguilar (2000) above. For other excellent perspectives and recommendations related to cultural awareness and diversity in the leisure services profession, consult the book, *Diversity and the Recreation Profession: Organizational Perspectives* edited by Maria T. Allison and Ingrid E. Schneider (2000).

PRINCIPLE 3: Keep a customer service orientation

Despite the efforts of consumer advocates, good customer service is not especially common. In any given week, most of us can probably recall more examples of poor customer service than high-quality service (Topping, 2002). From an agency or business point of view, customers are often perceived as "too demanding," with expectations that may be unreasonable. Placing community and participant satisfaction high on the agency's list of priorities, however, generates good will and can yield tremendous benefits for the entire community.

When an organization is truly committed to customer satisfaction, every member of the organization—the receptionist, activity leader, maintenance person, program director, executive director, and the chairperson of the board of directors—can share in the effort to demonstrate exemplary service (Bolman & Deal, 1997). Consider the "inverted pyramid" model discussed earlier in this chapter and how all employees are involved in customer service activities.

Customer service is the manifestation of an agency's vision, mission, and values. Customer service means group members respond to concerns pleasantly, respectfully, and efficiently. They anticipate people's concerns and proactively address them. They engage in actions to meet the needs of all their customers regardless of age, ability, race, culture, ethnicity, or sexual orientation (see suggestions for meeting the needs of culturally diverse groups in the previous section). They go "the extra mile" to show their willingness to assist and serve the customer.

PRINCIPLE 4: Focus on quality improvement

Closely related to customer service is an organization's commitment to quality improvement. An organization that is values-driven, and continually takes stock of its progress toward fulfilling its mission and vision, will ask itself the following kinds of questions to improve the quality of its services:

The way management treats the associates is exactly how the associates will then treat the customers.

Sam Walton

- Are there needs in the community that are not being met?
- What areas, services, and programs can we improve?
- What progress have we made in reaching the goals set forth in our mission and strategic plan?
- Are we moving in the right direction, or do we need to shift gears?
- What feedback have we received from our stakeholders—consumers, participants, board of directors, and staff?
- How can we partner with other community agencies to improve services?
- What community resources and models can we utilize to strengthen our services?
- What innovative practices can we utilize to better respond to community needs?

An organization that is serious about improving services is open to self-assessment. It is also a learning-oriented organization. The data necessary to make good decisions are gathered, and decisions are driven by the data rather than subjective impressions (Topping, 2002).

Organizations that continually seek to improve the quality of its services value innovation. Creativity and the generation of diverse ideas are encouraged, which means that, at times, agencies will need to be willing to take risks to respond to problems that are particularly challenging (Bruno, 1995). See Chapter 6 for a comprehensive discussion of creativity and innovation in problem solving.

PRINCIPLE 5: Build on strengths, capacities, and assets

The first step of the problem solving model presented in Chapter 3 involves assessing strengths and searching for problems in the organization. In this section, we introduce two approaches relevant to leisure, recreation, and park services that focus on building communities around strengths and assets: (a) appreciative inquiry and (b) the *Forty Developmental Assets* proposed by the Search Institute.

Appreciative inquiry. A traditional response to addressing concerns in the community typically focuses entirely on needs, deficiencies, and problems (Kretzmann & McKnight, 1993). A problem is identified, defined, dissected, analyzed, and eventually "fixed." Using this approach can be problematic, however, because it tends to reinforce deficit finding and encourages communities to look at what is not working well in an organization as opposed to what is working well (Hammond, 1996). Focusing on problems and deficits alone tends to create service-dependent communities rather than communities that are actively involved in meeting community needs by drawing on their own strengths and resources (Kretzmann & McKnight, 1993).

As an alternative to this traditional approach, the concept of *appreciative inquiry* was developed, first articulated by Cooperrider and Srivastva (1987). Appreciative inquiry submits that organizations change according to the direction of their inquiry. That is, if an organization inquires into problems, it will continue to find problems; if, on the other hand, an organization appreciates and inquires into what is working well, it will continue to discover the good within an organization and build upon it. Focusing on what works well in an organization affirms the people and practices that give life and creative energy to the organization. (See Table 4.7 for a comparison of appreciative inquiry and the traditional organizational development approach.)

> *It is not the employer who pays the wages, Employers only handle money. It is the customer who pays the wages.*
>
> Henry Ford

Table 4.7
Traditional Organizational Development Process versus Appreciative Inquiry (Hammond, 1996)

Traditional Organizational Development Process	Appreciative Inquiry
• Define the problem	• Search for solutions that already exist
• Fix what's broken	• Amplify what is working
• Focus on decay	• Focus on life giving forces
Asks: What problems are you having?	*Asks: What is working well?*

For certain problems that require immediate action and a concrete solution, such as during budget cuts or when key personnel leave an agency, the traditional problem-oriented model for solving problems may be the preferred approach. In other situations, in which one has the opportunity to look holistically and systemically at the organization, the appreciative inquiry model offers a viable alternative. Instead of focusing directly on specific problems, appreciative inquiry seeks to generate solutions to problems by validating and building upon people's contributions, creativity, and empowerment. Appreciative inquiry revolves around the following eight assumptions (Hammond, 1996):

1. Within every organization, something is working well.
2. What we focus on becomes our reality.
3. Reality is created in the moment and is composed of multiple realities.
4. Asking questions of an organization influences the organization is some way.
5. When people journey into the future (the unknown) carrying with them parts of the past (the known), they are more comfortable and confident in moving forward.
6. The parts of the past that we carry forward should be our best parts.
7. It is important to value differences.
8. The language we use creates our reality.

Applying these assumptions, appreciative inquiry allows people to recognize the good within an organization and to build upon its strengths. Instead of emphasizing what people are doing wrong and what they should stop doing, appreciative inquiry invites people to answer questions such as

"What is going well?"

"What ideas do you have that I can share with others?"

"How are you documenting your excellence?"

Helping people discover the good within an organization helps them create a future in which the life-giving practices become commonplace, and the practices that are not working well can eventually fade away (Hammond, 1996).

Forty Developmental Assets. Another example of a strength-based model relevant to leisure, recreation, and park services comes out of the Search Institute, an independent nonprofit organization in Minneapolis, Minnesota. The mission of the Search Institute is "to provide leadership, knowledge, and resources to promote healthy children, youth, and communities" (see http://www.search-institute.org).

Based on extensive research on adolescents, grades six to 12, the Search Institute identified *Forty Developmental Assets* that support the growth of young people into "healthy, caring, and responsible" adults. These assets, summarized in Table 4.8, are categorized as either *external* or *internal* assets. *External* assets are those that exist within families, park and recreation departments, schools, and other neighborhood resources. *Internal* assets, on the other hand, are those qualities and attributes that are developed within the young person.

> **Table 4.8**
> **Forty Developmental Assets for Youth Development**
> **(Search Institute, Minneapolis, Minnesota)**
>
> 1. **External Assets**
>   - *Support:* Family support, positive family communication, other adult relationships, caring neighborhood, caring school climate, parent involvement
>   - *Empowerment:* Community values youth, youth as resources, service to others, safety
>   - *Boundaries and Expectations:* Family boundaries, school boundaries, neighborhood boundaries, adult role models, positive peer influence, high expectations
>   - *Constructive Use of Time:* Creative activities, youth programs, religious community, time at home
>
> 2. **Internal Assets**
>   - *Commitment to Learning:* Achievement motivation, school engagement, homework, bonding to school, reading for pleasure
>   - *Positive Values:* Caring, equality and social justice, integrity, honesty, responsibility, restraint
>   - *Social Competencies:* Planning and decision making, interpersonal competence, cultural competence, resistance skills, peaceful conflict resolution
>   - *Positive Identity:* Personal power, self-esteem, sense of purpose, positive view of personal future

We were not meant to stand alone. We need to belong-to something or someone. Only where there is mutual commitment will you find people prepared to deny themselves for the good of others... Loneliness may be the real disease of the next century [sic.], as we live alone, work alone, and play alone, insulated by our modem, our walkman, or our television.

Charles Handy

The Search Institute's developmental assets focus on providing services that enhance the resiliency, competency, and empowerment of youth. Many of these assets may be addressed proactively through leisure, recreation, and park services, as illustrated in the following examples:

- Provide leisure education programs designed to
  - Build self-awareness
  - Enhance leisure awareness
  - Clarify values
  - Increase social competencies
  - Develop a positive identity
- Inform youth and their families of asset-building leisure programs and resources available in their neighborhoods. If no resources exist, develop services specifically designed to strengthen developmental assets.
- Encourage youth to participate in community recreation activities that build confidence, leisure competencies, and the constructive use of free time.
- Develop teen leadership programs that provide youth with mentors and opportunities to develop a sense of empowerment and optimism for a bright future.

Problem solving of this nature takes a positive, proactive approach to youth development that involves—and strengthens—the assets of the entire community.

PRINCIPLE 6: Build a sense of community

No one really knows enough to be a pessimist.

Norman Cousins

Many of the ideas contained in the previous principles are summed up by this guideline—to build a sense of community. A study described by Ray and Anderson (2000), authors of *The Cultural Creatives: How 50 Million People Are Changing the World*, reports that 83 percent of Americans believe that the top priority of this country should be to rebuild community.

Ray and Anderson (2000) note that the word community is derived from the Latin words, cum munere. Cum means "among each other," and munere means "to give." Therefore, community translates as "to give among each other." A community, in which people give among each other, provides a solid basis for problem solving. The organization that values and nourishes relationships will be committed to work out differences and move beyond them.

PRINCIPLE 7: Recognize change as opportunity

Fear is a natural response to change. The organization that views change as opportunity, however, holds tremendous advantage. Change allows community members to join together and re-commit themselves to—or, if necessary, amend—the organization's values, vision, and mission. They may reassess what is important to them. They may build upon the hidden strengths of their people and resources. They may experiment with innovative practices that can breathe new life into the organization.

Implicit in this principle is an attitude of optimism. Pessimism perpetuates an attitude of learned helplessness and fatalism within an organization, while enthusiasm is contagious and encourages optimistic thinking (Dinkmeyer & Eckstein, 1999). See the section, Change as Opportunity, in Chapter 6 for a continued discussion of these ideas.

Leadership to Support Inclusive Organizations

We live by encouragement and we die without it, slowly, sadly, and angrily.

Celeste Holme

Administrative leaders set the tone for the prevailing culture and climate of an organization. Many books have been written about leadership and organizational management. For the purposes of this chapter, we close with some thoughts taken from Don Dinkmeyer and Daniel Eckstein (1996) in their book *Leadership by Encouragement*. Their thoughts on leadership integrate many of the concepts in this chapter related to cultivating an organizational culture and climate that is inclusive and participatory—the "inverted pyramid" model, if you will. Their thoughts also suit the profession of leisure, recreation, and park services, which serves many kinds of people across diverse communities.

As the name of their book implies, Dinkmeyer and Eckstein (1996) propose a model in which administrators serve as encouragers. They quote *Webster's Dictionary* for the definition of encouragement, "the act of inspiring others with renewed courage, renewed spirit, or renewed hope" (p. 1). The essence of "leader as encourager" is presented in Table 4.9.

Table 4.9 **The Essence of the Encouraging Leader (Dinkmeyer & Eckstein, 1996)**
Encouraging Leaders = Encouraged Employees = An Encouraged Organization = Appreciated Customers

Good management is largely a matter of love. Or if you're uncomfortable with that word, call it caring, because proper management involves caring for people, not manipulating them.

James Autry

Discouragement, Dinkmeyer and Eckstein (1999) observe, occurs when circumstances involve "high standards, expectations of perfection, feelings of inadequacy, and doubt in one's abilities" (p. 8). Encouragement, on the other hand, gives people courage and enhances their self-acceptance and self-esteem. When encouraged, people are motivated and empowered to draw upon their own abilities and resources to find solutions. They take risks. They are energized and move forward with a spirit of optimism. According to the authors (p. 8), encouraging leaders

1. See situations as challenges and opportunities instead of problems
2. Identify the positive potential in every person and every situation
3. Respect and value uniqueness and individual differences
4. Communicate recognition of individual movement, progress, and contributions
5. Communicate openly and honestly
6. See themselves as equal to others in worth and dignity and therefore treat bosses, colleagues, and subordinates as equal participants in the process
7. Provide positive performance reviews
8. Communicate in a language of equality through collaboration, cooperation, agreement, and win-win relationships
9. Facilitate open communication of short- and long-term company goals or mission statements
10. Are committed to giving and receiving feedback

The encouraging organization, led by the encouraging leader, exemplifies the seven organizational principles presented in this chapter. The organization is built upon trust and open communication. A horizontal rather than a vertical hierarchy encourages input at all levels. Employees are empowered to pursue a shared vision. Teams are identified rather than individuals. Group members believe in and practice equality.

Bibliography

Aguilar, L. (2000). Customer service in a culturally diverse world. In M. T. Allison & I. E. Schneider (Eds.), *Diversity and the recreation profession: Organizational perspectives* (pp. 197-205). State College, PA: Venture Publishing.

Allison, M. T., & Schneider, I. E. (2000). *Diversity and the recreation profession: Organizational perspectives.* State College, PA: Venture Publishing.

Barry, B. W. (2001). *Strategic planning workbook for nonprofit organizations.* St. Paul, MN: Amherst H. Wilder Foundation.

Bolman, L. G., & Deal, T. E. (1997). *Reframing organizations: Artistry, choice, and leadership* (2nd ed.). San Francisco: Jossey-Bass Publishers.

Bruno, G. (1995). *The process analysis workbook for government.* Milwaukee, WI: ASQC Quality Press.

Cooperrider, D. L., & Srivastva, S. (1987). Appreciative inquiry in organizational life. In R. W. Woodman & W. A. Pasmore (Eds.), *Research in organizational change and development* (Vol. 1, pp. 129-169). Greenwich, CT: JAI.

Cummings, T. G., & Worley, C. G. (2001). *Organizational development and change* (7th ed.). Mason, OH: South-Western College Publishing.

Dinkmeyer, D., & Eckstein, D. (1996). *Leadership by encouragement.* Delray Beach, FL: St. Lucie Press.

Gilbertson, B., & Ramchandani, V. (1999). *Developing effective teams: Proven methods for smoother and more productive teamwork.* St. Paul, MN: Amherst H. Wilder Foundation.

Greenleaf, R. (1977). *Servant leadership: A journey into the nature of legitimate power and greatness.* New York: Paulist Press.

Hammond, S. A. (1996). *The thin book of appreciative inquiry.* Plano, TX: Thin Book Publishing.

Krause, R. G., & Curtis, J. E. (2000). *Creative management in recreation, parks, and leisure services.* Boston: McGraw-Hill Higher Education.

Kretzmann, J. P., & McKnight, J. L. (1993). *Building communities from the inside out: A path toward finding and mobilizing a community's assets.* Evanston, IL: The Asset-Based Community Development Institute.

Lumsden, G., & Lumsden, D. (2000). *Communicating in groups and teams: Sharing leadership.* Belmont, CA: Wadsworth/Thomson Learning.

Napier, R., Sidle, C., & Sanaghan, P. (1998). *High-impact tools and activities for strategic planning: Creative techniques for facilitating your organization's planning process.* New York: McGraw-Hill.

Enthusiasm is contagious. It's difficult to remain neutral or indifferent in the presence of a positive thinker.

Denis Waitley and
Remi Witt

Office of Human Resource Development. (1993). *Project team training: Course outline.* Division of Management Support and Quality Improvement. New York State School of Industrial and Labor Relations, Ithaca, NY.

Parker, M. (1990). *Creating shared vision.* Clarendon Hills, IL: Dialogue International Ltd.

Ray, P. H., & Anderson, S. R. (2000). *The cultural creatives: How 50 million people are changing the world.* New York: Harmony Books.

Schein, E. H. (2000). Sense and nonsense about culture and climate. In N. M. Ashkanasy, C. P. M. Wilderom, & M. F. Peterson (Eds.), *Handbook of organizational culture and climate* (pp. xxiii-xxx). Thousand Oaks, CA: Sage Publications.

Topping, P. A. (2002). *Managerial leadership.* New York: McGraw-Hill.

PROBLEM SOLVING IN A CONTEXT OF CHANGE

Most individuals seek familiarity, consistency, and some degree of predictability, both within their home life and within their work environment. A certain level of comfort and regularity is essential for people to maintain a sense of psychological equilibrium to function effectively in their lives. Even in dysfunctional situations that are personally harmful, people sometimes prefer the comfort of familiar, predictable circumstances to venturing into an uncertain, though potentially liberating, future (Topping, 2002). Consider the words of Pogo, the comic strip character created by Walt Kelly,

The certainty of misery is better than the misery of uncertainty.

There's nothing constant in the world, all ebb and flow, and every shape that's born bears in its womb the seeds of change.

Ovid

Change may be difficult on many fronts, and the personal response to change by community members, participants, employees, and administrators is key to addressing issues of change within leisure, recreation, and park services.

Despite the human need for homeostasis, in today's world, change is the constant. Change is a relentless force both within and outside an agency, continually shaping and reshaping the organizational culture and climate (Topping, 2002). The impact of change has long been a concern of leisure, recreation, and park administrators and, with recent technological advances and the fast pace of modern living, this issue has taken center stage. Planning, delivering, and evaluating programs is challenging in itself—add to the mix the sensation that the ground is continually shifting under one's feet, and the difficulty of arriving at sound solutions to organizational dilemmas is compounded considerably.

Change, in its simplest form, is something different in an environment from that which was previously perceived. Change may be positive or negative, simple or complex, mild or radical. Change may evolve naturally, or it may be intentionally initiated. Change may solve problems or it may create them. Change can challenge the ability of community members to communicate, test the organization's aptitude to reach satisfactory solutions to problems, and confront the overall resiliency of an organization.

Responses to change vary, of course, from individual to individual, from culture to culture. Change may be viewed as an unfriendly, negative force that gives rise to fear, resistance, and stymied thoughts and feelings; or, at the opposite end of the spectrum, change may be viewed as an opportunity to breathe new life and spirit into an organization. Let us look first at the resistive responses to change within an organization and how administrative leaders might address them.

Resistance to Change and Problem Solving

You must be the change you want to see in the world.

Mohandas Gandhi

Resistance to change, which can take many forms to block an organization's ability to problem solve, is evident in almost any workplace. If we, as administrators or future administrators, are aware of and understand resistive responses, we can better recognize them when they occur, acknowledge underlying concerns and fears, and work with people to move the organization forward.

Topping (2002) explains why people resist change within organizations and recommends techniques that managers can use to respond in each instance. The following resistant patterns, summarized in Table 5.1, and suggestions for handling them, are adapted from Topping's work.

Table 5.1
Resistance to Change: Six Common Patterns

1. Fear of the unknown
2. Fear of failure
3. Not understanding the need for change
4. Disagreement with the need for change
5. Losing something of value
6. Inertia

Fear of the Unknown

Change, as noted earlier in this chapter, is often accompanied by an element of uncertainty. When people are unsure what to expect and what life will be like for them after a change is instigated, they may become anxious, stressed, and fearful of the future. Resistance is a natural coping mechanism to reduce one's anxiety about an unknown and uncertain future.

Managerial response: Acknowledge the individual's feelings and concerns, and attempt to shift the person's fearful reaction to an orientation that envisions an optimistic future. Explain why the change is needed, and articulate the vision that will lead the agency or unit in a positive new direction. As the person understands the reality of the negative consequences of maintaining the status quo, he or she can begin to move toward accepting the different path. Describe, in as much detail as is needed, how the proposed changes will lead to a positive future for the agency, its employees, and its constituencies.

Fear of Failure

People who function competently in an existing culture and climate may worry they lack the necessary skills to perform well in a new and different order. Consider, for example, the advent of word processing to replace traditional typing and how, at the time, some administrative assistants resisted using computers.

Managerial response: Change requires new learning. People may be asked to learn new procedures, to operate new equipment, to adapt to a new location, or even to assume an entirely new role within an organization. In these instances, encourage employees as they tackle new learning and support them as they work their way through the learning curve. Steady encouragement will build people's confidence in their capacity to adapt, learn, change, and grow. As people acquire new skills and competencies, point out their accomplishments. Recognition and praise ease the fear of failing and reaffirm people's sense of self-efficacy to learn new skills and handle new situations.

Not Understanding the Need for Change

If an organization is experiencing success on some levels, employees may not perceive a need for change. The attitude, "If it ain't broke, don't fix it," may prevail. This form of resistance is most common in organizations that make decisions at the executive and board levels, with little or no input from individuals who work at other levels.

Managerial response: This type of resistance is minimized, of course, when people who are involved in all capacities of the organization are consulted in the decisions an organization makes. When an "executive decision" is warranted, however, communication is a key factor. Face-to-face communication from top administrators is almost always meaningful to employees. Personal communication also reduces the possibility that the message will become distorted as it is passed along the supervisory chain of command.

Try to understand how people will hear your message, and communicate in ways that match people's different communication styles. For example, appeal to people's reason by identifying and analyzing the problem, presenting the advantages and disadvantages of the proposed change, and providing a logical rationale for the change. Also remember to appeal to people's emotions by connecting the change to the agency's underlying values and convictions.

Disagreement with the Need for Change

People may understand the need for change; however, they may think the proposed solution is the wrong one. This form of resistance often occurs when an organization sets in motion frequent new initiatives that are ill conceived, poorly implemented, and for which buy-in has not been established adequately. These practices tend to lead to skepticism among employees, as they react to what appears to be the latest fad in organizational management. In these cases, people tend to develop an attitude that "this too shall pass," blocking their openness to investing in new ideas that actually might work.

Managerial response: Aside from making certain the proposed initiative is the wise solution to a problem and asking for people's input along the way, the key to addressing this form of organizational resistance is listening to people. Give people an opportunity

Out of every crisis comes the chance to be reborn, to reconceive ourselves as individuals, to choose the kind of change that will help us to grow and to fulfill ourselves more completely.

Nena O'Neill

to express their opinions and acknowledge that their views are important. Listening empathetically builds trust and sends the message that administrators care about the people in an organization and what they think. Listening to others is time-consuming and may slow down the change process, yet it can also yield valuable information that may be incorporated into how change is implemented.

Sometimes an administrator may listen to a person's views and communicate the advantages of the proposed initiative, yet the person persists in disagreeing with the need for change. In these instances, as a last resort, gently point out that the person's support is required to move the organization forward and, if he or she cannot provide it, the person may need to look for a more compatible organization.

Losing Something of Value

If people believe they have something to lose personally from change, they will naturally resist as a form of self-protection. Change could imply that a person will lose a familiar work setting, schedule, structure, co-worker, supervisor, role, or responsibility. A person may lose a portion of his or her salary. He or she may lose a position of rank or power. The larger the perceived loss, the greater the resistance a person is likely to feel.

Managerial response: Be honest about the situation. If no real risk of loss is imminent, then assuage people's fears. If, on the other hand, a person does stand to lose something of value in the transition, it is important to tell him or her so. Identify what is being lost: Is it power, position, responsibility, money, security? Ascertain the person's sense of the loss, and acknowledge it. Then encourage her or him to shift from focusing on the loss to seeing what might be gained by engaging positively in the change process.

Listen or your tongue will make you deaf.
Native American
Proverb

For example, Topping (2002) describes the transition supervisors were required to make in an agency that moved from a traditional model of authoritative decision making to a model of teamwork and cooperation. After working their way up the organizational ladder by following orders from their bosses, the new supervisors perceived they were not really needed, saw the change as a ploy to get them to quit, and had no idea how to be effective team leaders. As this situation was investigated more deeply, the supervisors expressed their concerns, managers listened, and ultimately training was provided to build the supervisors' skills in managing teams and facilitating team decisions. The supervisors indeed lost a familiar role, but they also gained by developing a new perspective within an organization that emphasized communication, cooperation, and the notion that everyone's contribution counted.

Inertia

We all have a personal threshold for the amount of change we can withstand. A person may understand the need for change and see the potential gain of moving in a new direction but lack the energy to become enthused, invested, and involved in the change process. Change takes tremendous effort, intellectually and emotionally. Whether a person is tired, burned out, or feeling drained from external demands, fatigue may take over and manifest itself as resistance to change.

Managerial response: External factors often contribute to a person's sense of inertia, which may be beyond a manager's influence and control. A manager who energetically shows his or her enthusiasm for a new initiative, however, can open the pathway for others to get on board. If administrators do not openly express their support for change, employees cannot be expected to show much interest or commitment either. Employees learn from a manager's example, and a positive attitude can go a long way toward motivating and energizing others.

Change as Opportunity

An administrator's empathetic response to people's resistance to change is instrumental in reshaping how employees and constituents perceive change. While change may justifiably bring about feelings of fear and uncertainty, change may also be viewed as an opportunity for personal and organizational growth. That is, change, formerly viewed as a threat, may be reframed as opportunity—an opportunity to renew and revitalize an organization.

Even times of extreme upheaval and stress can be turned into situations where people's strengths and assets are cultivated, nurtured, and redirected to contribute to a new order or realize a new vision. In fact, change is essential to sustain a dynamic, vital organization. Change presents organizations with opportunities to

- Clarify what is important to the organization
- Strengthen people's commitment to the agency's values, vision, and mission
- Identify individuals' strengths, which may have been underutilized
- Clarify people's points of view and beliefs
- Encourage dialogue about the important issues facing the organization
- Empower people to invest in rebuilding the future of the organization
- Reenergize an organization

Optimally, administrators will be on the watch for internal and external forces that impact the organization and make whatever small adjustments are needed along the way to maintain a healthy organizational culture and climate. As in personal relationships, if the small adjustments are neglected, they tend to accumulate over time. The emotional and psychological confusion that accompanies neglected problems can lead to misunderstanding, resistance, and conflict within the organization, often requiring radical changes to correct them, which is felt on many levels. Sometimes needed changes are ignored to the point that the agency nearly breaks apart—employees leave, the agency develops a bad reputation, participants seek services elsewhere, funding is lost. Even in these situations, however, great op-

Example is leadership.

Albert Schweitzer

When nothing is sure, everything is possible.

Margaret Drabble

portunity exists to rebuild an organization around strongly felt values, assets, and the strengths of the people within the organization to impact communities in positive ways.

The things we fear most in organizations—fluctuations, disturbances, imbalances—are the primary sources of creativity.

Margaret J. Wheatly

Bibliography

Dinkmeyer, D., & Eckstein, D. (1996). *Leadership by encouragement*. Delray Beach, FL: St. Lucie Press.

Schein, E. H. (2000). Sense and nonsense about culture and climate. In N. M. Ashkanasy, C. P. M. Wilderom, & M. F. Peterson (Eds.), *Handbook of organizational culture and climate* (pp. xxiii-xxx). Thousand Oaks, CA: Sage Publications.

Topping, P. A. (2002). *Managerial leadership*. New York: McGraw-Hill.

CHAPTER SIX

FACILITATING CREATIVE THINKING

What Contributes to Creativity?

As the importance of creativity to organizations becomes more apparent, the question becomes "Can creativity be increased in this organization?" Most creativity specialists today believe that creativity is not a special activity of which only some individuals are capable. In fact, creativity is considered to be a common cognitive process and one that can be enhanced through training. Csikzentmihalyi (1996) offers a number of ways to enhance one's personal creativity, including cultivating curiosity and interest, cultivating flow, developing habits of strength, and developing personal traits. These are described further in Table 6.1.

Table 6.1
Enhancing Personal Creativity (Csikszentmihalyi, 1996)

Cultivate Curiosity and Interest
- Seek to be surprised every day
- Surprise someone every day
- Keep a daily diary of what surprised you and how you surprised someone
- When something sparks your interest, pursue it

Cultivate Flow
- Start each day with a specific goal
- Match your skills to the challenge of the activity
- Increase the complexity of the activity

Develop Habits of Strength
- Control your schedule
- Allow time for reflection and relaxation
- Make day-to-day experiences more vivid and enjoyable
- Create an environment pleasing to you
- Identify your likes and dislikes
- Engage in more of what you like and less of what you dislike

Develop Personal Traits
- Strengthen the personal traits that you lack
- Shift your perspective back and forth from open and receptive to focused and hard driving
- Aim for a complex personality

Enhancing Personal Creativity

Csikszenmihalyi suggested ways in which individuals could enhance their personal creativity. Amabile (1998) has identified three components of creativity that have great relevance to the facilitation of creativity among organizational employees. These three factors—motivation, expertise, and creative thinking skills—determine the ability of individuals to be creative. All of these factors can be enhanced among the employees within an organization.

Motivation. An individual's level of motivation may be the most significant component of creativity. People who are intrinsically motivated are excited and engaged by the challenge of the problem and the work itself. They invest freely in the process and are committed to the task at hand. As a result of extensive research, Amabile has found that intrinsic motivation is central to creativity. She summarizes this work (1990):

> We find our results sufficiently compelling that we now refer to the intrinsic motivation principle of creativity: Intrinsic motivation is conducive to creativity, but extrinsic motivation is detrimental. In other words, people will be most creative when they feel motivated primarily by the interest, enjoyment, satisfaction, and challenge of the work itself-and not by external pressures (p. 65).

Csikszentmihalyi (1996) supports this connection between creativity and intrinsic motivation. He suggests that individuals who enjoy engaging in problem solving for its own rewards will persevere and thus have a higher probability of developing creative solutions.

Intrinsic motivation occurs in contexts in which individuals experience self-determination and perceive themselves to be competent (Deci & Ryan, 1985). Individuals are also intrinsically motivated to be in relationships with others (Deci, 1975). In some situations, extrinsic rewards are detrimental to intrinsic motivation (Deci & Flaste, 1995). There have been research results that have supported the perspective that extrinsic rewards have a negative effect on intrinsic motivation in the workplace and those that have refuted these findings. It has been suggested that intrinsic motivation and extrinsic rewards interact in a complex fashion that is not yet fully understood (Hennessey, 2000).

What is becoming clear is that any reward that undermines self-determination will reduce intrinsic motivation. Intrinsic motivation will be undermined by external rewards or conditions that are used to manipulate, control, constrain, or even motivate employee behavior. External rewards that are perceived by individuals as bonuses, rather than coercive management techniques, can serve to increase involvement in the creative process (Hennessey, 2000). Creativity will flourish in an environment that promotes free and autonomous engagement and choice. Likewise, any external reward that reduces the perception of competence will reduce intrinsic motivation. Although rewards that are provided in a group context may reinforce the perceived competence of the "winner," they can just as significantly undermine the perceived competence of those who do not come in "first." For example, although an external reward structure may enhance the intrinsic motivation of the "most creative," by enhancing their perception of competence, the social comparison may close down the creativity of those who believe themselves to be less capable.

Expertise. Although intrinsically motivated employees may want to engage in the problem solving initiative, if they do not have the expertise or tools, the creative undertaking will not be effective. In an organization, expertise refers to the level of work-related knowledge an individual possesses. Expertise encompasses the technical procedural and intellectual elements of the job and the organization. This expertise is captured in the job specifications listed within the employees' job descriptions. Job specifications describe the knowledge, skills, abilities and other characteristics (KSAO) that enable an individual to carry out those tasks (Byars & Rue, 2001).

Knowledge consists of a body of information (conceptual, factual, and procedural) that is required to perform work tasks. Skill refers to an observable competence to perform a particular task or closely related set of tasks. Ability is an underlying capacity to perform a task. Other characteristics include factors that do not fit neatly into the previous categories, such as certification requirements or personality characteristics. Certifications identify the minimum competencies of leisure services professionals or other specialized employees.

An individual who possesses the necessary KSAOs has foundational expertise. However, not all individuals with foundational expertise can contribute creatively. Most problems and attempts at creative solutions involve complex situations and information. Individuals who can engage in higher levels of complex thinking may offer more creative benefits. Bloom (1956) has offered one of the most widely used and respected hierarchical taxonomies of cognitive ability. The taxonomy consists of six levels starting at the least complex and moving to the most complex. At the highest level of complexity is synthesis and evaluation. Synthesis is the ability to integrate and combine information to form new ideas. Evaluation is the ability to judge the value of these new ideas and their potential for practical implementation. Synthesis and evaluation are critical skills in creativity and problem solving.

The evidence is clear that individuals will most enthusiastically approach tasks or situations that they value and in which they feel capable of succeeding or are self-efficacious (Bandura, 1997). Individuals will most readily engage in the creative process if they believe that they have the expertise necessary to solve the problem or successfully address a challenge. Individuals can gain confidence in their own ability by previous mastery experiences, viewing the success of other people perceived to be similar to themselves, or the verbal support and encouragement of others. In order to engage in the creative process, individuals require the knowledge and skills necessary to be effective and a belief in their ability to apply that knowledge and skill to the accomplishment of the task at hand.

Motivation is everything. You can do the work of two people, but you can't be two people. Instead, you have to inspire the next guy down the line and get him to inspire his people.

Lee Iacocca

Creative thinking skills. Creative thinking skills shape the way individuals approach problems. Key creative thinking skills include flexibility, imagination, perseverance, and the ability to reflect or incubate on a problem over time. Flexibility alludes to an individual's ability to process information from multiple perspectives fluidly. Imagination refers to the ability to see, in one's mind's eye, alternative realities. Perseverance is required to stay with a challenging and complex process and task. The ability to reflect or incubate on a problem over time, without prematurely foreclosing on a solution, is also an important creativity skill, and it requires a supportive environment.

The use of processes and techniques to promote creative thinking within organizations is becoming more common. Chapter 7 presents specific techniques, such as brainstorming and nominal group technique, that are widely used as a backdrop to encourage creative problem solving.

Stages of Creativity

A number of models have articulated the stages that individuals actually go through in the creative process. While they are not in complete agreement, many of the models are similar and involve a four- or five-step process. Amabile and Tighe (1993) developed a model that is representative of much of the thinking by fellow researchers. Their model consists of four stages and is depicted in Figure 6.1. While the creative process is presented in linear fashion, individuals move back and forth between the stages as necessary to clarify the problem, gather additional information, and generate and test ideas and solutions. The authors have also linked the stages in the creative process to the three components of creativity—intrinsic motivation, expertise, and creative thinking skills.

Stage 1: Problem presentation. As the first stage in the creative process, problem presentation places creativity in the context of an organization. In organizations, individuals and groups are often presented with problems to solve in addition to deciding to take on a problem that presents itself. Intrinsic motivation is critical to the problem presentation phase of creativity. Those who are intrinsically motivated will be more enthusiastic and receptive to attacking the problem. Involving them in the identification of the problem initially and letting them know that they are valued members of the problem solving team will increase their intrinsic motivation.

Stage 2: Preparation. In the preparation phase of the creative process, individuals gather the necessary information and resources to engage the problem. Preparation is heavily dependent on the expertise of the individual. The more expertise and competence the individual has related to the problem, the better prepared he or she will be.

> *The very essence of the creative is its novelty, and hence we have no standard by which to judge it.*
>
> Carl R. Rogers

Figure 6.1
The Stages of Creativity

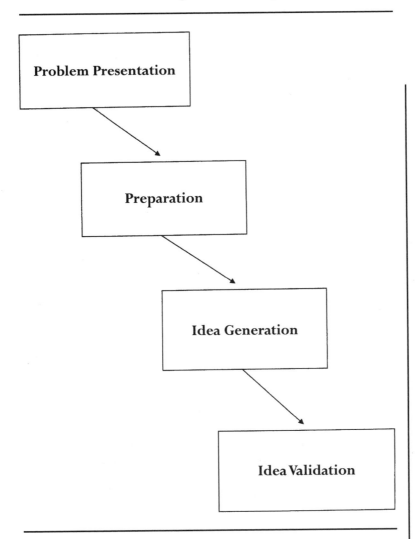

Problem Presentation

Preparation

Idea Generation

Idea Validation

Stage 3: Idea generation. Individuals in this phase of the creative process generate ideas that may be useful in solving the problem. Ideas are more likely to be creative if the individual has strong creative thinking skills as well as a high level of intrinsic motivation.

Stage 4: Idea validation. In the final stage of the creative process, individuals validate their ideas against criteria. Validation provides a means of sorting out the best creative ideas that may be successfully applied to the problem. The level of an individual's expertise dictates his ability to effectively validate ideas and determine the most salient problem solutions.

The four-stage model provides the link between the creative process and the factors that contribute to one's creative ability. Clearly, each of the creativity factors, intrinsic motivation, expertise, and creative thinking skills are important in the creative process. As mentioned earlier, intrinsic motivation may be the most important factor in creativity. Amabile (1997) suggests that to some extent intrinsic motivation can ameliorate deficiencies that an individual may have in expertise and creative thinking skills.

Bibliography

Amabile, T. M. (1990). Within you, without you: The social psychology of creativity and beyond. In M. A. Runco & R. S. Albert (Eds.), *Theories of creativity* (pp. 61-91). Newbury Park, CA: Sage.

Amabile, T. M. (1996). *Creativity in context: Update to the social psychology of creativity.* Boulder, CO: Westview Press.

Amabile, T. M. (1997). Motivating creativity in organizations: On doing what you love and loving what you do. *California Management Review, 40*(1), 39-58.

Amabile, T. M. (1998). How to kill creativity. *Harvard Business Review, 76*(5), 76-89.

Bandura, A. (1997). *Self-efficacy: The exercise of control.* New York: W. H. Freeman.

Bloom, B. S. (1956). *Taxonomy of educational objectives.* New York: Longman.

Byars, L. L., & Rue, L. W. (2001). *Human resource management* (6th ed.). New York: McGraw-Hill.

Csikszentmihalyi, M. (1996). *Creativity: Flow and the psychology of discovery and invention.* New York: Harper Collins.

Deci, E. L. (1975). *Intrinsic motivation.* New York: Plenum.

Deci, E. L., & Flaste, R. (1995). *Why we do what we do: The dynamics of personal autonomy.* New York: Grosset/Putnam.

Deci, E. L., & Ryan, R. M. (1985). *Intrinsic motivation and self-determination in human behavior.* New York: Plenum.

Hennessey, B. A. (2000). Rewards and creativity. In C. Sansone & J. M. Harackiewicz (Eds.), *Intrinsic and extrinsic motivation: The search for optimal motivation and performance* (pp. 57-78). San Diego, CA: Academic Press.

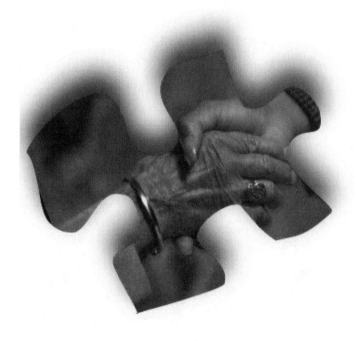

CHAPTER SEVEN

PROBLEM SOLVING APPROACHES AND TECHNIQUES

This chapter discusses various approaches and techniques often used to solve problems. The techniques included in this chapter are brainstorming, nominal group technique, focus groups, role play, mathematical models, fishbone diagrams, and decision trees (see Table 7.1). Related approaches for conflict resolution and mediation may be found in Chapter 8. Creative thinking, which was addressed in Chapter 6, is an important component of the problem solving process. This section will highlight several techniques that may stimulate ideas and potential solutions to the problem under investigation.

Brainstorming

Osborn (1963) developed the technique of organized ideation in 1938 while employed as an advertising executive. Participants involved in Osborn's organized ideation meetings quickly coined the phrase "brainstorm session," reflecting the application of the brain to storm a problem. Brainstorming is perhaps the most widely known and utilized group technique for generating creative ideas that lead to problem solutions. For example, at IDEO, a leading product design and development firm, brainstorming is a practice that employees engage in almost every day as shown in the following excerpt (Kelly, 2001):

> Brainstorming is the idea engine of IDEO's culture. It's an opportunity for teams to "blue sky" ideas early in a project or to solve a tricky problem that's cropped up later on. The more productive the group, the more it brainstorms regularly and effectively. We call the sessions "brainstormers," which to us sounds more like an active, engaging event. The buzz of a good brainstormer can infect a team with optimism and a sense of opportunity that can carry it through the darkest and most pressure-tinged stages of a project (p. 56).

Brainstorming is a method of enhancing creative thought through divergent thinking. The goal of a brainstorming session is to generate as many ideas as possible that may serve as potential problem solutions. There are two important principles of brainstorming. First, ideas are generated with deferred judgment. That is, group members may not criticize an idea when it is presented. The underlying premise of deferred judgment is that individuals are more creative in a group if they are sure that their ideas will not be attacked or criticized. Second, it is desirable to generate as many ideas as possible. This principle rests on the premise that quantity breeds quality. That is, the more ideas that are generated during a brainstorming session, the higher the likelihood that some of the ideas will be valuable (Vreede, Briggs, Duin, & Enserink, 2000).

Table 7.1
Problem Solving Techniques

TECHNIQUE	DESCRIPTION	PURPOSE	OVERVIEW	WHEN TO USE
Brainstorming	Brainstorming is the rapid pooling of all and any ideas that a group of people can come up with before any discussion or judgment takes place.	To allow members of a group equal opportunity to generate ideas and then determine which idea(s) best solves the problem.	Leader poses question to group or defines the problem. Group offers possible solutions or ideas without being evaluated or judged. Evaluation of ideas takes place to find solution(s) to the problem.	Brainstorming works best when you have a larger group (6 to 12) of varied people. Use this technique when a variety of creative ideas are needed and you want people to build off one another s ideas.
Nominal Group Technique (NGT)	NGT is a structured meeting that identifies and ranks the major problems or issues affecting the group. Individuals work alone yet in a group setting.	To allow a group of individuals to come to a decision when a consensus is not possible. NGT is used to get balanced participation from group members, or to get the group unstuck during the decision making process.	The group silently generates ideas and writes them down. A round-robin feedback session takes place to concisely record ideas. Each idea is discussed, clarified, and evaluated. Individuals then vote privately on the priority of the ideas, and a group decision is made based upon the ratings.	This technique takes advantage of pooled judgments. Thus, the ideas of a variety of people with varied talents, knowledge, and skills will be used together. NGT reduces the conforming influence common to most face-to-face group meetings.

Continued

Table 7.1 Continued
Problem Solving Techniques

TECHNIQUE	DESCRIPTION	PURPOSE	OVERVIEW	WHEN TO USE
Focus Groups	Focus groups are carefully planned discussions designed to obtain people s perceptions on a particular topic (Krueger & Casey, 2000).	To understand what people think and feel about a particular issue, service, program, or product.	A skilled moderator conducts a series of focus group interviews using pre-determined questions. Each focus group includes 5 to 10 participants who share common attributes but may have differing viewpoints.	Focus groups may be used to assess needs, improve service quality, or gather input before, during, or after programs. They may also be used to identify problems, generate solutions, or for strategic planning and marketing purposes.
Role Playing	Role playing requires individuals to act out the problems.	To integrate the distinction between thinking and doing, and to develop sensitivity to the feelings of others.	Generally there are two forms of role playing: (a) multiple-group (everyone participates), and (b) single-group (one group acts while the remaining people observe). When role playing ends, all members participate in discussion.	Use multiple-group role playing when the leader wants everyone to participate and when the objective does not focus on sensitivity to others; use single-group role playing when the objective is to increase sensitivity to the feelings of others.

Continued

Table 7.1 Continued
Problem Solving Techniques

TECHNIQUE	DESCRIPTION	PURPOSE	OVERVIEW	WHEN TO USE
Mathematical Model	Mathematical models use equations to describe the real, physical world.	To create a mathematical representation of some phenomenon in order to gain a better understanding of that phenomenon.	When modeling, the goal is to find an equation that reflects the real behavior of a system and that is simple enough so that it can be solved or approximated in a reasonable amount of time and effort.	Use the theoretical model to predict how a system will behave when experimenting in the real world is unfeasible (e.g., fish population).
Fishbone Diagram	The fishbone technique, also known as "cause-and-effect diagramming," focuses on the causes and effects of a given problem. This is one of the most widely used tools of quality control in the world today.	To permit the group to speculate on the root causes of a problem, explore a wide variety of causes, and roadmap what must happen to get a desired effect.	Select an effect to study and enter the effect in a block on the right side of the diagram (the fish head). The backbones and ribs are designed to demonstrate the causes which will be used to determine the roadmap to achieve the desired effect.	The fishbone technique is used to determine the causes of a problem by using a visual (fishbone diagram) to see the desired steps needed to achieve an effect.

Continued

Table 7.1 Continued
Problem Solving Techniques

TECHNIQUE	DESCRIPTION	PURPOSE	OVERVIEW	WHEN TO USE
Decision Tree	Decision trees are highly effective structures within which you can lay out options and investigate the possible outcomes of choosing those options.	To provide an effective structure in which alternative decisions and the implication of taking those decisions can be laid down and evaluated. To provide a balanced picture (visual) of the risks and rewards that can result from a particular choice.	Start with a decision that needs to be made and write it in a box. From the box, draw out lines to indicate solutions; consider the results for each solution in order to determine the best option.	Use decision trees when you need to choose between several courses of action, or when you need to make financial or number-based decisions where a lot of complex information needs to be taken into account.

Brainstorming sessions consist of approximately 6 to 12 employees who are at the same level in the organizational hierarchy. The session begins with the leader presenting the problem statement, as simply and specifically as possible. This is followed by group members contributing anything that comes to mind as a possible solution to the problem. The brainstorming approach by Osborn (1963) requires facilitation by a group leader. The leader explains the guidelines for participant involvement in the brainstorming session, ensures that each group member adheres to the guidelines, and keeps them focused on the task. Osborn developed guidelines for conducting a group brainstorming session:

Analysis kills spontaneity. The grain once ground into flour germinates no more.

Henri Amiel

1. *Critical judgment is ruled out.* Most adults think critically rather than creatively due to their education and experience. As a result, they tend to impede the fluency of ideas by applying their critical power too soon. By deferring judgment during the idea generation stage, it is possible to unleash creativity and to generate substantially more and better ideas. Although open criticism and evaluation is not allowed, individuals may very well censor their own ideas before sharing; therefore, while judgment is not completely ruled out, it is minimized.

2. *Free-wheeling is welcomed.* The wilder the ideas, the better for creative thinking; it is easier to tone down than to think up.

3. *Combination and improvement are sought.* In addition to contributing ideas, participants are urged to suggest how the ideas of others and their own ideas can be turned into better ideas; or how two or more previous ideas can be joined into still another idea.

4. *Keep discussion to a minimum.* There should be very little, if any, discussion during the brainstorming activity. Talking about the ideas will take place after the brainstorming is complete.

5. *Predetermine length of time for the activity.* A fixed amount of time should be announced for the session, and the leader should ensure that no train of thought is followed for too long.

Although brainstorming is considered an informal group process, the above rules are generally followed and reiterated as necessary. Group members are encouraged to piggyback, elaborate, combine other group ideas, and create radically new ideas. The group leader records all ideas that are generated.

Narrowing Down the Ideas

The following process will help to narrow down the ideas generated through brainstorming:

1. Once you have finished brainstorming, go through the results and begin evaluating the responses. Some initial qualities to look for when examining the responses include

> look f or any answers that are repeated or are similar
> gr oup like concepts together
> eliminate r esponses that definitely do not fit
> discuss the r emaining responses as a group

2. Number all ideas left for consideration. Let each member vote on the ideas by making a list of the numbers of the ideas he or she thinks are important or should be discussed further. This list should contain no more than one-third of the total number of ideas.

3. After counting the votes, cross out ideas with only one or two votes. Then vote again until only three or four ideas remain. If there is no clear-cut winner, then vote again or discuss the remaining ideas and determine which idea best answers the original question.

Table 7.2 provides an example of how to use the brainstorming process in a recreational setting (adapted from *The Step-by-Step Guide to Brainstorming* by Baumgartner, 2001).

Table 7.2
EXAMPLE OF THE BRAINSTORMING PROCESS

PROCEDURE	EXAMPLE
STEP ONE: The leader should review the topic of the brainstorm using "why," "how," or "what" questions.	The topic for the brainstorm activity is developing an orientation manual for newly appointed board members of the recreation and parks department. What should we focus on as the content for this training manual?
STEP TWO: Everyone in the group should think about the question silently for a few moments. Each person might want to jot down his or her ideas on a sheet of paper.	The content for the manual may include mission and vision statements, policy and procedures, and the roles and responsibilities of board members.
STEP THREE: Everyone suggests ideas by calling them out. Another way is to go around the room and have each person read an idea from his/her list until all ideas have been expressed.	Rotate around the room so each person may contribute. The leader may make comments such as "Everyone may participate; if you do not have an idea to share I will simply move on to the next person. Remember, there is no right or wrong answer during this activity, and we are not here to discuss your ideas at this time."
STEP FOUR: The leader writes down each idea on a board or flipchart until all ideas have been shared with the group.	To avoid the fear of misspelling a word in front of the group, you may want to joke that "This board comes with an automatic spell-check; therefore, anything I write down is spelled correctly whether it is or not!"

Brainstorming has received a great deal of investigation and, despite the popularity of this creativity-enhancing technique, the research evidence has not supported its use. At issue has been Osborn's contention that brainstorming in a group setting stimulates individuals to produce more ideas than individuals working independently. Some research would conclude just the opposite. For example, Debold (1996) concluded that when the same number of individuals, as comprise a group, work independently and their ideas are pooled (also referred to as a nominal group), individuals produce a greater number of high-quality ideas than the group.

There are several social psychological phenomena at work in the group brainstorming session that contribute to lower productivity in terms of idea generation. According to Vreede, Briggs, Duin, and Enserink (2000), brainstorming leads to synergy that may raise the number of quality of ideas that are generated; however, *production blocking* (participants are unable to share their ideas because someone else is talking), *evaluation apprehension* (individuals who experience anxiety when sharing their ideas in fear of being evaluated on those ideas), and *social loafing* (when individuals reduce their effort in the belief that others will compensate for them) may be counterproductive to idea generation. Ratzburg (2003) explains that when individuals within a group perceive that they can neither receive a fair share of rewards nor the appropriate blame, they frequently hold back and do not contribute to idea generation. Despite the warnings often associated with this technique, brainstorming continues to be one of the most widely used group techniques for generating ideas because it is relatively easy to employ, efficient, and yields beneficial results.

Electronic Brainstorming

The pervasive use of computer technology in the workplace offers the opportunity to utilize electronic brainstorming. Electronic brainstorming has the potential to directly reduce the problems associated with traditional verbal brainstorming such as production blocking, evaluation apprehension, and social loafing. There are two ways to apply computer technology to brainstorming. The first approach is to have individuals generate a list of ideas independently and then pool the results. The second approach is for individuals to be interconnected and to interact with each member of the group (e.g., an internet chat room).

One of the advantages to using electronic brainstorming, via e-mail for example, is that the participants can "dwell on the problem in the comfort and privacy of their desks and even their home" (Siau, 1997, p. 2) thus reducing production blocking. Additionally, electronic brainstorming can directly reduce the problems of social loafing. Social loafing, noted in the previous section, is the phenomenon in which participants who work together often generate less effort than do participants who work alone (Siau, 1997). Thus, the electronic nature of the session requires individuals to participate.

Individuals should always be given feedback on their performance at the conclusion of the brainstorming session (Siau, 1997). In addition, participants should be made aware they will receive feedback prior to the brainstorming. Feedback improves motivation and performance by creating a standard of comparison. Waiting until the conclusion of the brainstorming session to provide feedback creates uncertainty, which keeps people engaged in idea generation.

Brainstorming with Trained Facilitators

Osborn's classic approach to brainstorming incorporated a trained facilitator to assist groups in idea generation. The facilitator's contribution to idea generation has only been investigated in recent years. Offner, Kramer, and Winter (1996) investigated whether a trained facilitator could stimulate group members to produce as many ideas as possible, keeping the group moving forward on the idea generation task while still maintaining order. Their findings indicated that a trained facilitator does contribute to the productivity of brainstorming groups. Specifically, groups with a trained facilitator outperformed groups without a facilitator. In addition, groups with a facilitator produced a comparable number of ideas to nominal groups.

The use of a facilitator was taken a step further in an attempt to decrease the effects of production blocking, social loafing, and evaluation apprehension. Oxley, Dzindolet, and Paulus (1996) trained facilitators to interrupt group members when they strayed from the topic (blocking), to call upon group members who are not participating (loafing), and to remind group members of the "no criticism" rule in brainstorming (evaluation apprehension). The results again found that groups with a trained facilitator were superior to those without a facilitator.

A trained facilitator, therefore, may alleviate the detrimental effects of production blocking, social loafing, and evaluation apprehension during group brainstorming. In addition, a facilitator may contribute to group member satisfaction through the process of interaction. This interaction results in group members developing a higher level of cohesiveness. Perhaps this is the "buzz" that is experienced at IDEO. Kelly (2001) describes what happens after brainstorming, "People talk after brainstormers, sharing wild or practical ideas that may have come out of a particularly vibrant session. A great brainstormer gives you a fantastic feeling of possibility, and an hour later you walk out of the room a little richer for the experience" (p. 62).

Stop thinking in terms of limitations and start thinking in terms of possibilities.

Terry Josephson

HELPFUL INTERNET RESOURCES FOR BRAINSTORMING

Brainstorming (University of Brighton)
http://edweb.sdsu.edu/people/bdodge/scaffold/BS/Brainstorming.html

Brainstorming Guide #1 by Dan MacDowell
http://projects.edtech.sandi.net/staffdev/tpss99/processguides/brainstorming.html

Brainstorming Rules by Alan Levine
http://www.mcli.dist.maricopa.edu/authoring/studio/guidebook/brain.html

The Step-by-Step Guide to *Brainstorming* by Jeffery Baumgartner
http://www.jpb.com/creative/brainstorming.php

Nominal Group Technique (NGT)

Research in group dynamics indicates that more ideas are expressed by individuals working alone, but in a group environment, than by individuals engaged in a formal group discussion (Basden, Basden, & Thomas, 1997). Perhaps this is why the nominal group technique (NGT) remains a very popular problem solving tool. The nominal group technique was developed by Delbecq and Van de Ven (1974). The specific objectives of this process include (a) assuring different processes for creative activity, (b) providing for balanced participation among group members, and (c) incorporating voting techniques to determine overall group judgment. The NGT has been embraced by administrators and planners in developing, revising, and implementing human service programs under complex or particularly challenging circumstances.

There are several benefits and limitations to using NGT, as identified by Dunham (1998).

Benefits of NGT:

1. Balances participation and influences across individuals
2. Produces a greater number of ideas and creative ideas than traditional interacting groups
3. Reduces the conforming influence common to most face-to-face group meetings
4. Encourages participants to confront issues on a problem solving basis rather than on a personal-assault basis
5. Results in greater satisfaction for participants and leads to a greater sense of closure and accomplishment

Limitations of NOT:

1. Requires extended advance preparation, which means that it can not be a spontaneous technique
2. Tends to be limited to a single-purpose, single-topic meeting; it is difficult to change topics in the middle of a meeting
3. Needs agreement from all participants to use the same structured method, which some people might resist

Leading a Nominal Group Technique Session

Once a NGT session begins the first task of the nominal group leader is to welcome the participants and to impress upon them the importance and relevance of the task to be undertaken. It is essential that the leader create an atmosphere in which every member will feel comfortable and motivated to actively participate in the NGT session. Once the members have been introduced to the NGT purpose, the leader follows a series of steps to implement the session. These steps and their benefits are discussed below:

Step 1: Independent Written Generation of Ideas. The purpose of this first step is to generate a large number of ideas or solutions related to the problem statement. The group process begins with the participants brainstorming independently. This serves to reduce competition and the need for conformity, as well as provides the time necessary for reflection.

The group leader presents the problem statement in a question format by both reading it aloud and by providing a written copy of the question to each group member. Working independently, each person generates a list of sentences or phrases that represent his or her ideas or responses to the problem statement. The leader provides time limits, for example 5 minutes, for this step. It is important that the leader curtail interaction or distracting behavior among group members. The leader should also engage in the silent generation of written ideas along with session participants and refrain from providing content-related feedback to participants. The leader should serve as a role model for participants.

Step 2: Round-Robin Recording of Ideas. This step involves writing the responses of group members on a flip chart. Round-robin recording consists of asking sequentially each group member for one response from his or her list. If an individual has the same item on his list as another member, it should not be restated unless the person considers it somehow unique. The leader should encourage "piggybacking," which is the building upon or expanding upon the ideas of other group members, throughout this step. A group member may "pass" on her turn to present an idea while not losing the opportunity to reenter the next cycle of the round robin.

The round-robin recording guarantees that all members have the opportunity to contribute their idea(s), disassociates ideas from the individuals who presented them, and provides a written record of the group's efforts or problem solutions. The round robin is strictly

> *Do not follow where the path may lead. Go instead where there is no path and leave a trail.*
>
> Unknown

limited to the sharing of solutions from participants' initial lists or piggybacking; discussing or debating ideas is prohibited at this step of the NGT process. This concludes the nominal phase of the group process.

Step 3: Serial Discussion for Clarification. Each response that has been recorded on the flipchart is discussed in order by the group members. The leader points sequentially to each item, reads it aloud, and asks group members for clarification, questions, and agreement or disagreement. The purpose of this step is to ensure that all group members understand the intent and nature of the proposed solution and to openly discuss different perspectives. The leader must be careful to maintain a balanced discussion and to move on once the salient points have been made. It is important that all the proposed solutions be discussed without an inordinate amount of time being dedicated to any single solution. The discussion and clarification should not be allowed to degenerate into partisan debate on the merits or drawbacks of a particular solution.

Step 4: Preliminary Vote on Item Importance. In this step, the judgments of the individual group members are solicited in order to determine the relative value of the proposed solutions. The leader asks each group member to rank a specified number (e.g., five) of priority solutions from the list generated by the group round robin process. The group members write each of their priority solutions on separate index cards. Then, each member ranks his five index cards in order from the most to the least desirable solution. Taking all members' votes into consideration, a mean value is calculated for each solution. The item with the highest mean value would be considered the priority group solution. The NGT may be concluded at this point if the prioritized solutions have only minor disagreements, in terms of ranks, among group members. However, if there is great diversity among ranks, the following two additional steps may be warranted.

Step 5: Discussion of the Preliminary Vote. The purpose of this step is to discuss any dramatic inconsistencies among members' rankings. For example, if three participants ranked an item as the most desirable, and it was omitted from the list of the other group members, the discrepancy should be explored. It may be the case that certain group members have relevant information that others do not or biases that may impact their reaction to a solution.

It is important that this step focus on clarification, rather than attempting to persuade other members to change their positions. However, it is acceptable for members to change their ranks after clarification or additional information is provided.

Step 6: Final Vote. Once again, as in Step 4, the intention of a vote is to translate individual votes into a group decision. The same procedure of choosing priority solutions and ranking them on index cards may be used. The final vote will result in the selection of the problem solution and provide group members with a sense of accomplishment. It also serves to document the decision-making process.

There are several things to keep in mind when using the NGT. Research suggests that the NGT is best used for small groups, such as board meetings, for the purpose of fact finding, idea generation, or the search of problems or solutions. The technique is not beneficial for routine business, predetermined outcomes, or groups requiring a consensus. In addition, the more diverse the group, the more important clarification becomes to the process. And, finally, studies show that during early experiences using NGT, it is most difficult for people to keep from discussing topics or issues before all points are listed, clarified, and prioritized. The group leader or facilitator must prevent discussion from starting too soon—easier said than done!

HELPFUL INTERNET RESOURCES FOR NOMINAL GROUP TECHNIQUE

Guidelines For Using the Nominal Group Technique—Center for Rural Studies
http://crs.uvm.edu/gopher/nerl/group/a/meet/Exercise7/b.html

NGT: A User's Guide by Randall B. Dunham
http://www.instruction.bus.wisc.edu/obdemo/readings/ngt.html

Nominal Group Technique by Learning Technology Dissemination Initiative
http://www.icbl.hw.ac.uk/ltdi/cookbook/nominal_group_technique

The Nominal Group Technique by Robert DeBold
http://www.deboldgroup.com/TQM/nominal.htm

Focus Groups

Another group problem solving approach that has gained popularity among leisure, recreation, and park administrators in recent years is the use of focus groups. A technique first used by social scientists and later in marketing research, focus groups are used today in a wide range of settings in both private and public sectors, as well as by nonprofit organizations. There are several reasons focus groups are used so broadly across settings and disciplines (Krueger & Casey, 2000; Sharken, 1999):

- Focus groups provide direct, immediate contact with people who use a service or product, or who are concerned about a particular issue.
- Information may be obtained relatively easily, efficiently, and economically.
- Focus groups reveal the reasons why people think and feel the way they do.
- Focus group results reduce the risk of investing time and money in ideas that ultimately will not meet consumer needs.

- While focus groups are structured around predetermined questions, they are flexible enough to accommodate new information that arises. The moderator may follow up on comments that require more in-depth exploration and potentially uncover new insights.
- Exchange among group members can stimulate new ideas.
- Focus groups may be used with any age group—children, teens, young adults, and adults—and applied to any topic.
- When service providers listen empathically to people's thoughts and feelings during a focus group, trust is strengthened between the organization and its constituents, garnering buy-in for change or new initiatives.

The remainder of this section provides a definition of focus groups, explains their uses and limitations, and offers practical suggestions for planning, implementing, and evaluating focus group sessions.

Definition of Focus Groups

Krueger and Casey (2000) define the focus group approach as ". . . a carefully planned series of discussions designed to obtain perceptions on a defined area of interest in a permissive, non-threatening environment" (p. 5). The non-judgmental, relaxed atmosphere of a well-designed focus group encourages self-disclosure by the participants.

Led by a skilled moderator trained in group facilitation, focus groups provide an open forum where diverse viewpoints, opinions, and experiences may be freely expressed and discussed.

While focus groups vary in design and application, they share several common characteristics (see Table 7.3). Focus group participants typically share a mutual need, concern, or experience, yet do not know each other. Each focus group generally includes 5 to 10 participants who meet only once. If fewer than 5 participants are involved, the results may not be sufficiently rich and far-reaching; if more than 10 people participate, the group tends to splinter into side groups.

One would not conduct just one focus group; rather, a series of focus groups are facilitated to gain as diverse and representative a response as possible. Typically, three or four focus groups are initially conducted with each type of participant. When the point of saturation is reached—that is, little or no new information is being discovered—no more sessions are required. If, on the other hand, diverse views continue to be expressed, then more sessions should be conducted until a point of saturation is met.

We don't see things as they are, we see things as we are.

Anais Nin

Purpose and Uses of Focus Groups

The overall purpose of the focus group technique is "to better understand how people think or feel about an issue, product, or service" (Krueger & Casey, 2000, p. 4). The aim is not to reach consensus, though that may occur. Rather, the objective is to create an environment in which people are comfortable sharing their thoughts

Table 7.3
Characteristics of Focus Groups

- Participants share a common concern, need, or experience.
- Groups meet for a specific, time-limited purpose.
- A relaxed, non-judgmental environment is provided to encourage self-disclosure.
- Five to 10 participants are typically involved.
- Participants sit in close proximity.
- Moderator is knowledgeable in the subject area and skillful in handling group dynamics.
- Open-ended questions are used.
- Discussion resembles a group interview in which participants may respond to each other.
- The objective is to hear all sides, not to reach consensus.

When I listened most closely I could hear the unheard... To hear the unheard is a necessary discipline to be a good ruler. For only when a ruler has learned to listen closely to the people's hearts, hearing their feelings uncommunicated, pains unexpressed, and complaints not spoken of, can he [or she] hope to inspire confidence..., understand when something is wrong, and meet the true needs of his [or her] citizens.

C.W. Kim and Renee A. Mauborgne

and views, no matter how divergent they may be. Service providers must be prepared to truly listen to respondents as well as to use the information gathered to effect change related to the topic of discussion.

The focus group approach may be applied to a variety of situations in park and recreation administration, as illustrated in the following examples:

- *Needs assessment.* Input may be gathered related to community needs, interests, expectations, and preferences. For example, focus groups may be conducted to determine the need for inclusive recreation services in rural areas (Anderson & Heyne, 2000). Or one may gather information related to the need for youth programs, a community park, setting aside land for wilderness preservation, or another area of concern.

- *Program planning.* People with diverse roles but similar interests—such as consumers, group leaders, supervisors, and administrators—can be convened to dialogue about anticipated constraints, expectations, services, and facilities. Focus groups are a valuable means for checking assumptions and for considering the details of a program or service in a comprehensive manner.

- *Evaluation to improve the quality of services.* Focus groups may be used for either formative evaluation to monitor programs and address problems as they occur, or for summative evaluation at the end of a program to improve service quality. During programs, focus groups can be held to routinely involve program participants in the service delivery process, gain feedback on practices and policies, offer support, and let participants know their opinions are valued. After programs have been implemented, focus groups give administrators an opportunity to learn firsthand about the benefits of services, limitations and challenges, as well as recommendations to improve future programming. Additionally, focus groups may be held at any time to improve an agency's services. For example, Flood (2002) employed the focus group technique to gather visitor feedback to improve wilderness management practices.

- *Identify problems and generate solutions.* Bringing people together who are personally concerned about an issue can help identify problems and their root causes; brainstorm ideas, options, and opportunities; and spark creative solutions.

- *Marketing.* Focus groups can be effective mechanisms to recruit program participants, advertise a service or program, create good will between service providers and consumers, and establish connections with personnel from other community agencies.

- *Strategic planning.* Gathering input from key agency stakeholders—including participants, families, staff, the board of directors, advisory committee members, and external community agency representatives—is essential for developing a long-range vision and plan. A series of focus groups composed of each stakeholder group could be conducted to gain a complete picture of the agency's potential future directions. Public perceptions about the image of an organization could also be sought.

Clearly, focus groups may be adapted to serve a variety of purposes in leisure, recreation, and park administration, yet there are times focus groups should not be used. Focus groups should be avoided when consensus is desired (instead, use an approach such as nominal group technique). Nor should focus groups be used when a topic is emotionally charged, opinion is polarized, and group discussion could intensify the conflict (in these cases, use conflict resolution and mediation techniques, or a community forum). Similarly, focus groups are not intended to address sensitive topics that could harm an individual if discussed in a group (Krueger & Casey, 2000).

Focus groups have other limitations too. Because the sample size is typically small, generalizations, in a statistical sense, may not be drawn from the results. The advantage of focus groups, however, is that the information gleaned relates directly to a particular issue and circumstance—situations in which statistical figures are not especially relevant or illuminating. Other potential drawbacks of focus groups are that participants may be difficult to recruit, a biased moderator could influence group members' opinions, and results are often unwieldy and time consuming to analyze and interpret. Despite these limitations, focus groups have the potential to serve many functions and yield valuable information for leisure, recreation, and park administrators.

Focus Group Process

This section describes the basic steps involved in planning, conducting, and evaluating focus groups (Krueger & Casey, 2000; Sharken Simon, 1999). When planning a series of focus groups, a written plan should be developed that describes the problem, a statement of purpose, a plan of action, a timeline, and a realistic budget. The following guidelines are offered as recommendations that may be adapted to fit the needs and circumstances of particular groups and problems.

STEP 1: Define the purpose. Defining the purpose of the focus group and stating it in a straightforward manner is an essential, yet often challenging, task. A clear statement of purpose is important, because it helps to define the interview questions, identify the people who can best answer the questions, keep conversations on track, and evaluate whether the aim of the inquiry has been met. A straightforward statement of purpose also makes it easy for administrators to explain to others why the sessions are being conducted. Fully understanding the nature of the problem that led to the decision to conduct focus groups can help in clarifying the purpose.

In short, a purpose statement should be clear, concise, and specific, as indicated in the examples below:

- To gather feedback from park users about current programs and facilities to improve the quality of services
- To assess the recreational needs and interests of people who have recently retired so our agency can respond to their needs
- To gather information from stakeholders regarding the essential facilities and services that should be included in a new community center

Ultimately, a clear statement of purpose enables administrators to obtain the critical information they need to address the problem at hand.

STEP 2: Create a timeline and plan of action. Planning is the key to conducting successful focus groups, which includes allowing enough time to plan sufficiently. Planning should begin 4 to 8 weeks before the focus group sessions actually take place, depending on how difficult it may be to define the purpose, develop interview questions, recruit participants, find a moderator, and similar logistical factors. A timeline should include an overall plan of action that identifies the people who are responsible for carrying out specific tasks as well as due dates for task completion.

STEP 3: Develop a realistic budget. As previously noted, focus groups yield valuable information at a modest expense. Some budget items that may need to be purchased include audio-recorders and audiotapes, name tags, a flip chart and markers, notepads and pens or pencils, refreshments, and incentives, if they are offered. If an outside moderator is needed, there will also be a consultant fee.

STEP 4: Select and invite participants. Whereas survey research typically seeks a random sample, focus group research seeks respondents who are most knowledgeable and experienced in the topic area. Focus group participants are those who can best answer the questions related to the statement of purpose. Group members should be homogenous in the sense that they share a common attribute— for example, everyone uses a particular recreational service, is in a particular age bracket, or has voiced a similar concern. Group members should also be varied enough, however, to gather a spectrum of diverse viewpoints. While the viewpoints should be varied, they should not be highly controversial.

When participants are identified, contact information should be gathered. As a general rule, one recruits by over-recruiting. That is, two to three times more participants should be solicited than actually desired. For some topics, incentives such as money, food, gifts, or free passes may need to be offered to encourage participation. For other topics, people may be eager to participate purely out of personal concern and interest. (One should be aware that incentives could taint a participant's responses. That is, incentives might incline some people to say what they think moderators want to hear.) Personalized confirmation letters, with a concise explanation of the purpose of the meeting and clear directions to the site, should be sent prior to the session. One should also make follow-up telephone calls or send e-mail reminders to increase the chances of a satisfactory turnout.

STEP 5: Develop interview questions and a script. Interview questions should be built around the purpose of the study and the information that is sought. As a rule of thumb, about 10 questions are sufficient for a meeting that lasts 1 to $1^1/2$ hours. Here are some guidelines for developing effective focus group questions:

- Keep questions clear and short.
- Address only one issue per question.
- Ask questions that are open-ended. Avoid why questions, which can put people on the defensive. Instead, use questions that begin with how or what and encourage people to elaborate.
- Keep questions conversational and easy to state.
- Use the participants' own words.
- Avoid jargon, professional, or technical language. Use language most people will understand.
- Test out your questions beforehand. Revise them, if necessary, to be sure they are clear and will yield the information you want.

Because consultants are outsiders and they don't know the corporate culture, they can ask the dumb questions that no one else would dare ask.

Tom Ahern

Focus group sessions typically begin with simple questions that can be answered easily by the participants. For instance, group members could respond to one of the following inquiries: What is your name? What neighborhood do you live in? Which services do you use at our facility? Questions would then progress logically from general topics to issues of more specific concern. Questions that are central to the purpose statement would begin about one-third of the way into the session. Final questions would bring the discussion to a close, seek to clarify people's positions and opinions, and check that everyone's views have been expressed. Even though questions are determined in advance, moderators should seize opportunities to follow up on statements that are unclear or particularly interesting.

A script should also be developed which, in addition to the interview questions, includes the moderator's introductory comments, transitional statements, and closing remarks (see Step 9 below for specific information to include in the script).

STEP 6: *Choose a moderator.* A moderator should be knowledgeable in the topic area, sensitive to subtle issues that may arise, and comfortable leading a group discussion. Focus groups may be facilitated by an agency administrator or supervisor, program leader, advisory board member, community volunteer, recipient of services, or outside consultant. See Step 9 below and Table 7.4 for suggestions for effective moderators.

Table 7.4
Tips for Effective Moderators

- Create a warm, friendly, and relaxed environment. Emphasize that everyone's opinion is important.
- Be knowledgeable in the topic and sensitive to the issues that arise.
- Listen empathetically and with genuine interest.
- Ask how and what questions rather than why questions. Avoid questions that yield simply yes or no responses.
- Allow participants ample time to respond (wait at least 10 seconds).
- Memorize the interview questions, so you can look at and interact with participants.
- Probe participants' answers early so they will provide precise information.
- Maintain control of the group dynamics in a mild, unobtrusive manner.
- Avoid expressing your own opinion or evaluating participants' comments.
- Gauge when to move on to a new question. Be flexible, but keep the discussion on track.
- Dress similarly to the participants.
- Keep a sense of humor to maintain good will among the group members.

STEP 7: *Identify a location.* A good site is centrally located, architecturally accessible, easy to find, and has convenient parking. Locations might include community centers, schools, private homes, hotels, restaurants, churches or synagogues, libraries, or other public buildings. Discussion rooms should be clean, comfortable, and free from visual or auditory distractions. One large circular, square, or rectangular table that everyone can fit around comfortably is ideal for encouraging conversation and equalizing interactions. To ensure that the environment and accommodations are appropriate for one's needs, it's a good idea to visit the facility beforehand.

STEP 8: *Identify and gather necessary equipment and supplies.* To record comments accurately, an audiotape recorder is an essential piece of equipment. Audiotaping is generally considered less obtrusive than videotaping and more precise than note taking. Participants should always be asked for their permission to audiotape. Other useful materials could include notepaper, writing instruments, nametags, handouts, a flip chart, markers, and written surveys. Refreshments such as fruit, snacks, and beverages add a touch of hospitality and help put group members at ease.

STEP 9: *Conduct the focus group.* When group members arrive, the moderator should greet them in a friendly manner and engage them in light conversation. Taking note of potentially quiet or domineering group members, the moderator can invite shy individuals to sit across from him or her where eye contact can be established easily to encourage conversation. Domineering people can be invited to sit on the sides where eye contact is more easily averted.

When beginning the focus group discussion, the moderator attempts to create a relaxed, non-threatening environment. The moderator welcomes everyone, introduces himself or herself, and invites participants to introduce themselves. Opening comments may state the purpose of the discussion, clarify the agenda, and inform participants of any housekeeping concerns or ground rules. These introductory remarks may also address the confidential handling of responses, point out the necessity of an audio-recorder to accurately gather information, ask for participants' permission to audiotape the session, invite group members to ask questions, let participants know the location of restrooms, and indicate how long the discussion will last. Moderators can also remind participants that there are no right or wrong answers, and that the object of the session is to hear all points of view.

Facilitating the group discussion is accomplished through considerable mental preparation and practice (see Table 7.4). A good moderator is attentive to group dynamics, observes nonverbal messages, and anticipates the flow of the discussion. A moderator should take care not to talk too much, dominate the discussion, or bias people's answers. He or she must also temper personal reactions by appearing neutral to all responses, no matter how shocking or disconcerting.

A moderator should also memorize the line of questioning so he or she can be alert to shifts in the discussion and comments that should be explored more fully. One of the primary advantages of the focus group method is the flexibility the interviewer has to spontaneously seek deeper meanings and pursue new lines of inquiry. When comments require clarification or elaboration, a moderator could use one of the following probes: "I don't understand," "Would you explain that further?," "Can you tell me more?," or "Would you give me an example?"

When concluding the focus group, a wrap-up question is valuable for summarizing information and lending a sense of closure to the meeting. An open invitation for additional comments or questions can be useful to uncover any important, new information that may have been overlooked. The moderator or an assistant moderator can also summarize the key points of the discussion and present them to the group for verification. At the end of the discussion, participants are thanked for their time and contributions, and incentive payments are distributed, if appropriate. As group members leave, the moderator should be available to answer any questions the participants may have.

STEP 10: Evaluate the results. After conducting a series of focus groups, the wealth of information may make evaluating the results seem an overwhelming task. To make sense of the discussion and digest the information, the following questions may be asked:

- What was the general mood or tone of the meeting?
- What were the characteristics of the group members?
- What did the participants' body language, nonverbal communication, or other behaviors tell you?
- What common themes, comments, or opinions recurred through out the meeting?
- What divergent viewpoints were expressed?
- What shifts in mood, philosophy, or opinion occurred during the course of the meeting?
- What new questions or information emerged?
- How well did the discussion meet the original purpose of the meeting?

To reduce the possibility of evaluator bias, an assistant moderator may be present throughout the focus group process. Together, the moderator and assistant may then discuss observations and outcomes, and develop an evaluation report upon which both individuals can agree.

STEP 11: Translate results into action. A crucial aspect of the focus group approach is how the information will be used. Based on the focus group results, administrators should design a plan for translating the results into action. For example, recommendations could be incorporated into an existing or new program, or the results could be presented to the board of directors for further action. Whatever the outcome, it is important to communicate back to key stakeholders the results of the meetings and subsequent actions that will be taken.

Table 7.5
Checklist for Conducting Focus Groups

❏ Gain a full understanding of the problem to be addressed.

❏ Define the statement of purpose.

❏ Develop a written plan that establishes a timeline, plan of action, responsible parties, and due dates.

❏ Develop a budget and identify the funding source.

❏ Generate the interview questions.

❏ Develop the focus group script.

❏ Identify focus group participants.

❏ Develop a plan for recruiting participants.

❏ Gather contact information for participants.

❏ Write invitations and invite participants.

❏ Select a moderator.

❏ Choose a site to conduct the focus groups.

❏ Make room arrangements (e.g., reserve room, arrange seating, provide refreshments).

❏ Make telephone or e-mail reminders to participants.

❏ Gather materials for focus group sessions (e.g., audio-recorder, audiotapes, notepad, flipcharts, markers).

❏ Conduct the focus groups.

❏ Send thank you notes to participants.

❏ Transcribe the session audiotapes.

❏ Analyze and interpret the focus group results.

❏ Determine subsequent actions to be taken.

❏ Write the report.

❏ Send the report to relevant stakeholders.

In summary, focus groups are an effective means for obtaining direct feedback from people served by park and recreation agencies. Careful planning is the key to running successful focus groups. Table 7.5 presents a checklist of the necessary steps to planning a focus group, from start to finish.

HELPFUL INTERNET RESOURCES FOR FOCUS GROUPS

Conducting Focus Groups assembled by Carter McNamara, MBA, Ph.D., http://www.mapnp.org/library/grp_skll/focusgrp/focusgrp.htm

Groups Plus—articles by Tom Greenbaum
http://www.groupsplus.com/pages/articles.htm

Marketing Navigation, Inc.
http://www.mnav.com/qualitative_research.htm

Social Research Update, Department of Sociology
University of Surrey, Guildford, England.
http://www.soc.surrey.ac.uk/sru/SRU19.html

What are Focus Groups?—American Statistical Association Series
http://www.amstat.org/sections/srms/brochures/focusgroups.pdf

---

Imagination is more important than knowledge.

Albert Einstein

The Role Playing Technique

According to Simsarian (2003), role playing is "the practice of group physical and spatial pretend where individuals deliberately assume a character role in a constructed scene with, or without, props" (p. 1012). IDEO, a leading product design and development firm, introduced in the section on brainstorming, has used role playing at every stage of the design process. Simarian states, "With the dual properties of bringing participants into the moment and making shared activities physical rather than just mental, role playing techniques make the process more experiential and creatively generative" (p. 1012).

There are two key differentiating aspects of role playing. The first is being in the "moment"—an individual and group state that enables vivid and focused exploration of the situations. The second aspect is physicalization—using the entire body to explore generation of ideas that takes "brainstorming" to "bodystorming" (Simarian, 2003).

Role Playing With the Use of Case Studies

Role playing may also involve acting out the problems presented in case studies, thus increasing the "real-world" quality of the various exercises. The techniques of role playing are widespread in management education because they enable the instructor to focus on the human side of the organization. Managerial problems in the leisure service organization often arise in the areas of

Power and authority *Change and development*
Morale and cohesion *Norms and standards*
Goals and objectives *Interpersonal skills*
Group development *Decision making*

Using leisure service organization case studies that contain management problems, provides students with the opportunity to practice interacting with others in certain roles, including conflict resolution. According to Johnson (2003), role play provides an excellent tool for thinking while doing. Johnson uses case studies for role playing with her employees to help resolve employee conflicts within her organization. It is important that participants become more aware of, and sensitive to, others, especially when dealing with real issues of conflict.

There are two kinds of role playing that are generally used. These include multiple-group and single-group role playing. With multiple-group role playing, the entire audience participates in the role plays and is involved in as many separate groups as necessary. In single-group role playing, one group acts while the remainder of the audience observes, much like in the theater, except that those observers then participate in discussions.

When the instructor wishes everyone to act in a case study, and when the objective of the case study does not focus on developing sensitivity to others, multiple-group role playing is a better choice. With the multiple-group method, the audience forms role playing groups that role play the same case study simultaneously.

It is desirable to keep the groups sufficiently separated so that they do not disturb each other's discussions, but close enough so that the atmosphere stimulates the participants. There is no need to put groups in separate rooms; in fact, such separation might be detrimental. Finally, it is helpful to have written instructions, so that each group assumes consistent roles.

When using the multiple-group method, the participants are given a specific organizational situation and then are asked to react to a change in the situation. Details of a case are presented so that an emotional response can be elicited from the group. As the role playing progresses, additional information and actions are introduced into the case. This may cause a re-evaluation or a change of behavior by participants. This method of role playing is most effectively used for changing attitudes but requires a skilled leader.

The more widely used method is single-group. It is the preferred method when the purpose of a case study is to develop students' sensitivity to the feelings of others. The role play should be spontaneous and continue uninterrupted. However, the role playing instructor can interpret the dialogue whenever there is a need for explanation or interpretation for the observers. An example is students who act out a recreation and park board meeting while other students observe the action and the individual roles.

The advantages of the multi-group method are that everyone may role play and the groups can compare their results. For single-group performances, the advantage is that the actors are observed by interested outsiders. In later discussions, these observers and actors can share their viewpoints, thus enlarging the experience for all students. Both participants and observers become more sensitive to the feelings and conflicts of the players, much as in a theatrical production. It is not necessary for someone to be an actor to role play effectively. If a student is excessively shy or reluctant, he or she should not be coerced. The required experience is for the students to act as the persons they are playing would behave, not as they themselves might behave. If a student is to play the part of a busy, preoccupied supervisor, he or she should not transform this role into an ideal supervisor and defeat the purpose of the case study.

Role playing situations are usually unrehearsed; therefore, the participants may not anticipate the spontaneous dialogue that occurs. This gives the case study a more realistic atmosphere. For both participants and observers, seeing a lifelike drama can be more effective than simply reading a case. The inclusion of role playing makes discussions livelier and more productive.

Please note that some of the cases presented in this book do not lend themselves to role playing, nor was it intended that they should. Many, however, represent a framework for excellent role playing. Therefore, it is suggested that students and instructors study them carefully and together select those that seem most appropriate.

The following advantages and disadvantages to role playing are provided to better acquaint students and instructors with the benefits and hazards.

Disadvantages of Role Playing

- It is not an easy method to use, and it requires practice and the full cooperation of instructor and students.
- Students often place too much emphasis on their acting rather than on the problem.
- Unless the role players have been properly trained and coached, the result may be useless.
- It requires outgoing personalities. Persons who are shy, intro verted, or overly sensitive may not be successful at role playing.
- Unless well planned, role playing allows little time for discus sion. It is not advisable to use role playing unless ample time is scheduled for discussion.
- One person often may dominate the role play exercise. As a re sult, only his or her viewpoint is presented. This can be corrected by preparation before presentation.
- If a person gets too deeply involved in a role, it may be difficult for him or her to drop it.
- If role playing is not introduced properly, it might be treated by students as a "child's way of handling problems."
- The method is often used by those with little study or training in its use.
- The instructor must guard against role playing becoming merely entertainment for the students.

No problem can stand the assault of sustained thinking.

Voltaire

Advantages of Role Playing

- It is a spontaneous method for putting an idea or discussion into action.
- It reveals feelings and attitudes toward organizational problems that might not otherwise surface in class discussions.
- It dramatizes the situation being discussed.
- It brings "real world" situations and behavior into the classroom.
- It is an effective method of achieving participation by all students.
- It aids in developing personal characteristics, such as poise, self-assurance, speaking ability, argumentative logic, and self-control.
- It puts the actor in another person's place, thus giving a better understanding of others' behaviors.
- It gives participants an opportunity to demonstrate how they would handle problems encountered on a job.

Because role playing is only an aid to teaching problem solving skills, it should supplement other forms of training and educational experiences. As in using case studies alone, these aids are not intended to include the kinds of information needed by a student to recognize the demands of managerial problem solving. If used properly for achieving specific goals, for example, attitude or awareness training or increasing one's sensitivity to others, role playing of case studies will prove to be interesting, stimulating, and effective. Often it will be the highlight of a student's education in leisure service management.

USEFUL INTERNET RESOURCES FOR ROLE PLAYING

Find Your Role-Playing Stereotype by Free Webware
http://www.mutedfaith.com/quiz/q3.htm

Insights Through Role Playing by Pam Johnson
http://www.poynter.org/column.asp?id=34&aid=42524

Youth Leadership and Education Programs by Hospital Audiences, Inc.
http://www.hospitalaudiences.org/hai/pubs/news/winter04/3.htm

Mathematical Modeling

Models come in all shapes and sizes. One could model a playground with a miniature replica in order to study certain design features, or one could develop a conceptual model that predicts which conservation policies are likely to have the highest success rate. One mathematician insists that baseball teams would play better if coaches did away with the traditional batting line-up. His proven mathematical equation supports the theory that putting the best batter second, rather than the customary fourth, can substantially improve team performance (*Math Improves Baseball Line-up*, 2002).

Regardless of the various types of models, many of the most useful models are conceptual. These conceptual models consist of a collection of principles or rules that describe the behavior of the system under consideration. When the principles of a conceptual model are mathematically based, then a *mathematical model* is created. The success of a model depends on how easily it can be used and how accurate its predictions.

Models can be easily manipulated and changed when necessary. The goal with mathematical modeling is to use this tool when the real phenomena are too complex, excessively expensive, or impossible to analyze in their original setting. For example, how would one ever calculate the entire population of fish? Perhaps the terms of this equation may be found by counting the number of fish who are born and die in a given amount of time. In this case, the developed equation may be utilized to help estimate the entire population.

It is important to note that once a model has been developed and used to answer questions, it should be critically examined and often modified to more accurately reflect the observed reality of that phenomenon. Mathematical modeling is an evolving process and, as new insight is gained, the process begins again as additional factors are considered.

Given that mathematical modeling is a good way to predict how a system will behave when experimenting in the real world is unfeasible, one should start with the simplest model and then add more realistic terms. For example, researchers from Texas A&M in the Department of Wildlife and Fisheries Sciences have developed a mathematical model that predicts which conservation policies are likely to have the highest success rate. Several professors from various departments developed the "mathematical theory of landscape" by using equations to model the environment that will allow the researchers to investigate landscape patterns and to map the habitats and describe how they vary over time (Environmental News Network, 2001). The researchers began with the simplest model and continued to add more terms as their knowledge base grew.

The more you prepare, the luckier you appear.

Terry Josephson

Building a Mathematical Model

The following steps outline a general approach to the mathematical modeling process:

1. Identify the problem, define the terms in your problem, and draw diagrams where appropriate.
2. Begin with a simple model, stating the assumptions that you make as you focus on particular aspects of the phenomenon.
3. Identify important variables and constants, and determine how they relate to each other.
4. Develop the equation(s) that express the relationships between the variables and constants.

5. Check for accuracy by answering questions such as
   - Is the information produced reasonable?
   - Are the assumptions made while developing the model reasonable?
   - Are there factors that were not considered that could affect the outcome?
   - How do the results compare with real data, if available?

In answering these questions, the model may need to be modified. This process should continue until you have a model that represents closely with the real-world observations of the phenomenon that you have set out to model (*What is Mathematical Modeling?*, 2003).

HELPFUL INTERNET RESOURCES FOR MATHEMATICAL MODELING

New mathematical model predicts conservation's success by Environmental News Network
http://enn.com/news/enn-stories/2001/10/10232001/model_45329.asp

What is Mathematical Modeling? (Unknown)
www.ualr.edu/hxzhu/Modeling/ModelContent.htm

Women in Engineering Program - University of Colorado at Boulder
http://amath.colorado.edu/outreach/wie/2002/modelling.html

Fishbone Diagram

The fishbone diagram, also known as the cause-and-effect diagram, is another problem solving tool that attempts to identify the root causes for a problem or condition. The lines coming off the core horizontal line are the main causes, and the lines coming off those are the subcauses (see Figure 7.1).

To swear off making mistakes is very easy. All you have to do is swear off having ideas.

Leo Burnett

Figure 7.1
Fish-bone Diagram

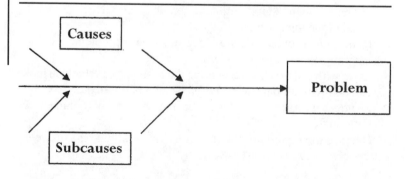

The fishbone is used to identify potential causes of a problem or issue in an orderly way (e.g., Why has enrollment in the arts program decreased? Why are there so many complaints about the phone in the park office not being answered on time?) and to summarize the major causes under specific categories (e.g., people, machines, methods, materials). This problem solving tool allows the group to focus on the causes and not the symptoms of the problem.

There are eight steps to constructing the fishbone diagram (*SkyMark Corporation*, 2003).

1. Clearly identify and define the problem, symptom, or effect for which the causes must be identified.
2. Place the problem or symptom being explored at the right, enclosed in a box.
3. Draw the central spine as a thick line pointing to it from the left.
4. Brainstorm to identify the "major categories" of possible causes (not less than two and normally not more than six or seven). You may summarize causes under categories such as
   a. Methods, Machines, and Materials
   b. People, Places, and Procedures
   c. People, Policies, and Surroundings
5. Place each of the identified "major categories" of causes in a box or on the diagram and connect it to the central spine by a line at an angle from the horizontal.
6. Within each "major category" ask, "Why does this condition exist?"
7. Continue to add causes to each branch until the fishbone is completed.
8. Once all the bones have been completed, identify the likely root cause(s).

Some points to keep in mind when constructing the fishbone diagram are to state causes and not the solutions, take note of causes that appear repeatedly, review each major cause category and then circle the most likely causes on the diagram, and finally, test the most likely cause and verify that with the data. Figure 7.2 illustrates an example of a completed fishbone diagram.

USEFUL INTERNET RESOURCES FOR FISHBONE DIAGRAM

Business & Charting—Org Charts and Trees—Smart Tree, Inc.
http://www.smartdraw.com/resources/examples/business/orgchart10.htm

Cause and Effect Diagramming by SkyMark Corporation.
http://www.pathmaker.com/resources/tools/cause.asp

Fishbone Diagram (Unknown)
http://www.sytsma.com/tqmtools/cause.html

Figure 7.2
Example of a Completed Fishbone Diagram:
The problem is: Why are there so many complaints about the phone in the park office not being answered?

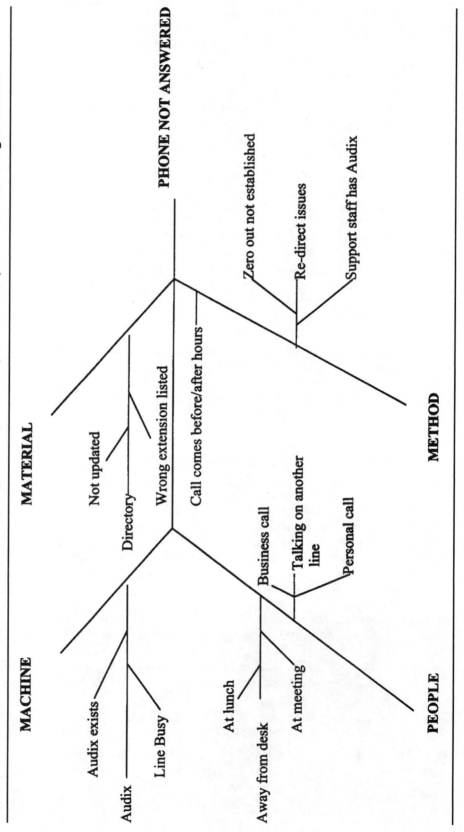

Decision Trees

Decision trees are diagrams similar to the fishbone diagrams; however, decision trees are used for making financial or number-based decisions where a lot of complex information needs to be taken into account. Decision trees can lay out options in order to investigate the possible outcomes of choosing those options. In addition, they also help form a balanced picture of the risks and rewards associated with each possible course of action (Mind Tools, 2003).

How to Draw a Decision Tree

1. Start a decision tree by considering a decision that needs to be made. This decision is represented by a small square at the top of a large piece of paper. Beneath this box draw out lines for each possible solution, and write the solution along the lines. Keep the lines as far apart as possible so that you can expand your thoughts.

2. At the end of each solution line, consider the results. If the result of taking that decision is uncertain, draw a small circle. If the result is another decision that needs to be made, draw another square. Squares represent decisions, circles represent uncertainty or random factors. Write the decision or factor to be considered above the square or circle. If you have completed the solution at the end of the line, just leave it blank.

3. Starting from the new decision squares on your diagram, draw out lines representing the options that could be taken. From the circles, draw out lines representing possible outcomes. Again mark a brief note on the line saying what it means. Keep on doing this until you have drawn down as many of the possible outcomes and decisions as you can see leading on from your original deci sion (Mind Tools, 2003).

Once you have done this, review your tree diagram. Check to see if there are any solutions or outcomes you have not considered. If there are, draw them in. If necessary, redraft your tree if parts of it are too congested or untidy. Now you should have a good understanding of the range of possible outcomes.

Decision trees provide an effective method of decision making because they clearly lay out the problem so that all choices can be viewed, discussed, and challenged. In addition, they help us to make the best decisions on the basis of our existing information and best guesses. As with all decision-making methods, though, decision-tree analysis should be used in conjunction with common sense.

**HELPFUL INTERNET RESOURCES FOR
DECISION TREES**

Decision Trees by Paul Utgoff, University of Massachusetts
http://www.aaai.org/AITopics/html/trees.html

Decision Trees and Evolutionary Programming by Kirk Delisle
http://ai-depot.com/Tutorial/DecisionTrees.html

Decision Trees: Tutorial Slides by Andrew Moore
http://www-2.cs.cmu.edu/~awm/tutorials/dtree.html

Bibliography

Anderson, L. S., & Heyne, L. A. (2000). A statewide needs assessment using focus groups: Perceived challenges and goals in providing inclusive recreation services in rural communities. *Journal of Park and Recreation Administration, 18*(4), 17-37.

Basden, B. H., Basden, D. R., Bryner, S., & Thomas, R. L. (1997). A comparison of group and individual remembering: Does collaboration disrupt retrieval strategies? *Journal of Experimental Psychology: Learning, Memory and Cognition, 23,* 1176-1189.

Baumgartner, J. (2003). *The step-by-step guide to brainstorming.* Retrieved March 22, 2004, from http://www.jpb.com/creative/brainstorming.php

Cause-and-Effect Diagramming (2003). Retrieved February, 1, 2004 from http://www.pathmaker.com/resources/tools/cause.asp

Debold, B. (1999). *The nominal-group technique.* Retrieved March 19, 2004, from http://www.deboldgroup.com/TQM/nominal.htm

Delbecq, A. L., Van de Ven, A. H., & Gustafson, D. H. (1974). *Group techniques for program planning: A guide to nominal group and delphi processes.* Glenview, IL: Scott Foresman.

Dunham, R. B. (1998). Nominal-group technique: A users' guide. Retrieved April 22, 2004, from University of Wisconsin, School of Business Web site: http://instruction.bus.wisc.edu/obdemo/readings/ngt.html

Environmental News Network. (2001, October 23). *New Mathematical Model Predicts Conservation's Success,* Retrieved January 14, 2004, from http://enn.com/news/enn-stories/2001/10/10232001/model_45329.asp

Films for the Humanities and Sciences (Producer). (2003). *Focus groups: Targeting the market* [DVD video]. (Available from Films for the Humanities and Sciences, http://www.films.com)

Flood, J. P. (2002). Using focus groups to improve wilderness management efforts. *Parks & Recreation, 37*(5), 24-31.

Greenbaum, T. L. (1998). *The handbook for focus group research* (2nd ed.). Thousand Oaks, CA: Sage Publications.

Greenbaum, T. L. (2000). *Moderating focus groups: A practical guide for group facilitation.* Thousand Oaks, CA: Sage Publications.

Heyne, L. A., McAvoy, L. H., & Schleien, S. J. (1994). Focus groups: Bringing people together in therapeutic recreation. *Palaestra, 10*(2), 19-24.

Johnson, P. (2003). *Insights through role-playing. Poynteronline*, 7. Retrieved March 19, 2004, from http://www.poynter.org/column.asp?id = 34&aid = 42524

Kelly, T., & Littman, J. (2001). *The art of innovation: Lessons in creativity from IDEO, America's leading design firm.* New York: Doubleday.

Krueger, R. A., & Casey, M. A. (2000). *Focus groups: A practical guide for applied research* (3rd ed.). Thousand Oaks, CA: Sage Publications.

Marcum, D., & Smith, S. (September 2002). Business think. *Executive Excellence, 19*(9), 12-13.

Maths Improves Baseball Line-up (2002). Retrieved April 10, 2004, from http://www.newscientist.com/news/news.jsp?id = ns99992559

McGregor, L. (2002). Improving the quality and speed of decision making. *Journal of Change Management, 2*(4), 344-356.

Mind Tools, Cardean Univerity (2003). *Decision-Tree Analysis.* Retrieved January, 14, 2004, from http://www.mindtools.com/dectree.htm

Mind Tools, Cardean Univerity (2003). *Decision Theory and Decision Trees.* Retrieved January, 14, 2004, from http://www.mindtools.com/dectree.htm

Offner, A. K., Kramer, T. J., & Winter, J. P. (1996). The effects of facilitation, recording, and pauses on group brainstorming. *Small Group Research, 27*, 283-298.

Osborn, A. (1963). *Applied imagination: Principles and procedures of creative problem-solving* (3rd ed.). New York: Charles Scribners.

Oxley, N. L., Dzindolet, M. T., & Paulus, P. B. (1996). The effects of facilitators on the performance of brainstorming groups. *Journal of Social Behavior and Personality, 11*, 633-646.

Ratzburg, W. (2003). *Social loafing.* Retrieved March 20, 2004, from http://www.geocities.com/Athens/Forum/1650/htmlobtoc02.html

Sharken, Simon, J. (1999). *Conducting successful focus groups: How to get the information you need to make smart decisions.* St. Paul, MN: Amherst H. Wilder Foundation.

Siau, K. L. (1997, April). Electronic Brainstorming. *Innovative Leader, 6*(4), 200-206.

Simasarian, K. (2003). *Taking it to the next stage: The roles of role playing in the design process.* San Francisco, CA: ACM Press.

Vreede, G., Briggs, R., Duin, R., & Enserink, B. (2000). *Athletics in electronic brainstorming: Asynchronous electronic brainstorming in very large groups.* Paper presented at the 33rd Hawaii International Conference on System Sciences. Abstract retrieved March 14, 2004, from http://www.informatik.uni-trier.de/ ~ ley/db/indices/a-tree/d/Duin:Ron_van.html

What is Mathematical Modeling? (2003). Retrieved March 11, 2004, from http://amath.colorado.edu/outreach/wie/2002/modelling.html

CHAPTER EIGHT

CONFLICT RESOLUTION AND MEDIATION TECHNIQUES

by Jean Greenwood

Conflict is inevitable. The only way to avoid conflict is to disengage from life. Most critical, therefore, are the skills and processes, attitudes and expectations we bring to a conflicted situation that encourage constructive or destructive outcomes. Inherent in conflict are both danger and opportunity. The costs of unresolved or poorly handled conflict are high; for example, alienation, anger, low morale, and loss of relationships, jobs, energy, and productivity. Conversely, the potential benefits of carefully addressed conflict are significant; for example, positive change, strengthened relationships, empowerment and resilience, improved communication, mutual understanding, and compassion.

The causes of conflict vary. Though tension is often attributed to personality differences, in fact, the actual source of conflict often pertains to other factors, such as the following:

- *Information:* Inaccurate or incomplete information, or differing interpretations

- *Structure:* Inequitable or ineffective distribution of power, space, time, or resources

- *Values and priorities:* Individual goals, ideological differences, or day-to-day focus

- *Relationship issues:* Unskilled communication, ineffective expressions of emotion, or unresolved problems from the past

There are, of course, various approaches to conflict. For many, conflict is competitive. Who can exercise the greatest power, whether physical, social, or positional, and, thus, prevail? This is a win/lose, adversarial proposition. Initially, it may be satisfying to win.

Jean Greenwood, M.Div., is an educator, with leadership experience in parks and recreation, a specialist in conflict transformation and restorative justice, and a Presbyterian minister. Jean is a community faculty member at the University of Minnesota and at United Theological Seminary, as well as a mediator for the State of Minnesota. She has also served as training coordinator for the Center for Restorative Justice & Mediation at the University of Minnesota. Jean provides training, consulting, mediation, and facilitation for nonprofit organizations and churches, and offers coaching for individuals, families, and groups.

The glory fades, however, as those who have lost the battle distance themselves from us, retaliate, or fail to cooperate. On the other hand, if we understood the interconnectedness and interdependence within communities, we might seek to resolve conflict in a collaborative way that restores and strengthens relationships, focuses on the good of all, allows everyone to win, and generates a good feeling in the community. Our approach then might grow out of the principles that follow.

The Principles

These principles grow out of the values we espouse in the field of parks and recreation, including the importance of community to healthy individual development, the dignity and worth of each individual regardless of ability, and the significance of physical activity, play, and social interaction in creating a healthy, holistic lifestyle.

Coming together is a beginning; keeping together is progress; working together is success.

Henry Ford

1. Build rapport, establishing genuinely caring, human connections. Everyone wonders, "Do you care about me and what is important to me?"

2. Establish a respectful climate that honors diversity and freedom of choice.

3. Build ownership by involving those most affected by the problem in designing processes and solutions.

4. Give everyone an equal voice.

5. Build on existing personal or organizational successes, assets, strengths, and resources.
   • Remember a time when you moved through a problem well: What was that like? What did you learn from that experience?
   • What does it look like when you are at your best?
   • What do you appreciate about others involved in this problem? What do you appreciate about their perspectives?

6. Go to the heart of things—the underlying needs, values, and desires that are generating this problem.

7. Integrate personal stories, which are often more potent than abstractions.

8. Seek and honor any shared values, perspectives, or interests.

9. Work creatively towards consensus and mutual benefit.

Guided by these principles, individuals may then engage in the following three-step process, which invites them to "Go to the balcony," "Go to the basement," and, finally, "Go to the table."

The Process

STEP 1: GO TO THE BALCONY: What do I bring to a conflict situation?

- Know yourself in relation to what you learned about conflict in your family of origin and your comfort with conflict. Understand your way of responding to conflict and how it affects others. How are your responses helpful, unhelpful?
- Bring your best self to conflict, practicing self-care, enjoying recreation and celebration, and tapping into your reservoir of energy and aliveness, serenity and wholeness.

STEP 2: GO TO THE BASEMENT: What is underneath this conflict? Why is it important?

- Know that reality is in the eyes of the beholder: Everyone has a story, believes in it, and has reasons for that story.
- What are the interests beneath the positions? What values, feelings, concerns, needs, desires, and life experiences have led you to your perspective? Similarly, what may have led others to their perspectives? (See Table 8.1 on *Positions and Interests*.)

STEP 3: GO TO THE TABLE: How can we engage in respectful dialogue that helps us resolve our differences?

- Create a welcoming, safe, and caring space that encourages everyone to have a voice, to speak their deepest truth in an effective, respectful manner. To that end, work together to shape a relational covenant regarding the way you will proceed with the dialogue. Guidelines for the conversation may include, for example: speak and listen with respect, allow everyone to speak without interruption, hold the conversation in confidence.

- Before speaking, listen first, with genuine caring and compassion, knowing that conflict often generates feelings of vulnerability. Listen in order to understand and empathize, inviting information about personal experiences and underlying interests.

- Speak from your own experience, rather than that of others, with authenticity and heart. Speak in a manner that others can hear you, understand you, and feel invited into collaborative dialogue. Use "I" Messages to explain why this issue is important to you and how your personal experience has led you to this perspective (see Table 8.2 on "I" Messages).

- Work together toward mutual understanding and benefit, highlighting any common concerns, values, or interests.

Table 8.1
Getting Underneath a Conflict: Positions and Interests

POSITION: A non-negotiable stance; a demand
  "Here I stand; here is my firm point of view!"

INTERESTS: Underlying needs, desires, concerns, values, or priorities
  "This is why I feel so strongly about this, why it is so important to me...."

When communication is focused on positions, it is difficult to achieve mutual understanding and work toward resolution of problems in a way that restores and strengthens relationships. More effective is communication that moves more deeply, honors the unique perspectives of each person, and uncovers the underlying issues and concerns.

EXAMPLE:
Position: "If you interrupt me again, I'm leaving this meeting."
Interests: "This work means a lot to me, and I feel very frustrated when I am interrupted again and again. It is important to me to hear what you have to say, and it is also very important to me to know that I am a valued and respected committee member, that I have a voice, and that my contributions are heard and taken seriously."

CONSIDER AND ASK:
- Why does this person see things this way?
- What is the need, the concern, the value, the vision, the longing underneath the position or demand?
- What personal experiences have led this person to this perspective and these feelings?
- Do I share any of this person's values, concerns, needs, or experiences?

Table 8.2
"I" Messages

"I" MESSAGE: Expressing what is important to me in a way others can hear and respond

GOAL: To be understood
- Express yourself as clearly and completely as possible
- Slow down and take the time to construct how to express yourself
- Give accurate information about your experience

BECAUSE: Whenever someone sincerely listens to you, a creative process goes on, as the listener reconstructs your experience. The more dimensions of your experience you share in clear statements, the easier it will be for your listener to understand what you are feeling and why.

Construction of an "I" Message:
1. When I saw/heard/noticed . . . [the facts-concrete and specific]
2. I felt . . . [the feelings-truthful, realistic, un-escalated]
3. because I . . . [describe the effect of the problem on you, why it's important to you]
4. and now I would like to… [what you'd like to see happen]
5. so that . . . [what positive results you are hoping for]

EXAMPLE:
"YOU" MESSAGE: I can't believe you failed to return all those phone calls you received. What were you doing all day? We don't pay you to sit around. You don't seem to understand the importance of what we do here. If you don't show more responsibility, I may have to take action!

"I" MESSAGE: When I saw that you had not returned all the phone calls you received today, I felt concerned because I know how important a prompt response is to our community participants. I realize you probably had a very busy day. I'd like to have a chance to discuss the situation with you, so that together we can find a way to meet the needs of the community, and the need all of us have for a reasonable workload.

"You" Message	**"I" Message**
• Listener feels judged or criticized	• Speaker states impact and desires
• Does not encourage resolution	• Speaker expresses feelings
• Threatening, accusing, demanding	• No blame, judgment, or threat
• Impolite, unclear	• Sends clear messages

CONSIDER AND ASK: What kind of message leaves the listener feeling more empathetic with the speaker and likely to help, as opposed to feeling criticized, threatened, defensive, or resistant?

Have you learned lessons only of those who admired you, and were tender with you, and stood aside for you? Have you not learned great lessons from those who braced themselves against you, and disputed the passage with you?

Walt Whitman

- Use a process that is consistent with your goals. If you desire to strengthen and preserve relationships, the following exercises and processes may be useful. These processes include a simplified problem solving process, a conflict de-escalation exercise, mediation, the circle process, and tough issues exercises.

Simplified Problem-Solving Process

Problems that arise in interpersonal relationships, for example, on the playground, during a game, or at a staff meeting, can often be resolved directly by the individuals, perhaps even at the time of occurrence or shortly thereafter. There may be no need for a third party to facilitate the discussion. When people bring closure to their own problems, they gain a sense of satisfaction and confidence because they have demonstrated and successfully utilized skills in working with conflict. They are also more likely to follow through with a plan for resolution because they provided input and assented to it.

Overview: This process, which is similar to the model used in many peer mediation programs, involves five simple steps that engage individuals in a process akin to mediation, but without a neutral facilitator. The process is easily self-directed, balanced, and fair. It encourages participants to demonstrate that they have been listening carefully, which enhances good will, and provides them with the opportunity to check their understanding for accuracy.

Uses: This process is well suited for two or more individuals, either children or adults, involved in a fairly straightforward conflict or misunderstanding. Perhaps there was disagreement about the rules of a game, or a misunderstanding about who was fulfilling which responsibilities for an event. It is helpful if the participants possess some positive communication skills and feel invested in the relationship. Language may need to be adapted to fit the needs of the participants if they are young or have a disability. If the conflict has become quite intense and escalated, it may be helpful to take additional steps before proceeding with problem solving (see the Conflict De-escalation Exercise in the section that immediately follows).

Method:

STEP 1: Person #1:
- Tell your experience of what happened.
- Talk about your feelings, underlying interests and values, what's important to you in this situation.

STEP 2: Person #2:
- Retell what the first person said, and ask if it is accurate.
- Tell your experience of what happened.
- Talk about your feelings, underlying interests and values, and what's important to you in this situation.

Every fight is one between angles of vision, illuminating the same truth.

Mahatma Gandhi

STEP 3: Person #1:
- Retell what the second person said, and ask if it is accurate.

STEP 4: Both:
- Suggest solutions.

STEP 5: Both:
- Agree to solutions.
- Set a time to check-in and make sure things are going well.

Conflict De-escalation Exercise

Overview: In intensely conflicted situations, where anger or distrust are strong, it may be helpful to initiate preparatory steps before suggesting a conversation focused on problem solving and dialogue. Perhaps someone has threatened to leave an activity, has verbally exploded in anger, or has shut down in sullen silence. Before proceeding, it is important to first create a climate that is conducive to mutual respect and understanding, in so far as that is possible.

Uses: The purpose of this exercise is to diffuse some of the intensity of the conflict by inviting others to vent, freely expressing what is important to them, and then listening well as they speak, seeking the meaning beneath the emotion. This can be done informally, without identifying your intention or strategy.

Method:

STEP 1: Inquire about a time and space that will allow for private conversation.

STEP 2: Begin the conversation by sharing your desire to understand better each person's perspectives.

STEP 3: Proceed with questions, shaping them in a way that seems appropriate to the moment. Sample questions appear below:
- Would you be willing to tell me about your experiences regarding this situation?
- What has it been like for you?
- What is important to you in this?
- What has led you to see things this way, to feel this way?
- What would you like to see happen in this situation?

STEP 4: Proceed with Step 2 of the Simplified Problem-Solving Process, summarizing what you have heard and checking it out, e.g., "Here's what I'm hearing . . . Is that correct?" Then explain that you would like to share with them how you see it. Ask if they would be willing to listen to you.

STEP 5: Move to Step 3 of the Simplified Problem-Solving Process by asking if they would share what they heard you say, just to make sure you are communicating clearly.

STEP 6: Continue with Steps 4 and 5 of the Simplified Problem-Solving Process.

Mediation

What is Mediation? Mediation is an informal yet structured, voluntary process of dialogue among two or more people, facilitated by a neutral third party.

Uses: Mediation has developed as a process primarily for the purpose of solving problems and resolving conflict. It is often used when attempts at direct resolution among the parties themselves have been unsuccessful, or when the conflict is simply too intense, complex, volatile, and important to be addressed comfortably without assistance. A mediator, then, offers the possibility of safer, more respectful and effective communication, by monitoring and guarding the process with an eye to balance an equal opportunity for speaking and making choices. While the focus of a mediation session may be decision making and problem solving, the practice of mediation has demonstrated that the interpersonal dialogue that occurs may, in itself, serve a very significant purpose, even when full and complete agreement is not reached. Thus, the goals of mediation continue to expand beyond problem solving and conflict resolution, as participants experience a breadth of benefits. The mediation process may resemble the kind of role played by a recreation director or coach, who attempts to resolve a dispute by facilitating a conversation between those in conflict.

Overview of the process: The mediation process begins with a preparation phase, which may involve a face-to-face meeting or simply contact by phone, after which a mediation session is scheduled. During the mediation session, participants describe their perspectives about a particular situation or issue, including facts and feelings that reflect their experiences. The mediator actively assists all participants in achieving meaningful dialogue, moving towards mutual understanding and clarity about perspectives, underlying interests, values, and needs. The mediator then guides them in exploring options for responding to the situation and resolving the issues and concerns. Any agreements reached by mutual consent are recorded by the mediator, and a copy is given to participants. If the participants so choose, additional sessions may be scheduled, to fully conclude the work and to follow-up on decisions that have been made.

Role of the mediator: The primary responsibility of a mediator is to facilitate dialogue among the participants, encouraging them to have a voice, to hear each other, and to be empowered to resolve their own problems by working toward outcomes that meet their needs and are mutually acceptable. To that end, the mediator creates a space where respectful conversation can occur, providing a simple structure for the mediation process that typically includes establishing guidelines for communication. Throughout the mediation session, the mediator guides and guards the process, listening and encouraging the participants to express what is important to them, assisting, as needed, by asking questions and summarizing what has been said. A mediator does not possess coercive power and, therefore, does not make decisions for the participants. It is not the mediator's role to judge, counsel, advise, philosophize, or advocate. Nor is it the mediator's role to be a fact finder, dominate the conversation, solve the problems, or compel agreement. A mediator does not take sides but rather supports all participants in achieving their goals.

Stages of Mediation and Purposes:

STAGE 1: Welcome and Introductions
  • to begin the process together in a respectful, hopeful way
  • to honor and acknowledge each person's presence

STAGE 2: Opening Orientation
  • to review the purpose of the mediation, the steps in the process, and the role of the mediator
  • to establish guidelines for communication by mutual consent (e.g., everyone speaks without interruption, every one speaks and listens with respect)
  • to address any questions about the mediation process before beginning

STAGE 3: Narratives
  • to discover what brings participants to mediation, including a concrete description of their experience of the situation, how they have been affected by it, how they feel about it
  • to explore the situation further by asking questions and making comments in response to what has been shared

STAGE 4: Brainstorming Possibilities
  • to generate options for moving forward, resolving the issues that need to be resolved, and repairing any harm that has been done
  • to explore the options in detail and negotiate what might be workable

STAGE 5: Agreement and Closure
  • to develop a plan of action based on options that are mutually acceptable
  • to schedule a follow-up meeting as needed
  • to offer any final words and bring closure to the process

Potential benefits of mediation: The potential benefits of mediation include the opportunity for safe, respectful dialogue about issues of personal significance, and the chance to exercise autonomy in decision making. With the assistance of a mediator, participants typically explore underlying needs and interests, which might otherwise remain hidden both to self and others, discover they have common concerns or interests, generate interesting and innovative possibilities for resolution, and then create their own solutions, tailored

Everything the Power of the World does, it does in a circle. The sky is round, and I have heard that the earth is round like a ball, and so are all the stars. The wind, in its greatest power, whirls. Birds make their nests in circles, for theirs is the same religion as ours. The sun comes forth and goes down again in a circle. The moon does the same, and both are round. Even the seasons form a great circle in their changing, and always come back again to where they were. The life of a man is a circle from childhood to childhood, and so it is in everything where power moves.

Lakota holy man in
Black Elk Speaks,
John Neihardt

to their particular situation, rather than imposed arbitrarily by an external authority. This leads to higher levels of compliance with agreements and greater satisfaction with outcomes. Questions are answered, and issues and concerns are clarified. Greater understanding of self and others may occur, along with the capacity to recognize the humanity of others and to empathize with their life experience. Because mediation is inherently collaborative, interpersonal connections are often reestablished or strengthened. In the process of being respected, having a voice, and exercising power in decision making, participants may grow in self-confidence and competence, learn skills in communication and conflict resolution, and gain a sense of empowerment and greater self-determination. Many also find that mediation creates an environment conducive to personal healing, as well as personal growth. These benefits resonate with the emphasis in parks and recreation on relationship building, competency development, resilience, empowerment, and self-sufficiency.

Best practices: The benefits of mediation are maximized for the participants when the model of mediation allows them to meet the mediator ahead of time, to begin to develop trust, to tell their stories in a comfortable environment, to learn about the mediation process, and to ask questions before making a decision about participating. This rehearsal of the storytelling also helps individuals to frame their narratives in such a way that others can hear and understand them. Secondly, an optimal model will focus on dialogue among the participants more than on settlement of the issues. This allows individuals to have a sense of shared ownership of the process, and thus, to address their own particular needs, which may be broader than simply settling the problem. Also, giving participants the opportunity to speak without interruption, a common communication guideline, enhances greatly the quality of the dialogue, fostering more thoughtful comments. In addition, the model of mediation will promote participant power by presenting opportunities for choice as much as possible. For example, participants may choose the time and place for the mediation session, identify support people they would like to invite to the session, create the mediation guidelines, decide who will speak first, and supply options for resolution. Finally, the optimal mediation model will encourage participants to move from their positions on the issues toward their underlying interests, which may include values, priorities, concerns, needs.

Accessing mediation: Because mediation is increasingly being applied to new situations, it may be possible to locate a mediator in a variety of contexts. Places to begin an inquiry would include: a community mediation center, peacemaking organization, mediation institute connected with a university or law school, association of professional social workers, peer mediation program within a school system, bar association, or restorative justice program, operating either as a nonprofit or as a division within community corrections.

Table 8.3
The Circle Process

THE CIRCLE: A WAY OF TALKING TOGETHER IN WHICH ALL OF US...
- are respected and treated equally
- have the opportunity to speak without interruption
- tell our own stories
- speak and listen from the heart

VALUES UNDERLYING CIRCLES
- respect
- shared responsibility
- consensual decision making
- personal accountability
- inclusivity
- equal opportunity
- voluntary direct participation
- spirituality
- interconnectedness
- holistic approach
- focus on interests
- flexibility

The Circle Process

The circle process creates a space for egalitarian dialogue, based on mutual respect and concern. In the circle, all participants, regardless of role or status, age or experience, are considered of equal importance, and are invited to speak and listen from their hearts, to reach out to each other in support, recognizing their mutual interdependence as they seek to live their lives in a good way. Table 8.3 presents the orientation and underlying values of the circle process.

Overview: The contemporary circle process draws upon an indigenous tradition common in North America, the talking circle, which utilizes a talking piece that is passed from person to person around the circle, signaling the opportunity to speak. When a participant holds the talking piece, they are given the opportunity to speak without interruption. This slows down the dialogue, encourages quieter people to have an equal voice, and allows for deeper conversation, more careful listening, and thoughtful expression. Ritual is typically used both to open and close a circle. This serves to create common meaning and set apart the circle process as a sacred space in which participants may experience themselves and others in a meaningful way that moves beyond the ordinary.

Uses: Circles can be used for a wide variety of purposes. The circle process is an effective tool for community building and consensual decision making, problem solving and conflict resolution, increasing mutual understanding and exploring complex situations, enhancing recreational experiences, facilitating transitions and supporting people through difficult times, grieving and celebrating, and healing individuals, relationships, and communities. A summary of the potential purposes of peacemaking circles appears in Table 8.4.

Stages of the Circle Process: The circle process typically follows three stages, as outlined below:

STAGE 1 - Initiation: The circle process begins with the initiation stage, in which decisions are made about who will participate in the circle, when and where it will be held, and additional details, such as selection of a talking piece, plans for opening and closing the circle, and, if needed, questions to shape the dialogue.

> *An apology is a good way to have the last word.*
>
> Anonymous

STAGE 2 - Preparation: In the preparation stage, circle keepers meet with the participants to learn about their perspectives and experiences, to familiarize them with the circle process, and to inquire about their concerns, feelings, thoughts, and hopes for the circle. Healing or support circles for individuals or groups may also be convened in preparation for coming together.

STAGE 3 - Circle Gathering: The circle gathering itself involves the following five phases:

Table 8.4
Uses of the Circle Process

Peacemaking circles can be used to
- build consensus
- make decisions together
- solve problems
- plan for the future
- achieve greater mutual understanding
- work through differences
- develop teamwork skills and attitudes
- build community
- enhance recreational experiences
- celebrate
- support each other through difficult times
- foster healing for individuals, relationships, and communities
- explore complex situations
- facilitate transitions
- discuss strong emotions in a safe, respectful way

1. Opening: Laying the groundwork for dialogue
2. Storytelling: Expressing values, interests, and needs
3. Exploring Options: Seeking alternative solutions
4. Consensus building: Finding agreement
5. Closing: Honoring the dialogue and the participation

Finally, agreements are implemented, and participants may gather again for a circle of review, celebration, and closure.

Role of Circle Keeper: The circle keeper is responsible for setting the tone for the circle and facilitating the process. A keeper seeks to create a climate of respect, openness, support, and hopefulness. The keeper also guides the process by offering questions to focus the circle's work, summarizing what has been said, and noting any common ground or progress that has been made. In addition, the keeper participates in the circle as a community member.

Potential Benefits of Circles: In addition to the potential benefits associated with mediation, the circle process can serve to strengthen a sense of connection, community, mutual caring, and shared responsibility, particularly because the circle typically includes a significant number of community members who contribute as equal and active participants. A circle may also result in holistic change, because circles intentionally integrate the broad dimensions of human experience, including mental, emotional, physical, and spiritual aspects, and draw heavily upon the resources of the wider community.

Best Practices: The principles outlined for best practices in mediation would also apply to circles.

Accessing Circles: The circle process is not as widely used as mediation, most likely because it has been more recently introduced as a contemporary process. In order to locate circle programs, contact resources familiar with mediation. See Accessing Mediation in the previous section.

Tough Issues Exercise

Tough issues often elicit fear because of the risks inherent in confrontation, such as escalation of the conflict and destructive outcomes. Thus, it is important to cultivate the skills to talk about difficult issues in an open, respectful, caring, and hopeful way. One way to develop these skills is to practice them first in a neutral learning environment. The following exercise provides that opportunity. In this exercise, participants have a chance to both listen and speak, though not necessarily expressing their own views initially. Working together, they seek to uncover the underlying issues, interests, values, and concerns pertaining to a particular controversy. A facilitator would lead the group in the exercise as follows:

STEP 1: Explain the exercise and its purpose, as described above.

STEP 2: Invite participants to suggest possible controversies to discuss. Then invite them to select one issue to address in the exercise.

STEP 3: Review the issue chosen and discuss with the group some of the reasons an individual might support or oppose a particular position on that issue.

STEP 4: Have group members number off by twos and partner with someone of the other number.

STEP 5: Identify ones and twos as either "for" or "against," and allow a few minutes for them to think through their assigned perspective.

STEP 6: The ones begin by explaining why they are opposed, for a period of 2 minutes, while the twos listen carefully to their partners.

STEP 7: The twos have 1 minute to share what they have heard, and check it for accuracy: "Here is what I think I heard, what seems to be important to you. Is this correct?"

STEP 8: The roles are then reversed, and the twos speak while the ones listen.

STEP 9: Together the partners seek to identify any possible common ground in their perspectives, any underlying values, interests, or concerns that may be shared, for a period of 1 minute.

STEP 10: Partners share with each other, if they wish, their own perspectives, why they feel that way, what is important to them, and their experience of the exercise, for a period of 2 minutes each.

After the tough issues exercise, the group is debriefed by asking questions such as the following:

1. How did you experience the exercise? What felt comfortable or uncomfortable?
2. What was it like to represent an opinion different from your own?
3. How easy or difficult was it to find common ground?
4. What did you learn from this exercise that might assist you in discussing tough issues?
5. Is it possible to respectfully agree to disagree? What does that look like?

Table 8.5 presents additional exercises that may be used to prepare individuals and groups to deal with difficult issues.

Table 8.5
Exercises to Prepare People to Deal with Tough Issues

- Draw a personal timeline, identifying your perspectives and feelings about a controversial issue, how they have changed over time, and then reflect about why they have changed.

- Meeting in small groups, develop one particular perspective on an issue. Without identifying your own point of view, draw out possible underlying interests, values, concerns for that perspective. Why might someone hold this view?

- Gather in small groups with people who hold similar perspectives on an issue. Then identify questions you would like to ask other groups who represent different perspectives, and record information you would like them to know about you and your perspective.

- As individuals, record and then share with others your response to these questions:
  — What are your concerns and fears about this issue?
  — What is at stake for you?
  — When you listen to a perspective that differs from yours, when do you feel uncomfortable, and why?

- Create a case study about a particular issue, describing the background leading up to a point of decision. Working individually or in groups, describe what you would do, and why you would make that decision.

- As a group, develop a list of questions to be used as starters for interviewing someone with a different perspective on an issue than yours. Individuals then conduct the interviews, focusing on listening for understanding and asking questions of clarification, meanwhile remaining silent about one's own perspective. Interviews are shared with the group.

- Remember a time when you discussed a tough issue with others and you felt good about it. Reflect about why you felt that way, record your reflections, and share them with others. Then, remember a time when you discussed a tough issue with others and you did not feel good about it. Reflect about why you felt that way, record your reflections, and share them with others.

**HELPFUL INTERNET RESOURCES FOR
CONFLICT RESOLUTION AND MEDIATION**

Appreciative Inquiry
http://appreciativeinquiry.cwru.edu

Association for Conflict Resolution
http://www.acrnet.org

Center for Restorative Justice and Peacemaking
http://ssw.che.umn.edu/rjpp

Conflict Resolution Information Source
http://www.crinfo.org

Conflict Resolution Network
http://www.crnhq.org

Cooperative Communication Skills
http://www.coopcomm.org

INCORE: An International Centre of Excellence for the Study of
Peace and Conflict
http://www.incore.ulst.ac.uk

National Center for Conflict Resolution Education
http://www.nccre.org

Victim Offender Mediation Association
http://www.voma.org

Bibliography

Domenici, K., & Littlejohn, S. (2001). *Mediation: Empowerment in conflict management* (2nd ed.). Prospect Heights, IL: Waveland Press.

Fisher, R., & Ury, W. (1991). *GETTING TO YES: Negotiating agreement without giving in*. New York: Penguin Books.

Hammond, S. A. (1996). *The thin book of appreciative inquiry*. Plano, TX: Thin Book Publishing.

Katz, N. H., & Lawyer, J. W. (1985). *Communication and conflict resolution skills*. Dubuque, Iowa: Kendall/Hunt.

Masters, M. F., & Albright, R. R. (2002). *The complete guide to conflict-resolution in the workplace*. New York: American Management Association.

Moore, C. W. (1986). *The mediation process: Practical strategies for resolving conflicts*. San Francisco: Jossey-Bass.

O'Hanlon, W. H., & Weiner-Davis, M. (1989). *In search of solutions: A new direction in psychotherapy*. New York: W. W. Norton.

Parry, D. (1991). *Warriors of the heart*. Bainbridge Island, WA: Earthstewards Network.

Pranis, K., Stuart, B., & Wedge, M. (2003). *Peacemaking circles: From crime to community.* St. Paul, MN: Living Justice Press.

Rosenberg, M. B. (1999). *Nonviolent communication.* Del Mar, CA: PuddleDancer Press.

Umbreit, M. (1995). *Mediating interpersonal conflicts: A pathway to peace.* West Concord, MN: CPI Publishing.

Umbreit, M., & Greenwood, J. (2001). *The handbook of victim offender mediation: An essential guide to practice and research* (Ch. 2, 3, 6). San Francisco, CA: Jossey-Bass.

Wilmot, W. W., & Hocker, J. L. (1998). *Interpersonal conflict* (5th ed.). Boston: McGraw-Hill.

Zehr, H. (2002). *The little book of restorative justice.* Intercourse, PA: Good Books.

CASE STUDIES

CHAPTER NINE

This section of the fourth edition presents case studies that represent the contemporary problems facing leisure, recreation, and park service professionals. Because individuals work in various kinds and sizes of organizations, we chose cases that represent problems that most, if not all, administrators would experience in the areas of administration, programming, personnel, finance, public relations, human relations, the environment, youth at risk, public policy, and facility management. Further, we chose to loosely categorize the cases into five themes, which consist of approximately 15 cases each, as follows:

- Human Relations
- Marketing and Publicity
- Planning and Policy Development
- Liability and Risk Management
- Financial Management

It is important to note that many cases could fit in one or more of the themes. For example, a case that depicts a recreation board in conflict with the recreation director because he shared confidential information and was quoted in the local newspaper could fit either a human relations theme or a marketing and publicity theme. Therefore, the designated themes, and the cases they represent, should be used quite loosely as they may apply to more than one issue of concern.

The case study method lends reality to the study of leisure, recreation, and park management, improves analytical ability, and increases the potential for learning. The case studies allow the student and the practitioner to gain a better understanding of the difficulties in applying concepts and principles to solving operational problems. They also give the student an opportunity to apply the problem solving model discussed in Chapter 3.

At the end of each case is a list of questions designed to provoke interest in and discussion of the problems mentioned in the case. It is not suggested that these are the only questions related to the case; each student may perceive the case in a different way. Also, you will note a sample of helpful, current resources at the end of each theme.

The cases are based on actual experiences and have been drawn from many sources: boards, practitioners, and students who have willingly shared their experiences, and from many newspaper accounts of stories related to the field. All names are disguised to avoid identification of organizations and individuals.

Finally, we wish to express thanks to the many administrators, supervisors, leaders, friends, and students who have contributed to this section of the book. Without their assistance, these cases could not have been included.

The role of the teacher [is] one of directing activity rather than actually teaching.

Terry Malloy

I am an idealist. I don't know where I'm going, but I'm on my way.

Carl Sandburg

THEME ONE:

HUMAN RELATIONS

Sexual Harassment: Pool Side

Problem Situation

You are the director at the Wind Valley YWCA. Brandon Smith is an 11-year veteran employee with a history of excellent evaluations. Last week during a Red Cross lifeguard training session, a participant accused Brandon of sexual harassment.

The participant, Mary Jones, claimed that during a backboard rescue, Brandon Smith touched her inappropriately while fastening the board's chest strap. Although this procedure is part of the requirements of a proper rescue, Ms. Jones has issued several complaints, including those to the American Red Cross, the Wind Valley YWCA aquatics director, and the YWCA Board of Directors. She also contacted local authorities.

Police reports indicate that Mary Jones's reaction was understandable but unable to be justified. There were no witnesses who came forward for Ms. Jones, and nobody appears to want to get involved with the incident.

The Wind Valley YWCA has a reputation as one of the best facilities in the area. There has never been a previous case of sexual harassment claims. Brandon Smith has a clean record that shows nothing less than being a professional. Some participants in the American Red Cross lifeguard training class have begun withdrawing from the rest of the training because of their uneasiness with the situation. Rumors are spreading in the locker rooms and at other activities now. The issue is dividing your staff at the YWCA, and employee morale has obviously decreased. Though Brandon Smith stands legally innocent, his behavior has changed dramatically. He is more withdrawn lately and tends to avoid speaking to others. The latest gossip implies that there is a petition being sent around the agency asking that the accusations be investigated further at an agency level.

Discussion Questions

Should Brandon be fired even though he has never been in trouble before? Would suspending him be helpful in keeping this agency running smoothly for the duration of the training? Should the police be involved again though the case has been dismissed?

On the other hand, should Mary's membership be suspended for harassing the staff and keeping the rumors alive? Will a staff meeting be enough to clarify the situation and stifle any developing rumors? Will ignoring the issue and letting it all "pass over" work in this situation?

Describe what you might do to protect this agency, its programming, and most important, its members and staff.

Helping Staff Deal with Park Drowning

Problem Situation

The local community owns a beautiful 20-acre park, which includes a reservoir with a swimming area. Four lifeguards staff the swim area during open swim, swimming lessons, and special events.

The public park is very popular among the local residents and nearby communities. Last summer over 65% of the community participated in some type of swim program offered by park personnel. Facilities within the park include barbeque pits, a skateboard park, playground area, basketball courts, picnic tables, and fishing in a stream adjacent to the park.

On one particular day, there was a large family reunion taking place at the park pavilion. Over 100 family members gathered to celebrate the special day. During the event, one of the younger boys (five years old) expressed a desire to go swimming but was told he had to wait an hour until his food digested. He asked if he could walk around the swimming area and go to the skateboard park to watch his friends skate for an hour. He was given permission to do so; however, he never made it to the skateboard park. Instead, he went down to the beach and in the water. Moments later an adult saw three boys screaming hysterically. The lifeguards were notified and immediately rescued the boy.

Unfortunately, the boy did not survive. All four lifeguards had correctly administrated first aid and CPR until rescue workers arrived at the scene. The boy was later pronounced dead at the hospital.

Discussion Questions

As supervisor of the lifeguards, how will you handle their emotional well-being? Do you recommend a counselor for the lifeguards? Will you give the lifeguards time off from work or make them "get back on the horse" right away? If you do give them time off, how much time will you allow? How will you deal with the negative publicity over this unfortunate event? Your lawyer does not think there will be a lawsuit and states that no lifeguard was at fault. However, your lifeguards are hurting emotionally from this tragedy. Develop a crisis management policy that you could implement in a situation like this one.

Civil Service Job Claimed "Tailor-Made" for Park Employee

Problem Situation

Tony DeMarco, a former campaign worker and cousin of the current mayor, had been doing odd jobs in the parks department for nine years. He had a high school education, no supervisory experience, and a history of disciplinary, driving, and criminal problems, including two prior arrests for assault.

Yesterday the mayor promoted DeMarco to the position of recreation administrative assistant with a starting salary of $55,000. He will be responsible for running the entire recreation program, which includes supervising more than 200 workers. DeMarco will be responsible for overseeing the teen and community centers, swimming pools, ice rink, and playgrounds. He will drive a city car and hold a job title that other city employees hold who have college degrees (and more supervisory experience) and earn thousands less.

Outraged by this promotion, a group of city workers investigated the situation and found that a civil service job description was tailor-made specifically for DeMarco's limited resume. Upon further investigation, workers were astounded to find that, for the past five years, DeMarco was the city's park equipment operator, earning a salary of $25,155. Since his involvement with politics (as of last year), he has become one of the leading figures in the city's recreation and parks department.

The local newspaper reported that DeMarco has a history of problems with the law and proceeded to report his criminal activities. In addition, the reporter received a copy of the job description, which required no supervisory experience, no high school diploma, and nine years experience within the parks department—the exact number of years DeMarco has been on the payroll of the city's parks department.

Discussion Questions

Realizing this is a political promotion on behalf of the mayor, is there anything the Recreation and Parks Commission can do about this unjustifiable hiring? What, if anything, can the current Recreation and Parks Director do about this hiring? Can the taxpayers do anything about this situation? What are the laws regarding civil service testing and hiring? How will this hire affect the reputation of the department?

Disciplining a Department Director

Problem Situation

The Newcastle Recreation and Parks Department employs over 200 employees in a rapidly growing county in a southern state. The department is relatively young in that around 20 years ago the city decided to relinquish its parks and holdings to the county park and recreation department. The director has been there since the merging of the departments. Until recently, the county manager had been the same since the changes

(Vertical left margin text:) HUMAN RELATIONS

were made. It has been universally recognized that the county manager and the director were friends both socially and through their business dealings. Under the director, the department grew through land acquisition, program development, and in the number of employees—from 30 to its current level. The department has been one of the jewels of the county organization.

The planning and budgeting of the organization has been driven by precise methods of development and goal setting. Employees have been well respected by the community. The operational policy had been developed by an extensive human resource team that has two levels—administratively at the county level and a team of five within the department itself. The policy has been developed and reviewed over the years into a very concise document.

"Director Arrested for Drunk Driving: Police Discover He Has No License"

This is what the headlines read in the metro section. This matter became the immediate topic of conversation throughout the department. Television coverage showed the recreation and parks director entering into the city/county office building with reporters hounding him for answers. The assistant director was immediately authorized to serve as interim director until further notice. As official word was released through the county manager's office, it became apparent that the director, a former marine, had left an officer's club when he was pulled over. He was charged with driving while intoxicated (DWI) and driving without a license (which he had lost in a previous DWI incident). The county manager had immediately placed the director on administrative leave with pay for 30 days and reserved a final decision on the case until the end of that period of time.

The following month it was announced in a staff meeting that the county manager had made his final decision. The director would be returning to work, and he would not be allowed to drive a county vehicle until he could regain his license and all legal obligations were fulfilled.

On the director's first day back on the job, he visited with all staff to formally apologize for his actions and any embarrassment he might have caused anyone. He insured that his commitment to the department was as strong as ever, and he would work for the continued success that had been experienced under his direction in the past.

Discussion Questions

Human resource policy states several conditions for employment that bring forth questions concerning the legitimacy of the final decision to reinstate the director. There is no doubt in most people's mind that favoritism was involved and a loophole exists in the current human resource policy as it pertains to this matter. How else could the director have been reinstated, and so quickly?

What public relations issues might surface with the decision to reinstate the director? What steps would you have implemented to reach the decision to reinstate the director? How do you think the decision effects human resources' ability to administer the operating and discipline policies? What effect will this have on the ability of the director to garner the support he has had toward new policies and the budgeting and development process? What effect will this have on the morale of the current staff? Identify a policy and procedure as it relates to this problem situation. How would you have handled this entire situation?

Just Enough Rope

Problem Situation

You are the director of a large outdoor education center with 30 full-time staff. Your agency serves adults and children as well as at-risk youth. Your program director, who has been working for you for seven years, tells you at dinner that she has just hired a friend from college to fill the position of challenge course manager. You are relieved. This position had remained vacant far too long, and the course has been consuming a lot of your other staff's time during the vacancy. You and the program director briefly discuss his qualifications, and you feel confident about the hire, especially knowing that this person was endorsed by your program director.

During the challenge course manager's annual review the following year, you realize that a criminal background check had never been completed on him. Your center's policy is that all employees must have a criminal background check prior to being hired. You talk to your program director. At first, she says it was an oversight on her part. As the discussion continues, however, she admits that it was omitted deliberately. The ropes course manager had been arrested eight years ago. The conviction involved providing alcohol to minors as well as driving while intoxicated.

This conviction aside, the ropes course manager has done an outstanding job. There have been no further issues (that you are aware of) involving alcohol, and he has been professional in all dealings with minors at your facility.

You feel that your program director has violated your trust as well as the ethics and values of your agency, not to mention agency policies and procedures. You feel that this incident has called her judgment into serious question, and you are unsure if you will be able to trust and depend on her in the future. As far as the ropes course manager is concerned, you would never have hired him had you known about the criminal conviction. While his behavior and job performance during the past year have exceeded your expectations, you do not want to condone his past behavior.

Discussion Questions

As the director of this agency, how would you resolve this problem? What legal responsibilities, if any, do you have to your clientele? What legal duties, if any, do you have to the ropes course manager and program director? What moral or ethical duties do you have to your clientele and your staff? What moral or ethical duties do you have to your board of directors or governing agency? Identify other areas of concern that you must address in resolving this problem. Will you terminate the program director and/or the ropes course manager? Why or why not? If you were to retain the ropes course manager, would you tell the board of directors or simply let it go?

Seven Months Notice—Still No Replacement

Problem Situation

You are the director of a comprehensive recreation and parks department. One of your recreation supervisors has decided to resign his position to pursue personal career objectives. He gave seven months notice to the department, out of respect for the agency's need for a full staff. The seven-month notice would allow a new supervisor to be hired and trained. The supervisor who is leaving is responsible for 50% of all programming during that time of the year (in which he will be gone). The other 50% of the programming responsibilities were distributed among the remaining three staff.

Five and a half months have gone by and a new supervisor still has not been hired. The old recreation supervisor wanted to leave the agency quietly; he wanted no interruption of programming to the participants. With less then two months left on the job, due to budget constraints, more and more responsibilities are being given to him. Unfortunately, this is the busiest time of the year, and he is about to leave his position without having trained anyone to replace him.

Discussion Questions

As recreation director, how would you handle the situation? If the job search has been unsuccessful, what changes should you make? If you do not hire a new staff before your supervisor departs, what will you do? How will you keep the employee morale up? How will you disperse 50% of the programming among your current staff? Time is running out, and you need to develop a plan for the job search, training, and increase in responsibilities for your staff. What will you do?

Getting the Park Board on Board

Problem Situation

Don Perkins, who is the president of the park board, opened the morning newspaper and read the headline, "Grand Jury to Investigate Park Board." Naturally, he was surprised, since he was unaware of any problem with the park board's operations. He immediately called an emergency meeting of the five-person board to discuss the situation.

Mr. Perkins appealed to Lisa Winters, a new board member, for cooperation instead of criticism while the board was trying to get going on a greatly expanded park program. Perkins' remarks came after Winters reported that she requested the state's attorney general to look into the activities of the board.

In a letter, Winters told the attorney general that a board member was receiving compensation for conflict of interest. Her reference was to a payment of $281.20 to Burt Sloan, an attorney and member of the board, for legal services in negotiations for an option on an 80-acre tract of land west of the city. Sloan performed this service for the board while the regular attorney was out of town on vacation. Perkins stated, "Sloan helped us out in a tight spot, and he certainly did not overcharge us for the service. I don't know why there is any fuss; nobody made any big money on this transaction."

Winters further said that she asked the attorney to investigate nine items relative to the park board's activities:

1. Minutes of board meetings are very seldom kept.
2. Board equipment and employees have been used for board members' own personal gain.
3. Checks are being written before the board meets to approve or disapprove the bills.
4. Board members are receiving compensation for conflict of interest.
5. A board member has been arrested in another city at 3 a.m. driving a park district truck.

6. The board does not keep a regular book or record of all ordinances.
7. Board funds are in the First National Bank and the Savings Bank; two park board members are currently serving on the board of directors at these banks.
8. The board does not use any formal bidding procedures.
9. Debts are being created without first issuing purchase orders.

Other board members are very upset that Ms. Winters did not discuss her accusations with the board prior to her writing a letter to the attorney general. All of them, however, indicated they would welcome the investigation and would cooperate fully.

Discussion Questions

Should Lisa Winters have discussed her letter with the board prior to sending it to the attorney general? Why do you think she requested an investigation? Do you feel that Burt Sloan had a conflict of interest? Should a board member be permitted to provide a service to the board for which she/he will receive compensation? What is the state law regarding this? What kind of records should be kept by the park board? Should employees be permitted to use board equipment for their personal use? What procedures should be established to permit the payment of bills? What bidding procedures would you recommend to the park board? Are there any state laws that affect bidding procedures? Recommend a purchase order and voucher system that would adequately facilitate park board business.

Little Leaguers Face "Lockout"

Problem Situation

You are the athletic director for a public park and recreation department in Blueberry, a town of 100,000. As a part of your responsibilities, you supervise the facilities used by the local Little League organization. However, you have no jurisdiction over the Little League Baseball Administration. A dispute between two boards of directors, each claiming control of the local Little League, is threatening to delay the start of this year's season for nearly 500 boys and girls.

The dispute began last autumn when a group of parents charged that the board of directors was violating Little League regulations by refusing to conduct annual elections. After much bickering, each player's family received ballots in the mail under the supervision of Leroy Vanderville, a county regional administrator for Little League. When Vanderville counted the votes, three long-term board members lost their positions.

Joe Wintworth, who founded the league in 1977, was among those who were re-elected, but he refused to recognize the new board. He split from Little League Baseball and started his own league. He also refused to surrender the Little League's bats, balls, gloves, and bases. In addition, he sued in State Supreme Court seeking to prohibit the new board from using the name, Blueberry Little League; however, his request was denied.

Wintworth contended that he founded the Wintworth Little League, incorporated it, and therefore was not bound by Little League rules governing the operation of the board. "Little League can just dictate things such as size of playing field, weight of ball, and circumference of the bat," he maintained.

The national Little League backs the new board, but has taken the position that the dispute is a local matter to be resolved by the parents. Ten-year-old Sarah Westervelt summed up the reaction of her teammates by saying, "They should get all this ridiculous stuff out of the way and let us play ball. We just want to have some fun."

Discussion Questions

Should you become involved in the dispute as the city's recreation director? If so, what should your role be? How do you personally think the crisis should be resolved? Do the feelings of the children matter? How much control should Little League maintain? What are the advantages and disadvantages of retaining the Little League logo and affiliation? Can the parents resolve the issue or should it be resolved elsewhere—in court, with an arbitrator, or by the national Little League office?

What is the central issue here? Why do you think the original board was against elections? If elections had been held annually, do you think the current crisis would have occurred? Does democracy have a place in sports administration? Does administration take the "fun" out of the game, or does it make the game more efficient and "more fun"?

Accusations and Misrepresentations

Problem Situation

Eight months after you were hired to shape up the long-troubled Waterville Parks and Recreation Department, you are facing many problems of your own. In a four-page letter sent to you this week, the executive committee of the parks and recreation advisory commission charged that you and your staff have misrepresented information to the City Council, used park issues to widen racial divisions, and have been unresponsive and insensitive to the commission and its duties. The letter complained that a commission memorandum on city playgrounds had been "aggressively and falsely characterized as an attempt by the Caucasian female outsiders to curtail or eliminate adult basketball for African American neighborhoods." The same memorandum was misrepresented to the City Council's parks committee, the letter said.

In addition, the letter claimed that you had not established good relations with the commission, and you have not kept members informed of community meetings and other activities. Commission Chair Rita Williams, in a published interview with a local journalist, acknowledged that the letter is critical, but it was meant to help resolve difficulties, not exacerbate them. She said that the full commission supported the letter, although only three of the commission members had signed it.

In the letter, Williams acknowledges that there has been a history of communication problems between the commission and the parks and recreation department. The relationship between the commission and the previous director had deteriorated considerably before the embattled director resigned last year.

As the director, you showed the commission's letter to your assistant for his comments, and he replied, "We're following the City Council's orders, which are to clean up the parks and recreation system. We have nothing to be ashamed of. My thought is that somebody's relative lost a job in the reorganization, and that person is now seeking revenge."

Commission member Mabel Rines also talked to you in private. She said the letter is "an outreach from the commission, and I want you to pay attention to these concerns. I'm disappointed that we didn't hire a parks and recreation director who can work with our commission."

Discussion Questions

What do you say in response to this letter? What are the concerns that are overtly expressed in the letter? What are the concerns that may be covertly expressed? Does one

H
U
M
A
N

R
E
L
A
T
I
O
N
S

issue underlie all of these issues? If so, what is it? How would you address each of the concerns stated in the letter? Would you address the concerns that are covertly stated? If so, how? Through what means should you respond? What are the advantages and disadvantages of (a) calling a press conference, (b) writing a letter in return, (c) calling an emergency board session, or (d) ignoring the letter? Should a response be immediate or should you wait a few days?

Is eight months enough time for the board to make a fair evaluation of the director? What must the board show to prove that the evaluation is unbiased? What criteria should be used in judging the effectiveness of the director? Should the director be held responsible for a "mistake" that a subordinate made? Why or why not?

Define communication. Diagram a model of effective communication taking place between the director and the board. Suggest ways that communication could be strengthened between the two parties. Which of the parties should be responsible for making sure that good communication occurs?

Farmer City Park Plan Raises Questions

Problem Situation
To the Editor:

The Farmer City Park Board should provide the community with detailed information about the proposed regional playground at Willowbrook Park.

To date, the board seems more interested in building a playground than considering the impact of these facilities upon the park's ecosystem and protecting this natural wildlife habitat and prairie area. I suggest that the board provide the community with the answers to the following questions and then give the community an opportunity to decide if the merits of building a playground outweigh the merits of protecting this open wildlife habitat.

1. What is the scope of the intended project and how does the project fit in with the overall long-range master plan for the park? Is this the type of project that was envisioned when the master plan was developed or is it different? If it is different, how is it different?
2. Is this project being developed as a community facility for the taxpayers or is it intended to be a regional facility that will attract people throughout the area? If it is to be a high-use regional facility, is such use in line with the intent for the park? Can the park support such use without detriment to the ecosystem?
3. What is the impact of peak use on the area wildlife habitat and the ecosystem?
4. What actions will be taken to mitigate the impact of the project on the natural habitat?
5. What is the impact, if any, of the project on the surrounding neighborhood and what actions will be taken to mitigate such impact?
6. Have public hearings been held on the project? What were the comments and concerns expressed at the hearings? What was staff's response?

There should be no further action on the playground until the park board provides the community with the answers to these questions.

Sincerely,
Hannah Turner

Discussion Questions

What will you and the Board do? Will you respond to this letter? If so, how will you go about answering her questions? Will you answer all of the questions? Will you write a letter or hold a meeting? How will you handle this letter to the editor at the next board meeting? Outline your plan to respond to this problem situation.

Board Seeks to Restrict Employee Use of Facilities and Outdoor Equipment

Problem Situation

You are the director of an outdoor program within a medium-sized metropolitan area. The outdoor recreation advisory board has suggested that a policy be implemented that would curb employee use of facilities, materials, and equipment. The proposal would permit employee use on the same basis as that authorized for the general public. The proposal also tightens language regarding the loan of outdoor equipment to other agencies and personnel.

Board members contend that this proposal is necessary to protect the board against lawsuits. "Our current policy has too many loopholes," said one board member. "We don't mean this to be a witch hunt against employees, nor is it a reaction to any specific employee."

The Outdoor Leadership staff is against the proposal. Trip guide Rae Porter said, "If an outdoor leader used her own equipment to show how to make repairs or adjustments, it would be a violation of the rules, because her personal property would be improved and she would personally gain from the situation. That's crazy!" Many other personnel, part-time and full-time, agree with Porter. The board has asked you to make recommendations.

Discussion Questions

Should a policy regarding the use of equipment be implemented? Is it possible to obtain a policy that is inclusive but not too restrictive? Should personnel have a voice in the forming of this policy? If you were to favor the policy, would you implement the policy immediately or give personnel the chance to adapt? Can the advisory board legislate a policy even if the director does not approve of it? Is the use of outdoor equipment for personal gain a legitimate benefit for working within the agency? Should there be exceptions to the policy, such as people with certain ranks or instructors of certain courses? Draft a policy that covers loaning equipment to other agencies and using equipment for personal gain.

County Board Officials Recommend Snowmobile Ban for Park

Problem Situation

The County Park Board has recommended banning approximately 20,000 snowmobiles that rumble through the county parks and preserves every winter. The move delighted environmentalists in the community but dismayed enthusiasts of the sport and local merchants who depend on snowmobilers for winter income. Observers say the County Commissioner is likely to follow the recommendation of the board when she makes a final decision about winter park use in November. However, it is an election year, so the board is not entirely sure of her stance.

The County Park Board claims that without snowmobiles, winter enthusiasts could enjoy the rural parks by using snowshoes and cross-country skis. Further, the ban would not take effect for another year—to give time for snowmobile-rental companies to switch over to snow-coaches for the rural parks in the area. The larger vehicles would have to meet emission and noise standards yet to be specified.

County Park Board members say that the snowmobiles spread noise and air pollution throughout the parks and preserves, startle animals, and create numerous safety hazards. The board states that by having fewer vehicles in the parks, and having more trained drivers, fewer problems will result. People who enjoy snowmobiling are saying this plan is extreme.

Again, some business people rely on snowmobilers for winter income. They fear for the future of their businesses and rural communities. For example, 28% to 30% of tax revenues are collected during the winter season.

One local resident claimed, "Snowmobile makers have failed to develop quiet, clean vehicles. The noise and the pollution take away from my leisure experience when I'm out in the preserves snowshoeing with my family. They can snowmobile in other areas, like the state parks. Get them out of our jurisdiction!"

Discussion Questions

Given that it is an election year, you are afraid that the County Commissioner may waffle with her intention to support the ban on snowmobiles in the county parks. In addition, you don't want to lose the businesses that cater to snowmobile enthusiasts. How will you gain the support of the local and county leaders? How will you deal with the business people who rely on the income generated from snowmobilers? You have been asked to address this situation at the next town meeting. Draft a plan that you intend to propose at next month's meeting.

Youth Center Director Fears for His Life

Problem Situation

You represent the Civil Service Commission for a large metropolitan area. Your first case of the day asks you to decide the case of John Dell, a youth center director. Dell was fired by his supervisor for insubordination when he failed to report to work downtown. He had held the position for nine months.

Dell claims that he had received death threats after he enforced an unpopular policy late one evening. The threat came from some teenagers who are reputed to be gang members. The teenagers said that they were going to get their knives and, if Dell was still at the center when they returned, he would not make it home alive.

The center is in a rough area of the city, and John Dell believes that the death threats were genuine. He claims that his life was in danger, and therefore he did not report for work the next day. Instead, he notified his supervisor of the situation. His supervisor, however, insisted that Dell report to work. Dell refused to go and was fired that day.

Discussion Questions

Should John Dell be reinstated? Do employees have the right to refuse to work in certain parks or community centers? Is the parks and recreation department responsible for its employees' safety? If so, what should be done about Dell's safety concerns? How would you investigate whether Dell is overreacting to what the teenagers said? If he is reinstated, should he be allowed to collect back pay? If reinstated, should he be sent to the same center or a different one in the city? Do supervisors have the right to remove an employee for insubordination in a situation like this?

Recreation Committee Considers Policy on Team Cuts

Problem Situation

The director of the recreation baseball and softball program sparked a debate at a recent recreation committee meeting when she said that 11- and 12-year-old players had been cut from a special traveling team.

Director Sally Wilson said the program for 11 and 12 year olds had too many participants to allow all children to play, and Coach Mel Fowler had considered cutting a handful of them from the team. Fowler later revised his plan, deciding to run a "tight ship" on the team, and those who were not as dedicated would simply weed themselves out, eliminating the need for cuts.

The team initially had 17 players, which Wilson said were too many to provide enough playing time for each player. "The kids were getting up to bat once during the game or maybe twice," she said. Ideally, the teams should have between 12 and 14 players to provide a good balance of playing time with a bench deep enough to provide enough players for all the games. Wilson told the committee that the proposed cuts were based on players' attendance, effort, and attitude through the regular season. "The kids know this is the way it's normally done," Wilson said.

The issue of cuts is a touchy one for the recreation committee. They had three basketball coaches quit last season due to this very subject. The coaches had resigned from their positions because of a conflict involving a special tournament team.

Recreation committee member William Henderson interrupted the heated debate by stating, "The board needs to create a policy statement on cuts, when they are and are not appropriate. I'm just uncomfortable when I hear the word 'cut.' I don't think it helps the kids." Board member Sheila Yaple argued, "I think it does more harm than good to keep kids on the team who aren't going to play very much."

The committee has by-laws, and members of the board have strong opinions, but the group lacks written practices and philosophies on controversial topics such as cutting players from sports.

Discussion Questions

What should the committee do? Should there be cuts at this level of play? What about the kids who do not make that cut? If no kids are cut, and the policy stands that all kids must play an equal amount of time, then kids may only bat once per game. Is this acceptable? How should the committee proceed with regard to developing a policy statement for this issue?

Should We Hire From Within the Organization?

Problem Situation

The Dassance Recreation and Parks Department, which has been in existence for three years, is in a suburb of a thriving metropolis in the Midwest. The suburb of Dassance has grown larger proportionally than the surrounding areas. The budget is large, acquisition of land has been increasing, programs are growing at a rapid pace, and the development of special facilities and large neighborhood parks has been on the upswing since the department was formed. This department is classified as one of the most rapidly growing and progressive in the state. The staff currently consists of a director of parks and recreation, a superintendent of recreation who has also been assisting the director for four years and is responsible for the supervisor of facilities and the supervisor of programs, and a superintendent of parks who supervises five maintenance workers. An organizational chart appears below:

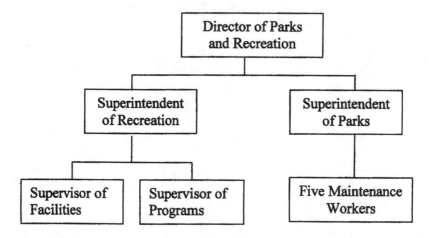

The director of parks and recreation recently announced that she is leaving the Dassance Recreation and Parks Department for a new position. She will be leaving in two weeks. The board of commissioners has been interviewing for her replacement for some time now. It is their intention to promote the superintendent of recreation to the director of parks and recreation. You, as superintendent of recreation for the past four years, look forward to the new challenges and opportunities with a tremendous amount of enthusiastic spirit and broad support.

One of the most important items on the list of goals for the next several weeks is to hold the personnel on a level that will enable you to continue the business of the department as usual. Although you may be shorthanded (because your position will be vacant), you still have to provide the services expected of a parks and recreation department. You have no problems with the superintendent of parks. He was not interested in securing the position of director, and he is fully supporting you in your new endeavors. As superintendent of recreation, you had an astute program supervisor and a capable facilities supervisor.

The key position that now must be filled is that of the superintendent of recreation. Needless to say, you have several thoughts running through your mind. Among them are the following:

1. Should you recruit from outside the department for the position of superintendent of recreation?

2. Should you promote the current supervisor of programs or facilities to the position of superintendent?
3. Should you eliminate the position and rethink the whole strategy?

Both of the supervisors have excellent credentials. You pride yourself on the fact that your recruitment for these two positions was a successful part of your job as superintendent of recreation. Either one would do an admirable job. There is one small problem, however. If you promote one over the other, will the one who is not promoted remain with the organization?

Discussion Questions

As the new director of parks and recreation, which decision would be in the best interest of all concerned and keep business as usual in the recreation and parks department? What affirmative action procedures must be followed? If you promote someone from within the organization, what problems would ensue? If you recruit and select an individual from the outside, what consequences would that have on dealing with the two supervisors and the other personnel?

If you promote one supervisor from within and the other leaves, what would be your short-term plan to fill that void? Are there economic factors that might be considered to help you reach a decision? If you are going to select someone outside, what qualifications will you be seeking?

With the current amount of growth in the area, would reorganization be worthwhile? You already know that the plans for the area call for additional special facilities such as ice rinks, swimming pools, outdoor tennis courts, indoor handball courts, and golf courses. If a reorganization plan is developed, how would you justify it to your board of commissioners, and how would you sell the idea to the rest of your staff?

Do you feel that as the new director of parks and recreation that this staffing dilemma may be one of your most important decisions? Why or why not?

THEME ONE: HUMAN RELATIONS RELATED WEBSITES

Boardsmanship: The Spirit of Cooperation by Dr. Ted Flickinger, CAE
http://www.lib.niu.edu/ipo/ip910906.html

Committees - Recreation Boards (Town of Springwater)
http://www.springwater.ca/committee.cfm?CatID=110&intUID=3889013428-WBAS
UGOEBZ

How to Work with Boards Even Though Boards Don't Work by Kim Klein
http://www.afpnet.org/ec_detail.cfm?folder_id=888&event_id=1821

Human Relations Area Files (Yale University)
http://www.yale.edu/hraf

Human Resources Learning Center (John McCarter)
http://www.human-resources.org

Methods and Strategies for Working With Boards 2004
http://www.ncvo-vol.org.uk/asp/search/ncvo/main.aspx?siteID=1&sID=5&documentID
=1687&viewType=6

Pennsylvania Human Relations Commission
http://www.phrc.state.pa.us

Working with Boards of Directors (Managing Community Health Services)
http://erc.msh.org/mainpage.cfm?file=2.3.1.htm&module=chs&language=English

THEME TWO:

MARKETING AND PUBLICITY

Table of Contents

"Family" Recreation Takes on an Alternative Meaning

Problem Situation

You are the Director of the local Recreation and Parks Department of a small town in New England. Since the tragedy of September 11, 2001, your department has been actively promoting family-based recreation programs. Given that many people prefer to participate in leisure activities close to home, your staff has created many types of recreation programs the whole family can enjoy. Further, as an incentive, family discounts apply to many of these newly created programs. The "family recreation" promotional campaign has been a tremendous success thus far.

Your secretary knocks on your office door and asks you to please come to the lobby area to meet with a woman who would like to sign up for some activities with the family discount option. The woman introduces herself and explains that she would like to take advantage of the family discount options to several of your programs. However, she is having difficulty filling out the "family discount" registration form and asks how your organization defines the term "family" in your promotional campaign. Not having thought much about the definition, you state that two parents and at least one child define the term "family," which is stated on the registration form. She explains to you that she has a family but not in the traditional sense. That is, she and her lesbian partner of 12 years, have two children, ages three and five. She wants to know, "Will I receive the family discount option?"

Discussion Questions

What do you do? The neighboring state (Massachusetts) acknowledges gay marriages and therefore cannot discriminate. Your policy statement is written for the traditional heterosexual family, however, is this discrimination? How about children who live with their grandparents? Would they qualify for a family discount? What impact does your decision have on other policy statements within your organization? How will you redesign the family discount registration form? That is, how will you define the term "family" so it reflects more diversity? How will the new definition impact public relations?

Obesity and Fast Food: Who's Responsible?

Problem Situation

You are the Director of Youth Services for the municipal parks and recreation department of a small city. You have just finished reading an article about the problem of children and obesity. The article highlights how fast food chains like McDonald's lure children into obesity. It indicated that trial lawyers are now targeting these chains and trying to hold them responsible for their marketing strategies. The article lists common causes of obesity such as the lack of physical activity. Television, computer games, and video games all contribute to a child's sedentary lifestyle, which contributes to the obesity problem.

The article caught your attention because you are the Director of Youth Services and interact with children and adolescents on a daily basis. In addition, you have noticed a tremendous increase in the number of obese participants in your programs.

One of your responsibilities as Director of Youth Services is to oversee the Youth Center. The Youth Center is a drop-in program that offers a safe place for children, ages 13 to 17, to go after school, but it also has a snack bar that traditionally does not offer healthy snacks. Your Youth Center also offers an Adventure Club in which youth go on overnight camping and hiking trips. They usually travel a moderate distance, and the ride home always entails a stop at a fast food restaurant. Another cause for concern is that you and your staff notice an increase in overweight adolescents in your facility during drop-in and family programs.

Attendance is at an all-time low for your drop-in program, and recently you have considered launching an expensive marketing plan and renovation of your facility to increase attendance. As a resident of this small city, you often see adolescents hanging out in front of the fast food restaurants. Your city has many fast food restaurants concentrated in a small area. There is also a high level of poverty in your community, which may lead to unhealthy eating patterns. These are all factors that you must consider before you react.

M
A
R
K
E
T
I
N
G

&

P
u
B
L
I
C
I
T
Y

Discussion Questions

As a professional in the area of youth services, you need to decide what kind of action you should take. The article you read is just one more piece of information that opened your eyes to this growing problem in our society. What should be your next move? Is the rate of child and adolescent obesity within your community significant enough to cause concern? How do you go about determining if you should act or not? What implications, if any, does the poverty level have on eating habits?

As the Director of Youth Services, is it your responsibility to take steps to help combat child and adolescent obesity within your community? Or is it the responsibility of the school or the parents? If it is your responsibility, or partly your responsibility, how can you get parents and the school district involved?

What types of programs or activities can you offer to get adolescents involved and active? Should the adventure club trips still include the standard stop at a fast food restaurant on the way home? If not, how can you offer healthy alternatives at a low cost? Should the snack bar that is operated within your youth center continue to offer ice cream and other unhealthy snacks? If not, how do you determine what food should be offered? Does the recreation department even have the budget or staff to launch an assault against obesity in your community?

After reading the article and considering all the factors, describe your plan of action. Write down what you would say about the situation at the next staff meeting.

Sport Sales Jog to Record High

Problem Situation

You are the director for a large sporting complex in your city. As you browse through your mail, you see that Wrona Shoes has sent you a news release. This news release presents findings from a national survey. The survey indicates that running shoes helped to push retail sales in sporting goods to a record high of $15.1 billion. Running shoes, included for the first time in an annual consumer survey prepared by the National Sporting Goods Association, showed an increase in sales of 110 percent over the previous year.

Another trend observed by the survey is that women constitute nearly one-third of the market for athletic shoes, snow skis, and athletic balls. Female participation was also cited for substantial sales increases in exercise equipment, racquet sports, basketball, and soccer. Twenty percent of all gloves sold were intended for a female hand. Thirty percent of all skateboards were intended for female feet. The survey also noted that the number of high-level female administrators at recreational and sporting facilities had tripled in the past year.

The letter from Wrona Shoes encourages you to seriously consider their product and, further, to prominently display the results of the survey to potential interested consumers. Permission is given to duplicate the survey. No reply is requested.

Discussion Questions

What should you do with the survey? Should you post it? Should you duplicate it? Should you use the information to justify offering more sports and equipment for women? If not, what other information would you need to make such a justification?

Does it make a difference that the survey was done by a national organization rather than by a shoe company? Why would a shoe company mail the results of the survey? Is the survey a marketing ploy or a public relations ploy? What is the difference between "public relations" and "marketing" in this situation? Do you trust the information presented? What could bias the information? How could you determine if the information is valid? What positive impact might this survey have on your sports complex?

Smoking and Recreation

Problem Situation

You are the owner and operator of large ski resort. The resort employs approximately 300 staff and is located in the northern Rocky Mountains. You recently had your marketing team come up with a new appealing commercial. The commercial has aired in local communities and in some of the neighboring states. The commercial was composed of quick flashes of different people skiing at your resort with a narrator describing the experience. The commercial was edited and produced by your marketing department and approved by you before being sent out to the television stations.

After the commercial had been played on television for about two weeks, a customer approached one of your ski instructors and told her how the commercial was unsettling to him. He explained that in one scene of the commercial a young boy can be seen smoking a cigarette at the outdoor café near the base lodge. The gentleman explained that the boy looked very young, perhaps underage, and that the image has stayed with him for days.

The ski instructor immediately shared this information with her supervisor who immediately shared it with you. As a result, you and the marketing department re-examine the commercial. After further examination it was found that the video did contain a young teenager smoking a cigarette for a split second before changing scenes. You ask your public relations manager how he thinks you should deal with this situation. The commercial has already been seen for at least two weeks around the state, and in bordering states. The commercial is scheduled to air several times a day for the next three months and further. You have already paid for these services.

Discussion Questions

What issues, if any, do you think this commercial could perpetuate? Would you spend the money to change the commercial, even though only one complaint has been lodged after several weeks of being viewed? Would you keep the commercial or pull it? How does this problem situation fit into your policies and procedures? Would you need to change your policies and procedures to deal with similar instances?

Dealing with the public could also be possible area of concern. Would you make your error publicly known and apologize for your actions and affirm your position on tobacco? How would you change the commercial for future viewing? Would you implement more training on editing and censoring the commercial? If so, how would you do this? Would you penalize any employee who could be, perhaps, in part responsible for missing the scene? If so, how would you deal with that employee?

Tourism Project Threatens Town's Attraction

(vertical sidebar text) MARKETING & PUBLICITY

Problem Situation

You have been hired by the Westernburg City Council to advise it about whether or not to approve a commercial recreation project. Mayor Dale Elks, the person who recommended hiring you, says he remembers the "good ole' days" in this riverside town. Nearly 30 years ago, just a few years before he was first elected mayor, Elks was chief of police. His own car served as the town's squad car, and he had no radio. A flashing beer sign at a local tavern or at the town's main office meant trouble.

"It was like Mayberry here," he told you. "People used to sit on the corner and whittle. But it can't stay that way. Times change, and you have to change with the times."

Right now, the biggest change facing this town of 1,050 people is a proposal to develop 1,200 acres of bluff-lined riverfront into a massive tourist attraction, complete with a water theme park, resort hotel, condominiums, private homes, and an 18-hole golf course.

The project is proposed by businessman Sam Jones on land his family owns. The first area scheduled to be built is a 20-acre water park. The Chamber of Commerce unanimously approved Sam Jones's plan last autumn, saying it could boost the city's sagging treasury by adding as much as $60,000 to the town's tax base—no small change to a town with a total budget of $230,000. The Chamber of Commerce hopes that Jones's plan is the first in a series of bluff front developments that could ultimately include a small museum, another hotel, a discount shopping center, and medical offices.

"What happens if the project doesn't go through?" supporters asked. "Nothing. Absolutely nothing. And we sit here like we have been for the past 20 years."

On the other hand, local environmentalists say the water park and the ensuing development will only denigrate the town's prime asset, which is its natural beauty. "We are extremely concerned about what this means for the scenic beauty of the area," said Sharon Beeler, who leads a local chapter of the Sierra Club. "It's the most scenic section of the Mississippi. Sure, we understand it's on private land, but the state and community have fought to preserve the area the way it is now. Sam Jones may own the property, but the heritage belongs to everyone."

Jones dismissed the importance of a Sierra Club petition of 8,500 signatures opposing the project, saying that many of the signatures are from tourists only passing through. Beeler acknowledges Jones's point of view, but suggests that Jones should heed the wishes of those who are drawn to the area for its beauty and who see development as a detriment.

Beeler claims that the construction will also have a tremendous adverse impact on wildlife because "a lot of species which currently inhabit the area, including the bald eagle, will be driven out." Jones counters this claim, saying that two-thirds of the area under development will remain "green."

Discussion Questions

What would you recommend to the City Council? Is Jones realistic about how little environmental damage his project will cause? Who should have the right to determine the fate of scenic land, the owner or the public? Could the town better market its current assets rather than seek to bring in new attractions? If so, devise a marketing strategy. Does the fact that you are being paid by the City Council influence your decision on whether you recommend this project? Does it influence how you word your presentation?

Public Relations Determines Success of Health and Racquet Club

Problem Situation

You have just been employed as a consultant to the Cape Elizabeth Health and Racquet Club, a private commercial recreation facility. Your principle responsibility is to design a public relations and information campaign that will attract new members six months from now, when the facility will open.

Cape Elizabeth is a community of approximately 100,000 residents with a median family income of $46,600. At present there are no other indoor health and racquet facilities in the community. Tennis is very popular due to the instructional programs and tournaments offered by the city's recreation department. The only exposure that the community has had to racquetball is through the use of three courts at the local YMCA. There are four radio stations in the community (one station devotes most of its programming to teenagers), a morning and evening newspaper, and three television stations, one of which is a public television station affiliated with the local university.

Upon accepting this assignment, the owner and builder inform you that the following facilities will be included in this new recreation development: Six indoor tennis courts; twelve air-conditioned racquetball/handball courts; a supervised nursery; an exercise room; carpeted locker rooms; furnished lounge area; a pro shop with the latest tennis, handball, and racquetball equipment; and a steam room, whirlpool, and sauna. A large room with a kitchenette for social activities is also being included. Annual membership fees have been established at $100 for an individual and $200 for a family. Persons wishing to use the tennis courts or the racquetball courts must pay an hourly rental fee of $10. The club will be open from 6:00 a.m. to 11 p.m., seven days a week.

You have been told that the maximum amount of money that can be spent on the campaign during the next six months is $9,000. Advertising on the radio, TV, and in newspapers, and any promotional brochures must come from this amount.

Discussion Questions

Plan a detailed promotional campaign for the opening of the racquet club, not to exceed $9,000. What would be the most effective way to spend the allotted money? Which of the available media would be most effective in publicizing the program? Develop a promotional brochure describing the club's facilities and why individuals should join. What promotional gimmicks can you suggest to encourage individuals to join before the club opens? Are there any public relations and information programs that require little or no expenditure of funds? What assistance would you need to carry out your proposed program? Outline your entire campaign.

Pineapple Paradise: A Resort for All?

Problem Situation

You are the business manager of Pineapple Paradise, a resort in the southern part of the United States. The resort name is a small chain that has 11 other beachfront resorts, which share the same philosophy: At Pineapple Paradise, you can escape to unspoiled beaches where the only footprints in the sand are your own. Rock each other gently to sleep in hammocks that sway to soft ocean breezes. Come to Pineapples, it's a paradise where love is all you need.

MARKETING & PUBLICITY

M
A
R
K
E
T
I
N
G

&

P
U
B
L
I
C
I
T
Y

One of the policies at Pineapple Paradise states that you have to be a heterosexual couple in order to secure a room at the resort. This attitude is expressed by spokesman Leo Lambert who says the resorts "cater expressly to the niche market of heterosexual couples. We believe that our opposite-sex, couples-only policy provides an atmosphere which many clients demand in a vacation experience."

Because of this publicity, some companies such as Microsoft and Yahoo no longer promote Pineapple Paradise and will not maintain a promotions or advertisement affiliation with them. Other companies such as U.S. Airways, Travelocity, and American Airlines still promote and advertise for Pineapple Paradise but do not support their policy.

When Pineapple Paradise learns that someone is inquiring about reservations for same sex couples (platonic or not), they will not send information about the resorts. However, today a young gay couple approached the reservation desk only to learn they will not be granted a room because they are two males. They explained that they made reservations online and used both names, Jamie and Dani. They specifically reserved rooms at this resort because of the "no kids" policy. They were unaware of the policy prohibiting same sex couples at the resort. As business manager, you need to make a decision immediately.

Discussion Questions

Will you permit the couple to stay? Will you try to change the policy of the resorts to meet the needs of possible future customers or take this as a one-time request and not try to change anything? You are aware that same-sex marriages are being allowed in some states and countries. Civil unions are becoming more prevalent, too.

The board of the resort is very opposed to changing the policy, but you are beginning to see things differently as the world becomes more progressive as it relates to gay and lesbian rights. How would you handle the publicity that surrounds this case? Would you reconsider working for an organization that has a policy like this? How will you attempt to persuade your board into changing this policy?

Logos Do More Than Whet the Appetite

Problem Situation

You are the chief executive officer for recreation in a metropolitan area with a population of 400,000. As the softball season prepares to open, a beer company distributor approaches the recreation board about letting the beer company distribute free merchandise to softball patrons. The company representative claims that he will pass out T-shirts, footballs, and other miscellaneous items with a popular brand of the beer's logo imprinted on them. He emphasizes that he will not be distributing free beer. The board decides to turn him down, because, as one board member put it, "Allowing beer logo distribution will encourage drinking at softball games. He knows that, or else he wouldn't be here."

After the representative's request is turned down, the board decides to proceed with other new business. The next item of business is approving softball sponsors. Billy's bar has decided to be one of the sponsors this year. The board approves the sponsorships and agrees to let Billy's logo be imprinted on the team T-shirt.

The beer company representative now claims that you are being unfair by allowing the bar to have its logo on the T-shirt while excluding his company's logo. How do you respond?

Discussion Questions

What do you say to the representative? How do you justify the decision that has been made? Is the justification likely to hold up in court? What is the recreation board objecting to regarding the representative's case? Would a beer company sponsoring a team be acceptable, or is there something greatly different between a national beer company with a local distributor sponsoring a team and a local tavern sponsoring a team?

Do either the beer distributor or Billy's Bar want to "do something nice for the community" or are both trying to make money through advertising? What is the purpose of a logo? Would the beer distributor's gifts be acceptable without the logo on them?

Do Late-Night Games Prevent Youth Crime?

Problem Situation

You are the superintendent in charge of overseeing seven public parks and community recreation centers. One of the programs that you decide to try at an inner-city center is a basketball league for teenagers. You have learned about the "Midnight Madness" program at a recent conference and would like to try it in your community. The goal of the league is to keep young men and women off the streets and on the basketball courts between the peak crime hours of 10:00 p.m. and 2:00 a.m. Players practice two nights per week and play games on two other nights during the week. The league has 16 teams with names taken from the National Basketball Association (NBA) and the Women's National Basketball Association (WNBA).

As you evaluate the program by watching a game, the community center director scans the players and spectators, pointing out which people belong to which gangs. "I'd guess that about one-third of the players are in gangs. It's very strange—the gangs are getting along really well. I can't explain it."

After each game, players are required to attend workshops on subjects such as job training, drug abuse, and parenting. Role models talk to the young men and women. Although the recreation director does not have actual proof of the success of the program, she makes a public statement that the program is benefiting the community—namely, that crime is decreasing in the area.

Discussion Questions

What sort of concrete evidence could the director give to support her "gut feeling" that the program works? Should community centers be "gang hangouts"? Should members from the same gang be allowed to play on the same team, or does this cause more "us" versus "them" feelings? What security precautions can you take to prevent gang fights?

Is it fair to insist that the players attend workshops after the ballgame? Are the workshops' topics appropriate? What other topics would you include? How long should the workshops be? What sort of teaching methods should be used? Who is qualified to teach these workshops?

Farmington Wants New Pool: Mayor Not on Board

M

A

R

K

E

T

I

N

G

&

P

U

B

L

I

C

I

T

Y

Problem Situation

Farmington residents will likely be able to celebrate Independence Day in a new outdoor swimming complex, which was approved by the village board last week. The Farmington Village Board voted four to two to hire an aquatics company for $250,000 to prepare plans, specifications, and bidding documents for a new family aquatic center to be built southwest of the local fitness center.

The outdoor complex would include a bath house; concession stands; an atrium area for parties and eating concession food; a large, grassy picnic area where families could spread out blankets; a sand play area for small children; a zero-depth pool to accommodate small children, the elderly, and persons with disabilities; a flume water slide; sand volleyball courts; and a pool mechanical and storage building.

The pool project faces one more possible roadblock, however. Mayor Sarah Terry said she will decide by Monday whether to veto the proposal. "That's an awful lot of money, and we still have a lot of people here in town on fixed incomes," Terry said.

Even if Terry issues the veto, the pool plan will probably go forward since the village attorney says it only takes four votes of the village board to override a veto. Plans call for awarding a building contract in August, starting construction in September, and opening the complex next summer. "I believe Farmington needs a new pool, and I believe we are going in the right direction," said one of the board members.

While the family aquatic center would cost about $3.7 million if it were all contracted out, it is hopeful the cost could be trimmed by having municipal employees do some of the electrical, landscaping, utility, and other work. One of the opponents to the plan stated, "I am opposed to spending this much money, and I'm opposed to the size of the pool. I think it is important that we have more time to study the figures before we proceed. I'm not worried about the design; I'm worried about the funding. I want a pool too, but I want to be responsible to the taxpayers of Farmington. I would have preferred to put this thing on hold while we looked at other options."

"But if we can't commit to this, how can we expect developers to commit money to Farmington? If the board delays the project by a year, inflation would boost the price of the aquatic center by $350,000," retorted another board member.

Plans call for building the pool without increasing taxes. The village board is considering using up to $600,000 of existing bond proceeds, $900,000 in tax increment financing district money, and/or $200,000 from the sale of surplus property toward the project. The rest of the money would most likely come from grants, bonds, revenue, and tourist development tax revenue.

Discussion Questions

How will you convince the mayor that this plan is a good idea? What happens if she vetoes your plan, but the project has permission to proceed? Will there be a political impact on you? What impact will this have on your recreation department? How will you convince the townspeople that this is a wonderful opportunity for everyone?

Editorial States That Parks Belong to People

Problem Situation

A recent editorial was published in your local newspaper concerning the future of our national parks. The editorial, written by a high school teacher, argued that the government should make parks accessible to everyone and not keep people out. After reading the editorial, the recreation and parks commission has asked you to write an editorial stating your thoughts about the future of our national parks—given that you are the recreation and parks director. The commission feels this opportunity would allow the residents to hear an expert in the field share her thoughts about the issues surrounding the national park service and their efforts to balance people versus the environment. The published editorial, in its entirety, is presented below:

All of our citizens, especially past and future visitors to our beautiful national parks, are devastated by the severe flooding that has closed Yosemite National Park. This act of nature is not uncommon in our parks and focuses our attention on the many risks and uncertainties that surround providing visitor services in the parks. It is shortsighted for the National Park Service (NPS) to leap on the tragedy at Yosemite as an opportunity for a "scouring action" leading to many restrictions of the people's right to visit, use, and enjoy a park that has been acquired, maintained, and paid for by the partnership of the U.S. taxpayers and the private-sector concessionaires over the past years.

Instead, we should be drawn into a realistic planning and construction effort, which will emphasize ways the lodging, food service, gift shops, and other "necessary and appropriate visitor services," can be provided. The fact is that all roads and visitor services in our parks take up only about one percent of the land area, with nearly all the rest being preserved in its natural state.

Why shouldn't the NPS, in conjunction with its concessionaires, plan carefully and creatively so that even more visitors can enjoy our parks without endangering the resources? This can and should be done to balance the dual role of the NPS in protecting the resources and, at the same time, allowing and enhancing the use and enjoyment of those resources by visitors eager to share in their wonder.

The founders of our present-day National Park System envisioned a partnership between the park service and its private-sector concessionaires, which would welcome visitors to these special places and provide for their comfort, enjoyment, and safety through carefully regulated visitor services.

That plan has worked well since 1916, when the NPS was formed, and even before, back to the time of the founding of Yellowstone National Park in 1872.

Let's not turn back the clock and discourage people from using and enjoying their national parks because government can't plan creatively to accommodate them. America deserves better than that.

Discussion Questions

The editorial is very well written and eloquently states the individual's frustration in the way the government is dealing with our national parks. Again, the board has asked you to state your opinion of the future of our national parks and acknowledge this published editorial you have just read.

What will you write? How will you go about writing a thought-provoking editorial much like the one you have just read? Draft a plan to help you get started with your editorial. That is, outline the steps you will take to complete a well-written editorial. Finally, write the final draft of the editorial that you will submit to the newspaper.

MARKETING & PUBLICITY

Developing the Ideal Boys and Girls Club

Problem Situation

Over the past decade, the directors, board of directors, and friends of the Boys and Girls Club have spent considerable time, money, and energy pursuing the goal of developing the "ideal club." This extraordinary effort has been justified not only in terms of the obvious needs in the community, but also in the belief that their success could and would serve as an inspirational model for other Boys and Girls Clubs to follow. To a great extent, the club has attained its goal of providing the "ideal club" when applying the criteria of success used within the Boys and Girls Club system. On the other hand, it is clear that the club has not provided a "model" widely embraced by other Boys and Girls Clubs in the metropolitan area.

The club is surrounded by one of the most economically and racially diversified neighborhoods in the city. It is frequently referred to as a major melting pot of social, cultural, economic, ethnic, and racial conglomerations. It is similar to, but unlike, any other neighborhood of its size in the city.

The club is a well-equipped modern facility, which has the outward appearance of a bank or medical building. It is a well-financed organization with the largest budget of any boys and girls club in the city. Although most of the board members of the organization live outside the neighborhood, many have their places of business in the area. For the most part, these are men and women who are very influential leaders; they not only contribute large sums of money toward the financial support of the club, they also take a serious interest in the problems of the community.

The present and former directors of the club are also key elements in the organization. Although both directors have been successful at managing the club, their greatest strength is in their charismatic personalities. They have been very successful in getting many people to follow them even when there is frequent disagreement with their methods. Also, both directors have been generally successful in maintaining continuity in staff over the years and this has contributed to the steady growth of the organization.

Strength of the organization has been the ability of the professional staff to maintain personal interest and concern for the individual boys and girls while conducting a comprehensive recreational program. Sometimes, however, the individual interest in the boys and girls is carried to the extent that some staff see themselves as counselors or therapists. Although the staff seem to perform the role of counselor well, the time demands required to adequately perform their roles have a deleterious effect upon their other responsibilities. Consequently, they do not have sufficient time to devote to the supervision of part-time employees and junior staff. This tends to contribute to a general deterioration in the quality of recreation programs and low staff morale.

Some of the attributes that have been pointed out as strengths of the club might also be considered weaknesses. For example, the increased emphasis on developing the "ideal club" has resulted in the displacement of some goals considered primary in terms of Boys and Girls Club philosophy. This has resulted in the down grading of importance of the recreational programs in the club and has tended to subvert the democratic social group work principles upon which Boys and Girls Club leadership is usually based.

As the club has become more like a comprehensive care taking service agency, the staff has tended to move more toward professionalism and the structure of the organization has become more rigid and formal. Regimentation has resulted in increased emphasis on conformity. Children have less involvement in the decision-making process, which affects their interest in the life of the club.

As the club director became more aware of the problems the club was facing, she tended to become more autocratic in her style of leadership. The more autocratic the director, the less her subordinates are able to make decisions that might improve the situation at the program level. Their frustrations have led to job dissatisfaction and some staff departures. Even though this club has all the outward appearances of success, there are some early signs of organizational deterioration.

Discussion Questions

The Boys and Girls Club is showing major signs of organizational deterioration. Recreation programs are no longer as much fun as they once were. Staff roles are conflicted between recreation and counseling. Three of five professional staff members have quit to take other jobs in the Boys and Girls Club system. Community support is rapidly decreasing. The board of directors fires the club director and you are hired as the new administrator to come into this situation and bring it back to its former position. How would you proceed to improve the situation? Identify the steps you would take to address the many problems facing the Boys and Girls Club.

If given the opportunity, how would you restructure the organizational flow chart (i.e., the chain of command)? What new recreation programs would you implement to increase popularity and enrollment? How would you address the leadership problem that exists in the organization?

Pressure-Treated Lumber Causes Playground Problems

Problem Situation

Two years ago the local recreation and parks department rallied the community to build Freedom Park, a barrier-free playground for persons with and without disabilities. Children with disabilities could enjoy the same playground activities as other kids, without the hazards a regular playground would pose. It was a day for rejoicing as the community came together to build this state-of-the-art playground.

Unfortunately, your department has just been informed that the wood used to build the Freedom Park structure is pressure treated, infused with chemicals to keep it from rotting and to keep insects out. You were told the pressure-treated lumber contains chromate copper arsenate (CCA), which is 22 percent pure arsenic. Arsenic is a poison and a carcinogen. It can leach from playground structures onto children's skin. It can also run into the soil, and end up in the mouths of kids playing in the dirt.

Upon further investigation of this information, you learn that the U.S. Environmental Protection Agency (EPA) has just announced that the pressure-treated wood industry will voluntarily phase out the use of CCA in residential products. By the year 2005, the EPA will ban the use of pressure-treated wood with CCA items such as children's play structures, decks, picnic tables, and landscaping timbers. The government has not called, however, for the removal of existing play structures. Your fear, of course, is that once this information hits the community, residents will be up in arms about the future of the Freedom Park playground structure.

At the next board meeting a heated discussion takes place regarding the future of the Freedom Park playground structure. One board member claims that CCA treated wood has been around for 30 years and it's been widely used in playgrounds for at least 25 years. "Millions of kids have played on them, and if there was a problem we would see an epidemic of cancer and cancer related illness. But we haven't."

However, not everyone on the board is convinced that leaving the pressure-treated structure in place is the right thing to do. One board member had read that short-term

M

hazards from inhaling the arsenic could include nausea, vomiting, diarrhea, abdominal pain, and irritation of the nose and throat. Skin and eye contact can cause irritation and burning. Another board member stated that long-term exposure is perhaps more troubling. "Inhaling it is strongly associated with lung cancer, and its ingestion has been linked to skin, bladder, liver, and lung cancers." Another board member chimed in to state, "We need to prevent our children's exposure to arsenic. I don't think it's something that we should play around with. I think we should remove the structure."

A

R

Discussion Questions

K

What are you to do? Should you remove the playground structure? Should you leave it alone and hope that it isn't too dangerous? What about the other 13 playgrounds within your jurisdiction? What will you do with all of those playgrounds? Do you have legal concerns? What about the public relations nightmare that might ensue? Develop an action plan of your intentions.

E

T

I

Body Piercing Doesn't Fly with Members

N

Problem Situation

G

You are a Program Director at a YMCA in a small conservative town. There are about 3,500 members in your organization and everyone knows just about everyone at the YMCA. You are responsible for supervising over 40 staff members and you have been the Program Director for seven years.

&

One of your strongest employees, Sue, has been the sports coordinator for many years. She is very well liked by the members and the community. Upon returning from her vacation, you notice something very different about her appearance. She dyed her hair red with black streaks and had her tongue pierced. At first you thought it was a joke, but then realized she wasn't about to change her hair or get rid of her piercing. One week later she arrived at work with her eyebrow and nose pierced.

P

Gradually members start to complain about her appearance. One mother states, "Great, now my kid wants to dye her hair and get a pierced nose!" More complaints are surfacing, but you do not feel as though there is a reason to take action. Her performance evaluations are excellent and the participants adore her.

U

The Director of the YMCA approaches you and says that something needs to be done. You read the policy and procedures manual and conclude that there is nothing you can do; the YMCA does not have a dress code policy. However, the complaints keep rolling in from parents.

B

L

Discussion Questions

I

What do you do now? Do you propose a new dress code policy? If so, will this action be expected every time a complaint is lodged against an employee? Her performance appraisals are outstanding. Does this count for something? What actions will you take to resolve this problem? What will you tell the members who are complaining? What will you say to Sue about the problem? If other staff members approached you with their concerns about personal freedom of expression, how would you handle the situation?

C

I

T

Y

A Program for Presque Isle

Problem Situation

Presque Isle is a community of approximately 8,900 people. Its per-capita wealth is relatively high, much of it being derived from the oil industry. The community maintains two small parks, a swimming pool, and it has the usual minimum indoor and outdoor sports and recreation facilities for use by the schools.

During past summers, two playgrounds have been operated for school-aged children with funds provided by the city. Up until recently, through the efforts of the Citizens' League (consisting of representatives from the different civic services, fraternal organizations, and patriotic organizations), a youth center was operated for the students of the middle and high schools. Due to overcrowding of the schools, facilities formerly used for recreation center purposes were returned to the school board for use as classroom space. Aside from the school program and the Boy Scout and Girl Scout activities, there is presently no organized recreation program for young people available in Presque Isle.

At a public meeting sponsored by the Citizens' League, most of the discussions revolved around the plans for developing a recreation center. Presque Isle is seriously thinking of building two new elementary schools and one middle school. In this respect, proper attention was given to the feasibility of designing the schools so they would be used by the community as well as for educational purposes. Nevertheless, the league wasn't too optimistic about the chances for using the school buildings for both purposes, particularly because the current population center of the teenage group does not coincide with the suggested location of the new schools, which will mainly serve the elementary school population.

A careful check of existing facilities in the community revealed absolutely no available space, resulting in the serious intention of the Citizens' League to construct an entirely new center. Land has been deeded to the league upon which a center might be built. It is located adjacent to the present high school, not far from the school's athletic facilities and overlooking the Lennon River. There seems to be little doubt in the community about the possibility to raise as much $50,000 or perhaps $75,000 to build the center. Many firms and organizations have already agreed to make large contributions in work, materials, or money, and some thought has been given to maintaining and operating the building through contributed funds. The pros and cons of financing the work in this manner as well as the potential of securing funds through taxation were discussed at great length.

The civic leadership in Presque Isle apparently realizes the importance of employing trained leadership to direct the program. At the meeting it was agreed that the following action would be taken:

1. The Citizens' League representatives would meet with the members of the board of education to consider the possibility of using the new school facilities for recreational purposes.
2. A committee would be appointed to explore the state enabling legislation for the establishment and operation of a recreation system.

Discussion Questions

What state enabling legislation is available that will permit municipalities to establish and operate a recreation and park system? What would be the purpose of meeting with the board of education? How can the civic and fraternal organizations play an effective role in promoting the establishment of a recreation and parks system? Should the Citizens' League embark on a fund drive to construct a recreation center? Why? State the pros and cons of financing a facility in this manner. Should the mayor and city council

M
A
R
K
E
T
I
N
G

&

P
U
B
L
I
C
I
T
Y

play an active role in promoting the recreation and parks program? Why? Should a teen center be located on or near school grounds? With the current emphasis on education, is a teen center really necessary? What type of programs should be offered? Who should supervise the program? How could the establishment of a recreation and park agency stretch school tax dollars?

THEME TWO: MARKETING AND PUBLICITY RELATED WEBSITES

A Definition of Marketing by Howard and Crompton
http://www.msu.edu/course/prr/389/Cromptonpublics.doc

Central Florida's Sport Marketing (Polk County All Sports Award and Hall of Fame Induction Ceremony)
http://www.centralfloridasports.com/content/default.asp

Marketing Recreation: Tahoe Ski Operators Moving into the Big Time by Tom Gardner
http://www.reviewjournal.com/lvrj_home/2000/Nov-24-Fri-2000/news/14885932.html

Marketing Specialist (City of Roseville)
http://www.roseville.ca.us/upload/files/marketing%20specialist%20i-ii.pdf

Phone & Targeted Publicity Campaigns (Outdoor Management Network)
http://www.outdoormarketing.com/marketing/campaigns.shtml

Promoting Recreation (Environment Agency)
http://www.environment-agency.gov.uk/subjects/recreation/345720/369071/?version=1&lang=_e

Sports and Entertainment Marketing (Ewing Township Public Schools)
http://www.ewing.k12.nj.us/EwingWeb/PRandComm/District/Curriculumpdfs/SportsAndEnterMktgfinal.pdf

Still Striving for Clear Communication by Barbara Eaton
http://www.lib.niu.edu/ipo/ip940722.html

The Attraction, Marketing and Publicity Toolkit Checklist - By Dr. Sheldon Nix
http://www.canadaone.com/ezine/dec99/marketing_checklist.html

Your Guide to Effective Marketing and Publicity (Griots.Net)
http://www.griots.net/downloads/riots.net%20Marketing%20and%20Publicity%20Brochure.pdf

THEME THREE:

PLANNING AND POLICY DEVELOPMENT

Snack Attack Hits Sporting Events

Problem Situation

Los Angeles, New York, Philadelphia and many other communities have banned soda, candy, and high-sugar snacks from school vending machines. Chicago has proposed to do the same for its schools. Moreover, a midwestern recreation district wants to take it a step further. It has asked all guardians to stop bringing snacks to the recreation-sponsored athletic events. It seems that too many adults are bringing chips, soda, juice, candy, and cookies to the games. It was a unanimous vote by the seven-person recreation and park board and applies to about 5,000 children who play soccer, football, softball, baseball, and basketball.

"We're looking at changing the mindset of our youth who are taught from an early age to associate athletic activity with caloric intake," said the spokesperson for the recreation district. "It's junk food—Oreos, chips, and soda. We would like people to start thinking healthfully."

There will be an attempt to enforce the rule at recreation and park-sponsored events, but parents and guardians worry about depriving their children and youth of a snack after so much running and jumping. "They have worked really hard, and I don't see a problem with giving them a snack after a hard fought game. I think the kids deserve a little reward," states one soccer dad.

Discussion Questions

As the recreation and parks director, you are responsible for developing the procedures for this new policy. How would you go about developing these procedures? Who would you include in this process? How do you intend to enforce this new policy? What if parents and guardians strongly oppose this new policy and the enrollment drops in these sporting events? What are the pros and cons of this new policy? Do you fear for your job if the parents complain too much? How will you persuade the community that this is a good policy?

Pilates Stretches Limits

Problem Situation

You are the recreation supervisor at a large community center. In your brochure of upcoming activities, you have listed a weekly pilates class. A week before the class is to begin, a group of picketers forms outside your building to protest the class.

"Pilates is a form of New Age mysticism that can lead to devil worship," said Larry McCoy, the organizer of the protest. "The people who signed up for the class are just walking into it like cattle to a slaughter. Half of this is a branch of Eastern mysticism and it has strong occult influences. As Christians, we must protest what you are doing."

While the protests continued, you called a professor of religion at a nearby university to see if what McCoy said was true. The professor replied that yoga has become a secularized form of exercise and relaxation. He admitted that yoga did have ties to Eastern religions, but stressed that Eastern religions and devil worship are far from being the same thing. As for Pilates, more research needs to be conducted.

The superintendent wants to know if you still plan to offer the class. He claims that the parks department cannot promote religion but that it should definitely promote health. He has given you until this afternoon to decide what to do. Pilates is new and needs to be explored more fully, he suggests.

Discussion Questions

Should the pilates class be offered? Why or why not? Does the fact that it has already been listed in a printed brochure influence your decision? Should the community have been surveyed prior to offering such a class? If so, discuss the survey procedure.

Should the protestors be allowed to influence your choice? How do you propose to deal with the protestors? What kind of power do protestors have?

Is this new wave of pilates a form of religion? What does "separation of church and state" mean? How does this phrase apply to the park district? Draft an outline of a "pilates class" lesson plan that could be presented to the park board.

Merriman Study

Problem Situation

The Merriman National Forest, stretching 500 miles up the southeast of Alaska, represents the largest remaining temperate rain forest on the earth. It is home to more than 300 species of wildlife, trees, and over 100,000 humans. It provides world class commercial, sport, and subsistence fishing. The Merriman National Forest has been a battleground between individuals who want to continue logging in the old growth forest and those who want to prevent it from ever happening. The real struggle is over jobs, economy, values, lifestyles, industry, and free market.

Recently there was a Land Management Plan approved by the United States Forest Service. The plan was to strike a balance, increase wilderness, protect old growth, protect wildlife, and make sure the area's economy still grows. The economic stimulation depends heavily on tourism, commercial fishing, and sport fishing over logging. Tourism and recreation are most important, and economic growth could be limited by logging.

A recent survey found that of the 437 bays and coves in the Merriman suitable for boat-based nature, 54 percent were impaired. Conservation groups want sustainable management rather than a ban on logging. Logging is not producing enough jobs in Alaska. They get four jobs per million board feet compared to 12 jobs per million board feet in California, Washington, and Oregon. The development of local wood processing could help eliminate job loss, but United States law allows only minimal processing on public lands.

Discussion Questions

If you were handling this situation, would you be lenient towards the loggers or the conservationists? Would you want no logging in the forest, or would you allow partial logging? How would you address the United States Forest Service's plan and what would you discuss? Would you try to work with federal agencies or private timber companies? If you had total control and power over the fate of the Merriman National Forest, what would you do? The problem has been going on for a long time, so what would you do differently?

Equal Access for Everyone?

Problem Situation

You are the new director in charge of children's programming at a public parks and recreation facility in Springville, a mid-size town in a southern state. Springville offers a variety of recreational programs for children including swimming lessons, gymnastics, sports leagues, theater, summer camp, and after school day care.

In April, Amanda Green approaches you requesting that her daughter be enrolled in the summer day camp. Mrs. Green tells you, "Tracy is eight years old and loves to be outdoors. And, by the way, she has cerebral palsy and uses a wheelchair. She also uses a communication board and has a slight cognitive delay. She's never been to camp before, but I'd like her to have the same opportunity to attend as her older brother, Sam, who doesn't have a disability."

You are caught off guard by Mrs. Green's request, yet you reply to her as you would to any parent, "Please fill out this registration card and camper information form. I'll respond to you as soon as I can." To yourself you think, "Mrs. Green is very cordial, but I sense she could cause trouble if her request isn't met!"

P
O
L
I
C
Y

D
E
V
E
L
O
P
M
E
N
T

The day camp facility is not architecturally accessible. In fact, in the past the agency has used environmental barriers as an excuse not to serve participants with disabilities at camp. You are aware of the Americans with Disabilities Act, however, and the right that participants with disabilities have to architectural and programmatic access in recreational activities. You personally support the spirit of this law but don't have much experience accommodating people with disabilities. Based on the agency's track record, you suspect your agency would prefer to avoid the whole issue—even though the published mission statement says the agency does not discriminate on the basis of ability.

Camp begins mid-June. You think there is sufficient time to work out the details to accommodate Tracy at camp, but how do you go about accomplishing this without much experience and amid a history of resistance at the agency?

Discussion Questions

What are Mrs. Green's and Tracy's rights in this situation? What recourse would they have if the request to attend camp were denied? How will you present this matter to your supervisor? What levels of the agency should be involved in the decision to allow Tracy to attend camp?

How will you respond to Mrs. Green? What accommodations and adaptations could be made for Tracy so she could participate as fully as possible? How would you go about gathering information about the supports Tracy would need? What would you do to make sure Tracy is included both physically and socially at camp?

What training would you provide the camp staff about including Tracy in the program? How will you respond to staff that don't think Tracy should be allowed to come to camp?

What implications might this case have on the agency's policies and procedures in the future?   Write a policy statement regarding equal participation and access by individuals with disabilities and their families.

Pristine or Chlorine?

Problem Situation

More and more we are faced with a question of irreversible consequences when it comes to the conservation of our natural environment. Creeks and lakes not only provide a valuable drinking source for the local communities, they also provide ample opportunity for the outdoor enthusiast to enjoy recreation activities. However, if valuable natural resources are neglected or abused, they will be forever subjected to an irreversible condition that may never allow for a return to its natural state.

Onondaga—the name itself implies historic values. Located in a northern state, there is a creek and a lake that have been the lifeline for the Onondaga Indian Tribe for hundreds of years. The creek and lake provide fresh water, in addition to unmatched fishing and an abundance of wildlife.

The population of Onondaga has outgrown the sewage treatment facilities, a problem that has faced many cities throughout the Nation. The city and county seem to have reached an impasse in negotiations for an alternative solution. Many representatives from the county, the city, the neighborhood, environmental groups, and the Onondaga Nation have worked out a collaborative and cost-effective engineering solution, namely underground storage. Although overall calculations show that both alternatives have comparable costs, the county is now claiming that the underground option is too expensive. A comparison study of environmental impacts shows that underground storage is clearly superior. The proposal that is supported by the county would do a poor job in treating the wastewater.

In the county's proposal, chlorine bleach is added to the partially treated wastewater to disinfect the sewage. This creates hundreds of toxic byproducts: chloroform, carbon tetrachloride, and trichloroacetic acid, to name a few. Many of these byproducts cause cancer and mutations in mammals and are no doubt bad for fish and other organisms in the creek. No chlorine is used in the underground storage system. Disinfections can be accomplished using ultraviolet light, which is currently a process in operation at the Metro facility. This is just as effective as chlorine, and avoids harmful byproducts. It is also much safer for workers and the nearby community.

Discussion Questions

What is the solution? How would you handle this very important environmental dilemma? What options are available to you? Why is there such a variance in opinions about the environment? How important is the conservation of natural habitat in comparison to the importance of controlling waste? How contaminated are our fresh water sources now? Should cost be a major consideration? Should conservation be a major consideration? Is it possible to find a middle of the road solution that would appease both sides? If so, how can any amount of toxins and byproducts not have an effect on the habitat?

If handled improperly, how will the contaminated fishing creek and lake affect tourism? Creek corridors have recently become hiking and biking paths. How would these recreational activities be affected? Is it possible to have a creek corridor fulfill the needs of wastewater treatment and recreation? What are the long-term effects of a waste facility? What are the long-term effects of a creek corridor for recreational purposes? What are the psychological effects on the public using a recreational ground with a waste treatment facility?

Curfew Considered to Curb Vandalism

Problem Situation

You are the parks and recreation director in the town of Waterville, a community of 150,000 people. The Waterville City Council is considering two actions to reduce vandalism in the town: establishing a curfew and closing one of the town's parks.

"We are giving serious thought to closing the park," said Council spokesman Steve Peterson. "Although the park has been open for nearly 10 years, it has recently been the site of rough and rowdy teenage parties. Police have been called to handle fighting, noise pollution, and teenage drinking on many occasions during the past two years, especially on weekends. Broken beer bottles are more prevalent than flowers in the park. We have recently received petitions from residents asking that the park be closed. Ironically, we have also received a petition from a group of teenagers who asked that the park be refurbished. The youth want new equipment, because the current equipment has been destroyed. Although I would like to help our youth, the town can't be babysitting people's children."

A City Council vote is necessary to close the park. Peterson said the vote is likely to come at next month's Council meeting. He also said the attorney would present a list of streets to include in a curfew ordinance at the meeting.

P
O
L
I
C
Y

D
E
V
E
L
O
P
M
E
N
T

Discussion Questions

Should the park be closed permanently? If not, should the City Council refurbish it? What are some other options? Is a curfew likely to keep teenagers out of the park? Is either the curfew or the closing of the park a good alternative? Can you think of a better one? Do residents living near a park deserve a voice in what happens in a park? Should the youth petition be ignored since it was submitted by "just a bunch of kids"? How can you balance the wants and needs of the residents near the park, the youth who party in the park, and the youth who merely utilize the park?

Heat Wave Leads to Overcrowding

Problem Situation

The meteorologists have stated that New York City is currently in a heat watch and will continue to be in one for most of the month. In addition to a heat wave, the city is also in a drought. The mayor is encouraging all residents in the metropolitan area to conserve water and energy. The Parks and Recreation Department have traditionally opened up the outdoor pool facilities located all over the city during the last week of June. The parks that have sprinklers usually do not have them on when there is a drought watch. The local parks are open from dawn to dusk, but the majority of the pools are open between noon and 6 p.m. All city lifeguards go through the city's lifeguard training even if they are certified through another organization. The pool is supposed to be vacuumed around 11 a.m. or before it is opened for public swim. Chlorine check is supposed to be done every two to three hours.

As the director of the City Parks and Recreation Department, you are faced with many problems. Due to the heat, the pools are overcrowded. Lines are forming around the block at 11 a.m. filled with eager kids, teenagers, and some adults waiting to get into the municipal pool. Many residents are turned away and highly frustrated at the situation. In order to cool down, the rejected people open up the street hydrants. This results in lowering the water pressure in the neighborhood and wastes water, especially in a time of drought. This scenario continues to play out for two weeks in a row. The mayor calls your office and demands a solution to the problems at stake.

Discussion Questions

Overcrowding in the pools is leading to opened hydrants on the streets. What can you do to help resolve this problem? What do you say to the mayor? What policies and procedures might you want to institute during this crisis? Is it your responsibility to solve the hydrant problems? How would you go about solving this entire situation?

High Premiums Lead to New Low

Problem Situation

You are the Director of the White Fox Preserve District. Your insurance has tripled in the last four years, primarily due to lake activities. To reduce insurance premiums, board member Paul Giguere has proposed that the risks of swimming at the lake be taken from the district and placed upon the swimmers. To transfer the risks, he suggests that the lifeguards be removed and that a swim-at-your-own-risk sign be established. He says that the injury cases that may surface could be evaluated on an individual basis but that, without a lifeguard on duty, the district could no longer be held responsible. "The more responsibility we assume for participation in a given activity," he argues, "the higher our risk insurance premiums are going to be."

To reduce insurance premiums in the past, the preserve board has previously taken out the waterslide, paddleboats, and diving board. The only activities that take place now at the lake are swimming, sunbathing, and beach-front activities. The board is indecisive.

One board member asks Mr. Giguere to show what he means when he refers to a sign being posted. When pressed for a description of an adequate sign, he draws the following:

Beach Rules
1. Swim at your own risk. No lifeguard on duty.
2. No person may enter the water or swim alone.
3. No bather, 16 years or younger, may enter the beach area without being super vised by a responsible adult, 17 years of age or older.
4. Swim in marked area only.
5. Stay within buoy lines.
6. All food or drink is prohibited in beach area.
7. No glass containers allowed in swimming area.
8. No diving or horseplay in the swimming area.

After Giguere has finished his presentation, the board members ask you for feedback.

Discussion Questions

What would you reply? Is Mr. Giguere right in saying that insurance would go down if you took away your lifeguards? Are more accidents likely to happen if the lifeguards are removed? Are more lawsuits likely to happen if you do not post lifeguards? Why or why not? Is his proposed sign adequate? What would you add or delete? Is the sign a good idea? How will the rules on the sign be enforced? What sort of penalties would the violators be assessed?

Many of the sentences are stated negatively (with a "no"), while others are not. Should these negative sentences be reworked? Are the cut-off ages of 16 and 17 reasonable? Why do you think he chose the 16- and 17-year limits instead of something else, such as 18 and 19?

What alternatives can you think of that would likely reduce insurance while keeping lifeguards at the beach? What is the purpose of carrying insurance? What would happen if you dropped insurance coverage? What other options are there besides purchasing insurance from a commercial carrier, or not having insurance at all?

Locker Room Lacks Privacy

Problem Situation

You are the recreation supervisor in charge of aquatics. One afternoon, as you tour one of the city's revenue generating swimming pools, a lifeguard approaches you.

"I'd like to talk to you," he said. "I'm Roland Henry, a 31-year-old swimmer. Yesterday I went swimming at this pool. While I was in the locker room changing into my swimming trunks, I turned around to find a 5-year-old girl staring at me! I later learned she had been brought there by her father, who was calmly drying himself after showering. The locker room was crowded with men in various stages of dress and undress. Some were completely naked. All were unaware that we were being observed by a wide-eyed girl.

"I found the pool manager and complained. She went to the father and asked him not to bring the child into the men's locker room again. The father got extremely angry. He said he had no one to leave his girl with and wasn't about to let her wait for him outside alone. When the father was informed that the other men in the locker room might not appreciate being observed by a young girl, he said that any man who is embarrassed to be seen naked in front of a 5-year-old girl must have something wrong with him.

"So I ask you, what are you going to do about the situation? And, while you're at it, what are you going to do about the pool manager who did nothing about the situation except talk to the man, and then point me toward you?"

Discussion Questions

What do you say to the man? Should a 5-year-old girl be allowed in the men's locker room? What other alternatives are there? Would your decision be affected if you were told the man was a season pass holder? Why or why not? Would it make any difference if the girl were 4 or 6 years old instead of 5? How much privacy should be guaranteed in a locker room?

What could be done to increase the father's trust in security so that he would feel comfortable leaving his child outside the locker room? Where should he leave her? Would you discipline the pool manager for the way she handled the situation? What discipline would be justified?

Off-Road Vehicle Park in Doubt

Problem Situation

The county planning commission soon will be asked to give its final verdict on a proposed off-road vehicle park, and supporters and opponents alike are sure the commission will reject the project.

Andy Bailey, Chairperson of the Santee Planning Committee, said yesterday he believes the commission will affirm its earlier 4-to-0 vote against the planned regional park. Although the commission's vote against the park in February was tentative, Bailey said he expects the vote to stand at the commission meeting on March 31.

"I'm not against off-road vehicles," maintains Bailey, who said his children number among the legions of off-road vehicle enthusiasts. "But there is a place for everything and, in this instance, it's not an urban area."

Bailey is not alone in his belief that the planners will veto the plan. The same opinion is held by Beth Cotter, a county park planner and a supporter of the county's off-road vehicle park proposal. "The die is cast as far as the planning commission is concerned, and it was cast at the first meeting," said Cotter. "I'm not even going to go to the meeting [on March 31]; I think it's all going to be routine."

Although the planning commission is expected to reject the Santee off-road vehicle plan, Cotter said she still believes that concerns over park noise can be resolved. Cotter did admit that there might be problems with air pollution, specifically the amount of dust generated from the park. Nevertheless, she said the emotionalism might have played a major role in turning the tide against the proposed Santee regional park.

A recent letter to the planning commission was one indication of the concerns and feelings of supporters of the proposed park. "Your commission has been deceived into believing that the Santee Park is worse than the West Nile virus," wrote Ivan McDermott, chairperson of the County Off-Road Vehicle Citizens Advisor Committee. "Problems suggested by staff are not nearly as bad as they are presented to be. It is very hard for me and a few other people on the committee to compete with perhaps as many as 50 persons in IPO [County Integrated Planning Office] who are working fulltime to do away with the ORV [Off-Road Vehicle] program" said McDermott, who called the Santee site "one of the best sites in the country."

Although April 17 and 24 are set as tentative dates for the county board of supervisors to decide the matter, Cotter said the board may not receive the matter until May or June. Regardless of when the supervisors hear the matter, supporters and opponents of the park are preparing for the next confrontation.

Although she did not identify people by name, Cotter said some "local heavyweights" are being lined up to appear before the supervisors. Meanwhile, Bailey said he expects residents of the nearby Eucalyptus Hills area to come to the board chambers "with their guns loaded." The Eucalyptus Hills section is situated east of the planned Santee Regional Park, to be built in northern Santee in an area just east of proposed U.S. Highway 125. About 400 of the planned 500 acres would be set aside for off-road use.

Discussion Questions

What provisions should be made for off-road vehicles in the park development plan? Should parks of this nature be allowed within city limits? Why or why not? What amount of land in relation to community total park land should be set aside for this type of activity? What criteria should be established for selecting sites for this type of activity? To what extent should the planning committee seek citizen involvement in this decision? How could they do this? Assuming that you are Andy Bailey, who is the chairperson of the planning committee, develop a strategy for addressing this problem.

Snow Dumping Procedure Has Residents in Dumps

Problem Situation

You are a member of the Jonesburg City Council. For years the city has been using city parks as wholesale dumping grounds during blizzards. At tonight's meeting, residents are upset because the piles of garbage and ice in the parks have begun to attract rats, and they fear the parks are a health hazard for children. The residents claim that the baseball and softball fields have been gouged by snowplows, which have left rivers of melted snow, chunks of earth, asphalt, and other debris in their wake. In addition, a local newspaper has just run a photo essay showing the parks to be marshlands of garbage and melting ice, with debris-packed snow mounds as high as six feet surrounding several baseball diamonds.

Park director Joan Marie claims that the park district does not have the necessary heavy equipment to clean up the mess. The district has only one giant vacuum truck available for clean-up work. Marie insists that the city should supply the labor and equipment to clean up the mess or provide her with the funds for more trucks and for salaries for extra personnel. "The city caused the predicament, and it must take the necessary steps to clean it up."

The director also said the park district would no longer allow the city to dump snow in the parks. "The city should begin planning now where to dump snow—other than the parks—in the event of another emergency situation."

P
O
L
I
C
Y

D
E
V
E
L
O
P
M
E
N
T

Discussion Questions

Does the city have an obligation to help the park district clean up the debris? If so, what should the city do to help? If the parks cannot be used as dumping grounds, what alternatives would you suggest for the placement of removed snow? What sort of compromise might the city and the park district reach regarding the dumping of snow? How would you handle the residents' complaints of rats resulting from the snow-dumping incidents? What would you say about the editor of the newspaper who published the degrading, but truthful, essay of the parks' condition? Should an ordinance be drawn up by the park board to prohibit dumping snow in the parks? If so, should the ordinance apply to anything besides snow?

This Place is a Zoo and Needs Help!

Problem Situation

Last week your hometown Department of Parks, Recreation, and Cultural Affairs hired you as a consultant. You are to review the evidence from a recent series of animal mishaps at the city's zoo. From these incidents, you have to determine administrative changes and present them to the mayor in 2 weeks.

The problems at the zoo began reaching public attention last May when the department reported the death of an elephant named Ellie in a press release. The press release indicated Ellie died on a farm outside of the city; however, it was later announced that the elephant apparently died while traveling with a circus.

Last week, a lioness and a tiger from the city's zoo were put to death at the local university where they had been taken for treatment. The zoo's own clinic was ordered to close down by the federal government last year due to incompetent employees. Authorities are also investigating the deaths of two bears that had been transferred from the zoo to a game ranch in upstate New York.

The mayor in your hometown has announced that the city is launching an investigation of the zoo's treatment of its animals and the claims of poor management and deteriorating facilities. As one of the consultants hired, you are expected to investigate orientation and training (and retraining) programs for the zoo. Your consultation with the mayor is in two weeks.

Discussion questions

What overall changes would you suggest the zoo make to rectify the situation? Is management to blame for the recent problems? If so, do you suggest that the management be fired or retrained? If you fire management, outline the employee selection process that you will recommend to the mayor. Next, outline an orientation program suitable for the zoo. Further, outline a retraining and/or training program that could meet the needs of management.

Your report to the mayor should be professionally written. You will not only distribute this report to the mayor, but the zoo management will also receive a copy to assist them with training and developing their employees.

Creating Wildlife Refuges Causes a Stir

Problem Situation

Plans to create two of the state's largest wildlife refuges are angering people in two respective counties. Not everyone opposes the plans, but residents are concerned about the loss of farmland, erosion of the tax base, and costly government purchases at a time of economic belt-tightening.

The state's Department of Conservation is buying 16,000 acres, and the land will become the state's largest park. Some residents are supportive, but they want the state to create a lake that would attract tourists and their money. Environmentalists claim this is a once-in-a-lifetime opportunity, and that it is very important to preserve some remnant of that ecosystem. Both parties (residents and environmentalists) agree that it's an important project environmentally and important economically for the Counties involved. Officials say the park area will provide a place for camping, hiking, hunting, picnicking, pond fishing, and horseback riding.

Elected officials in both counties are on record opposing the projects and local residents' feelings have run the gamut. Many support the projects, but opponents have been vocal. "Our worst fear is that the Department of Conservation won't develop the site. People hope they'll build a lake, open it up for hunting, and make it something great for everyone in the state. Don't just turn it into a prairie land," said one resident. But prairie is exactly what makes the land valuable to biologists. Another resident comments, "The frustration I hear is how the state can justify spending money like this when the government can't pay the nursing homes and Medicaid bills. They don't have money for teachers and they are closing state parks."

Discussion Questions

Although the land being purchased is not directly under your jurisdiction, you are a neighboring community that will be affected by the onslaught of predicted tourists to the new park. Your community will feel the effects of increased tourism, and you and your community need to be prepared for whatever happens. How will you prepare your recreation and parks department for this newly acquired park area? What new and innovative programs might you implement? How will you educate the community that this is a great opportunity for everyone? How will you convince those who are against the state purchasing the land?

The Tale of Creek Side Trail

Problem Situation

You are an associate professor at a local college in the Department of Environmental Science and Forestry. Recently, the issue has been raised about developing a recreational walkway along the creek that runs through the city. The state is trying to implement a plan for developing a trail that will celebrate two canals. One of the more difficult sections of the canal is the part that lies within your city limit. It is a difficult section because, years ago, the part of the canal that ran through your city was filled in. Many people in your community feel the city lost a major sense of identity when the waterway was filled. The city is fortunate to have another major waterway running through the heart of the city, but the same sense of identity is not linked to this waterway. Part of the reason for this may be the fact that the waterway has been tightly controlled over the last several decades. The waterway has also been neglected and has lost a lot of its natural state. With the right development, it has the potential to become a civic and environmental highway through your city.

The main problem is the fact that the city board and members of the community are split as far as what action to take. One side wants to turn the waterway into a recreational site. Restoration to parts of the creek would return it to a more natural state and establish pedestrian and bicycle paths. This side hopes to encourage people to traverse this city at a pace that will encourage interaction among members of the community. It will also give people the chance to see nature within the city limits in a way not seen in many years. The renovation to the creek would include interpretive/education displays; public places for gathering, sitting, and people-watching; gardens; and provide for recreational activities such as rollerblading and running.

The other side thinks the money that would be put into renovating the creek can be better spent. There is added pressure to conserve money particularly because of the effects of September 11th on the city and state. The board members of the city and some community members have approached your department to evaluate both sides of the proposal and determine which is the more logical course of action. You have been chosen to perform the research and evaluate the situation at hand.

Discussion Questions

Both sides of this debate are trying to persuade you to decide in their favor. You need to develop a plan of action. How will you conduct research? What course of action would be best for the community? What type of information do you need to find out? What benefits will result if the trail is built and the creek renovated? How will you determine the cost to the city taxpayer? What are the other cities along the canals doing, and how will you go about obtaining this information? Develop a list of pros and cons for the plan. Can you find examples of other creek side recreational trails? What type of process did those groups go through to come to a decision? What other pieces of information do you need to make a sound decision? How are you going to present your findings to the board and the community members?

Foes Aid Cagney Park Design

Problem Situation

You are a county commissioner for a rural town in the northeastern region of the United States. Based upon a comprehensive needs assessment, plans for a 50-acre park/sports complex were developed to meet the needs of the residents in the rural area. This idea made sense given the town has very little open space dedicated to recreation.

At a recent meeting, you learn that opponents, most of whom live very close to the intended site, are complaining that the soccer and baseball fields, tennis courts, and roller hockey rinks will generate too much traffic on the two-lane road, and disturb the neighbors with stadium lights, and damage a large wetland on the property. After learning of these complaints, you decide to have an open meeting with the public.

Over 100 residents attend the meeting. Some wear anti-park stickers while several children and youth wear their soccer uniforms. All total, about 40 speakers blast the park idea or demand playing space for their children to recreate. One resident stated, "I'm not opposed to a sports complex...but why in the world would you people consider a small, rural, residential, quiet community for this massive facility?" Another man argues, "I live right beside the proposed site, and it's going to drive me crazy having all that traffic near my house, not to mention all those flood lights out on the fields."

On the contrary, another resident argues, "My kids and I have traveled all over the county in search of soccer, in search of baseball, and just plain open space to play. There's nothing here for them. I don't want to have to travel all the way to the next county just so my kids can kick a ball around. I'm looking forward to being able to stay within two miles of home."

In a compromise move, you announce at the meeting that you have decided to appoint a committee to try to address the concerns of the development for the controversial $925,000 park. That is, neighbors as well as sports enthusiasts, will be able to help design the final product. You state, "It seems to me that it's appropriate to find some people from all sides of this issue to come together and work out something that could make this idea more palatable."

After the meeting, members of both sides say they are interested to see what the committee comes up with, although their outlooks were vastly different. "I think it's a good idea to form a committee," states a soccer coach. One of the opponents says, "I think it's a good idea too. It's a politically correct move by the commissioner—although I think they need to find the people who want a park and stick it in their backyard and not mine."

Discussion Questions

How will you form the committee? Who will be on the committee? How many will be on the committee? What are the goals and objectives for this designated committee? Develop a draft of policies that will determine who will comprise this committee. Also, develop the guidelines under which the committee should operate. How long will they have to reach an agreement? What happens if they can't agree on a design for the park? How will the meetings be run? How often are they required to meet? How will they reach a consensus?

THEME THREE: PLANNING AND POLICY DEVELOPMENT HELPFUL WEBSITES

Focus on Recreation Planning (Ministry of Sport and Recreation)
http://www.dsr.wa.gov.au/publications/focus/focus%20on%20recreation%20plan.pdf

Indiana Department of Natural Resources
http://www.in.gov/dnr/outdoor/planning

Open Forest Policy by Coillte http://www.coillte.ie/managing_our_forests/policies_plans/open.htm

Sport and Recreation Policy for New Brunswick
http://www.gnb.ca/0131/d-r/pol_sport_e.pdf

Town of Tillsonburg Land Use Policies
http://www.county.oxford.on.ca/cao/planning/pdf/OfficalPlan/Chapter_8_6.pdf

What are Policies and Procedures? (Center to Advance Palliative Care Manual)
http://64.85.16.230/educate/content/elements/whatarepolicies.html

What is Strategic Planning? (The Evergreen State Society)
http://www.nonprofits.org/npofaq/03/22.html

POLICY DEVELOPMENT

THEME FOUR:

LIABILITY AND RISK MANAGEMENT

L
I
A
B
I
L
I
T
Y

&

R
I
S
K

Table of Contents

No Pool Photos Policy Doesn't Click With Grandpa

Problem Situation

Even an unsuspecting grandfather can get into trouble these days. Grandpa's crime was videotaping his wife, daughter, mother-in-law, and granddaughter during noon swim at the local municipal pool. According to the newly enacted policy, no one is allowed to photograph or videotape at any of the local public pools. The intent of the policy is to protect the privacy of people who may not want to be photographed.

As the director of the local recreation department, you have maintained that there is a danger of some people who use digital cameras at the pool for not the best of reasons. Therefore, due to the increasing dangers involving persons photographing or videotaping participants, the recreation department adopted a policy banning the use of all cameras at the pool. The policy resulted from several complaints about the unwanted photographic attention at the pools. This policy has been in effect for three months without any problem.

But it is a policy that some say conflicts with constitutionally protected privileges, as well as the simple pleasures of capturing one's family on film for posterity. One angry grandfather states, "If we allow this type of infringement on individual rights to stand, one can see, say, city councils applying the same rationale to prevent members of the public from taking photographs or videotapes in any public place!"

Discussion Questions

Is this a good policy? Is it fair? Does the grandfather have a valid point? Is a blanket policy like this a good one? What rules should accompany this policy? That is, are there times when it is allowable to photograph or videotape? What if the grandfather went outside of the pool area to video (from beyond the fence)? Discuss the pros and cons of this policy. What suggestions or recommendations would you make?

Should Alcohol Be Permitted in the Park?

Problem Situation

You are the director of a public parks and recreation park district in an eastern city of 100,000. Two groups have approached the park district board about changing your liquor laws on the park grounds. One group wants alcohol allowed for "special occasions" such as weddings and reunions. The other group wants to allow alcohol at all times, especially for tailgate parties before softball games. The current policy forbids alcohol within the park premises.

One board member proposes that liquor can be served provided that the group obtain a $50 permit from the park for the evening. "This will make sure they are serious about wanting to have alcohol there. We shouldn't make it easy, but we should make it possible."

Another board member disagrees, "We've really had to clamp down on people tailgating before or after softball games. To be fair, we can't allow anybody to drink, regardless of the occasion."

A third board member suggests a compromise. "If they want to have a private party to celebrate a wedding or family reunion, for example, we should let them. That's a whole lot different than people tailgating before and after a game."

Discussion Questions

Should drinking alcohol be allowed in the public parks? Why or why not? Is there a difference between drinking at a wedding and tailgating? Explain the difference. How would you enforce your drinking policy? Is a permit system justified? If so, how should the money that is collected be spent? Create a drinking policy for the park.

High School's Earth Day Celebration Causes Uproar

Problem Situation

You are the public parks and recreation director for a medium-sized community. One afternoon, a principal from one of the four local high schools telephones asking your assistance to help him deal with the aftermath of the school's Earth Day celebration. To celebrate Earth Day, the high school dimmed its lights and asked for a moment of silence in memory of the earth.

Citizens for Educational Accountability are calling the event "a humanistic New Age celebration to the Goddess Mother Earth." They claim that this celebration "tends toward a religious practice that is not allowed for other religions."

"I don't believe in the school manipulating our children. Children at the high school age are very responsible," said one activist. "I'm not saying I'm against all Earth Day activities. However, I think the kind of celebration that took place in the high school can lead to other similar celebrations of a less palatable theme than conservation. I believe in God, but I also believe in a separation of church and state. The school conducted a religious ritual, and that was inappropriate."

The principal informs you that the idea to turn down the lights came from a national environmental group. He adds, "We did not make a big deal about the moment of silence; we just sort of let the kids sit there and think. We didn't want to make it a religious activity. It was intended to be a reminder that energy conservation was a dimension of Earth Day. It was nothing more than that."

Discussion Questions

What do you tell the principal? How can you help him? If he suspected that some people might claim that his celebration was a religious ritual, should he have gone ahead with it? Can a ritual take place outside of religion; can there be a religion without ritual? What is the purpose of Earth Day?

How would you have advised the principal to celebrate Earth Day? Should local schools follow national trends if local citizens are likely to object? What can be done to pacify the activist? Will the issue die if no action is taken? Is no action sometimes better than action?

Stealing Causes a Moral Dilemma

Problem Situation

You are the director of a state park. The park has many facilities on the property which offer a wide range of services. One of the many services provided are swimming lessons. The pool facility is supervised by five staff at all times. Two staff work as life guards, one staff works the entrance gate, and two more staff supervise the male and female locker rooms.

There is an admission into the pool, and a head count is calculated using a clicker. The number of people admitted and the amount of money collected every day are recorded in a log. All staff have a pretty good idea of how many people visit the pool each day. One day one of the lifeguards, upon leaving the facility, checked the books to see how much money was made that day. The lifeguard knew it was a particularly busy day at the pool, and he was eager to see the total profit. He was shocked to see how little money was made that day. Further, he was disturbed that the recorded number of people who entered the facility that day was way off.

The lifeguard did not mention this to the admissions staff, although he did mention it to his supervisor the next day. The supervisor checked the books and saw the number of admittance matched the amount of money; however, she noticed the number of admittance was very low compared to previous weeks.

The next day the director tallied her own head count and noticed a different admittance number at the end of the day. The staff working the entrance was notified of this miscalculation by the director the next evening at an emergency meeting.

Discussion Questions

How will you address this situation? Should the admissions staff been made aware that there was a problem with his numbers? Should he have been given an opportunity to explain?

Did the lifeguard handle the situation appropriately, or should he have talked to the admission staff first? Maybe someone else had access to the money and changed the log accordingly. What would be your decision as the director? Should the admissions staff be notified, warned, or fired? Identify procedures you might implement to avoid this type of situation again.

Playing by the Rules

Problem Situation

You are the director of parks and recreation in a medium-sized city. One night at a board meeting, an irate resident demands to know why her fun must be regulated. "I got to the park to break free of constraints and restrictions, but I find that I cannot enjoy myself because of the numerous rules."

Upon the request of a board member, she specified the rules that infuriated her:

- No parking on the grass.
- No alcoholic consumption on park grounds.
- No dogs without a waste disposal bag.
- No entering the park after 11 p.m.
- No parking vehicles in the park after 11 p.m.
- No picking flowers.
- No standing on swings.
- No fishing except in designated areas.

"Everywhere you turn, there are rules, rules, and more rules. There's a sign here, a sign there, a sign everywhere. How can we enjoy the beauty of the park with so many negative signs? How can we enjoy our freedom in the park with so many rules?

Discussion Questions

Explain why rules are needed if a park is to be enjoyed by everyone. Is it possible to have too many rules? Should all rules be posted, or should some be assumed? Is it better to have one huge sign indicating all of the rules or many signs with one rule each?

For each rule she objected to, provide a rationale for why that specific rule is needed. Do you think that providing a rationale for a rule makes it more palatable? If so, should the rationale be available on a brochure for the park patrons? What is the real problem here? Is it the clutter of signs? Is it the numerous rules? Is it the desire to have input about things that affect one's life?

L
I
A
B
I
L
I
T
Y

&

R
I
S
K

Hot Springs Can Burn

Problem Situation

You are a manager of the Bureau of Land Management (BLM) in the southwest. The outdoor recreational area you manage is known to many people as Lee Hot Springs. People visit the springs to hike, relax, and spend time with family and friends. Most of the people are aware that Lee Hot Springs is a hot spring, with extremely hot temperatures. The public has unrestricted access to the hot springs. As manager of this area, you provide literature to inform the public of the natural hazards at the hot springs, and there is a sign posted at the main entrance warning people of the hazards.

Recently there was an incident at Lee Hot Springs. A family was on a camping trip for the Fourth of July. They had just recently moved to the area and were not familiar with the hiking trails as they came across Lee Hot Springs. Lee Hot Springs consist of a small spring and pool with a narrow, shallow stream that flows south into a marshy area with grass, brush, and trees. The reported temperature of the stream that day was about 160 to 180 degrees Fahrenheit. Other times the temperature has been reported to reach as high as 200 degrees Fahrenheit.

As the parents and their 2-year-old son were walking towards the area there were no signs identifying the area as a hot spring, nor were there fences or any other warnings of any kind. The only signs they read were "United States Department of the Interior-Bureau of Land Management" and "Entering Public Lands—Help Maintain Your Property."

Concluding that the area was safe, the boy and his parents followed what appeared to be a footpath that crossed the stream. Although the stream was very hot, the high temperature was not visible to the naked eye. There was no steam, hissing or smell to indicate that they had entered a hot spring. The father noticed a pool and told his son, who was lagging behind, to stay away from it. Within seconds they heard screaming and saw that their little son had fallen in the stream and was in tremendous pain. After recovering the boy from the hot springs, they rushed back to their car and found the nearest hospital. You read about the incident the next day in the local paper.

Discussion Questions

Are you or BLM responsible for the accident? Are you required to post danger signs from all angles of the open recreation area? Describe the immediate action you will take. How could this situation have been avoided? How can you better inform the public of the dangers of the hot springs? Identify a risk management plan that will help you to avoid this type of situation from happening again. Will you contact the family to express your sympathy?

Halloween Fracas Causes a Disturbance

Problem Situation

You are the director in the division of campus recreation at a large university with an enrollment of over 30,000 students. Many of the students have established a tradition of going out to the campus town bars dressed up in Halloween costumes. Perhaps, as a release from mid-semester tension or as an opportunity to shed their student image, the Saturday night Halloween observance has grown in popularity and attracts thousands of masked students into the campus town.

When the bars close at 2 a.m., many students are not ready to retire for the evening and leave the festival atmosphere behind. Rather, most of the masqueraders linger in the streets with really nothing to do. A few students seeking entertainment begin to block traffic in the streets and "rock" cars. The resulting traffic jam attracts not only an even larger crowd, but also the police. Police bring out riot sticks and dogs. Students reply with bottle and can throwing and verbal abuse. Before the area is cleared, there has been a substantial amount of vandalism, several minor injuries to both students and police, and about 15 students are arrested. This confrontation between students and police has been repeated for the last five years.

A special university committee for campus-wide programming, comprised of university representatives and administrators, has been formed to discuss the problem. The decision has been made to plan a special nighttime program that will preserve the festival ritual of dressing up, but will avoid another police-student confrontation. You and your campus recreation staff have been given the responsibility of creating a challenging program that will provide activity for the Halloween enthusiasts.

Discussion Questions

What do you think are the main causes of the Halloween disturbances? Outline your idea for the programmed activities for the evening and be ready to present this plan to the committee. Do you feel that scheduled activity alone can solve the problem? What form of police patrol would you recommend for the evening? What special arrangements could you make with the town businesses? Do you feel it will be necessary to close off the streets? Why or why not?

Nativity Scene Barred from Public Park

Problem Situation

You are the public parks and recreation director of a large metropolitan area. For three weeks before Christmas each year, your staff sets up a sparkling Christmas tree in the park downtown. In addition, you also fence off a corner of the park and allow reindeer to graze in that portion of the area. The scene is breathtaking, and thousands of people come to view it each year. The local Chamber of Commerce, recognizing the numerous people your department attracts into town with the exhibit, underwrites most of the costs.

Because you are a public agency, you have attempted to avoid any reference to the religious connotations of the holiday season in the park. Make sure that groups that might promote controversial religious ideas do not have access to the park during December. In fact, your agency has adopted a policy that no group should be allowed to use the park during the holiday season. All groups are treated equally by the parks department by the policy of not allowing any group access.

Jesse Fredericks, president of the Prince of Peace Foundation, wants to install a nativity scene in the park. He claims that the three-fourths of the park that is not being used for the town display is public land, and that he has the right to utilize it. He contends that to forbid him from using the land denies a First Amendment right to free speech on public ground.

Discussion Questions

Does Frederick have a right to use the park to set up a nativity scene? Would he have a right to use the park if he wanted to set up a scene that had no religious overtones?

Is the park policy of denying all groups access even-handed? Is not being able to use the park as a group a form of censorship? Can the parks department legally tie up public land for an extended period of time for display? Can private citizens tie up public land for an extended period of time for display?

Do your personal religious values play any part in this situation? If so, how? How can you vouch for the fact that you are being fair, realizing that your own religious views color your interpretation of the situation?

Park Officials Won't Arrest Topless Bathers

Problem Situation

State parks officials said they will not arrest women who go topless at the state's parks or beaches, but will ask them politely to cover up. Officials said they are awaiting clarification on this week's state Court of Appeals ruling that a state law prohibiting women from baring their breasts should only be enforced if the act is lewd or for profit.

According to a lawyer for the state Department of Parks, Recreation and Historic Preservation, in the past, police would arrest women who went topless at a state beach or park. Recently, in a 6 to 0 ruling, the Court of Appeals threw out the convictions of two women who were arrested for going topless in a state park to protest the state nudity law, which they claimed discriminated against women.

The state Department of Environmental Conservation, which operates several state campsites, said its regulations prohibit the exposure of intimate body parts "in a lewd manner." The department is waiting to read the ruling before making any policy changes.

Yesterday the state's highest court ruled that women in fact could go in public with breasts bared and, therefore, not be arrested in state parks and beach areas. The laws that require women to clothe their chests were found to be unconstitutional because it singles out women only. That is, men were not similarly required to hide their chests from view in public places.

Discussion Questions

Obviously you need to rewrite the policies and procedures addressing this situation (since arresting the women is no longer an option). In the meantime, you have instructed your park workers to politely ask topless women to cover up. If the women refuse, no further action is to be taken at this time.

How should park officials deal with this situation? If park officials are not allowed to arrest women who bare their breasts, what are some other possible solutions in dealing with this problem? How might you balance the interests of people out there—those who wish to go topless and those who are concerned about seeing topless women at the park?

Skate Boarding Into Trouble

Problem Situation

You are a member of the Bailey City Council. One of the problems in the community is skateboarders who attempt reckless stunts at the parks and who have harassed pedestrians on public sidewalks. The issue was brought up by police officer Joe Riley at the city council meeting. "If you are a resident and you are trying to walk down the street, all it takes is one skateboarder for it to be a nuisance," said Riley. He also noted the property damage done by the skateboarders, the injuries that had resulted by youth flipping off of public steps, and the liability the park currently assumes for the skateboard accidents. He proposed several solutions, including

1. Pass legislation requiring that skateboarders wear protective gear.
2. Assess fines for breaking laws that restrict skateboarding. Riley suggested that the fines start at $10 and run as high as $500.
3. Restrict skateboarders from the streets and steps, but build them a challenge course. The estimated cost for the course would be approximately $8,000.
4. Confiscate skateboards of those skateboarders who violate the law.
5. Pass a law that would limit the use of skateboards to particular streets and facilities.

Also at the meeting, however, were members of the group SKATE, Students Keeping American Transportation Efficient. The group claimed that skateboards were the only way that many students had to travel and that restricting the use of skateboards restricted their freedom. The SKATE president was especially defiant. "Kids love to do whatever they can't do. The bans are not one bit a threat. Skateboarding is a sport. We should be free to participate in the sport if we choose."

Discussion Questions

Which, if any, of Officer Riley's suggestions do you think the board should pursue? If you do adopt one of Riley's suggestions, how would you answer each of the objections submitted by SKATE? If someone does violate a skateboard ordinance should the person be treated "like a criminal"—arrested, jailed, and forced to stand trial? If fines were to be assessed, would you agree with Riley that they should range depending on the circumstances, or argue that they should apply to everyone at all times?

Open Culvert Repairs Raise Questions

Problem Situation

You have been hired as a consultant for your state's Department of Conservation. Your assignment is to determine whether the state should spend over $44,000 for repairs in a park that nobody can use.

The 27-mile hiker-biker trail has been closed for several years in a squabble between landowners and conservationists. Farmers who live along the trail claim that increased use by hikers and bikers would increase liability, litter, and noise. The farmers also worry that the state might condemn adjacent farmland in the future if it chose to enlarge the park. The 27-mile strip had been a railroad right-of-way before being acquired by the Rails to Trails Foundation and then turned over to the Department of Conservation for use as a park.

A section of a stone arch drainage culvert 15 miles into the trail recently collapsed, partly blocking the flow of a tributary of Wesley Creek. The lowest bid solicited to repair the damage is $44,000.

Farmers argue that the fallen bridge is a potential safety hazard and the cause of a drainage problem. They claim that the bridge belongs to the state and therefore the state has an obligation to maintain the bridge. The farmers insist, however, that no further development of the park take place.

L
I
A
B
I
L
I
T
Y

&

R
I
S
K

Discussion Questions

Who is responsible for the bridge repairs? Is it legally and morally correct for public money to be spent on land the public cannot use? Should the bridge repair be a high priority? If the state allows the water to back up onto a farmer's land, could the state be sued? Suggest ways of obtaining the farmers' backing for the Rails-to-Trails project. Are the farmers' objections reasonable? What could be done to overcome these objections? What benefit might the farmers find in a Rails to-Trails park?

Coydogs Go Bad on the Links

Problem Situation

You are the executive director of a major public golf course. One day you are in your office going over plans for next week's celebrity charity event when a young caddy comes running into your office and says, "Sir, we have a problem. A woman was just attacked by a pack of coydogs."

Prior to the situation, it had been known that the pack of dogs had visited the golf course regularly. The dogs, traveling in a pack of five to seven, had been seen on the golf course late one afternoon just last week. On this occasion the dogs appeared to be scared and, as soon as they saw humans, they retreated back into the wooded area. However, just yesterday you were told that another pack of coydogs was seen walking on the fifteenth fairway, and one dog snarled at an 18-year-old boy who threw a golf ball at the dog to scare it away. No serious issues have resulted with the coydogs, and you have not taken any action at this point.

Today presents a very different problem. After making sure that someone had called an ambulance, you immediately drive out to the course to aid the victim. Upon investigation, you learn that the dogs attacked a 73-year-old woman. Apparently she was near the wooded area waiting for her husband to finish putting when three dogs attacked her from behind. Her husband managed to scare off the coydogs by screaming and waving his putter at them. Fortunately, it was not a fatal attack, however the woman was bit several times and appears to be in shock. Within minutes the victim is transported to the hospital. The husband turns to you and says, "You haven't heard the last of this. I have complained about those dogs all summer. I hope you have a good lawyer."

Discussion Questions

How could this situation have been avoided? What actions could you have taken to warn people of the coydog situation? What actions could you have taken to get rid of the dogs? Now what do you do? What about the celebrity golf tournament next week? How about the safety of all players? How about the negative publicity that will be published in the local newspaper tomorrow? What comments will you make to the reporter? What actions will you take with the victim? How can you ensure this will never happen again? How will you prepare to defend yourself in a lawsuit?

THEME FOUR: LIABILITY AND
RISK MANAGEMENT RELATED WEBSITES

Campus Recreation Risk Management Plan (University of Texas at Stephen Austin)
http://www.utsa.edu/compliance/Riskassmnts/StudentAffairs/CampusRec/
FcltsMngmntPln.htm

National Park Service
http://www.nps.gov/parks.html

National Parks Conservation Association
http://www.npca.org

Risk Management (author unknown)
http://www.explainplease.com/risk-management.htm

Risk Management for the Recreation Professional by Rachel Corbett
http://www.sportlaw.ca/articles/other/article1.htm

Risk Management and Claims (District of Saanich)
http://www.gov.saanich.bc.ca/finance/riskmgmt.html

Sport and Recreation (Municipal Association of Victoria)
http://www.ourcommunity.com.au/files/sport_and_recreation.pdf

LIABILITY & RISK

THEME FIVE:

FINANCIAL MANAGEMENT

Movie Production May Close Down Club Temporarily

Problem Situation

You are the director of the well-established Emerald Fitness and Spa. Universal Pictures has approached you requesting the use of your facility to shoot an upcoming blockbuster. This involves shutting down the facility to the members for 6 to 8 months along with unemployment of your current staff. Universal Pictures has offered you a large amount of money to compensate your loss of business while the movie is in production. The amount of money you will be given will allow you to renovate areas in need, build new annexes to the building, and purchase land for another spa in the immediate future. Realizing that the money from Universal Pictures will benefit you and your members more so than declining the offer, you and your lawyer set up a meeting with Universal to accept their offer.

There are numerous rumors going around the club, and members are coming to you demanding that you do not shut down the facility or they will terminate their membership. Your staff is threatening that they will be forced to quit and find work elsewhere if you shut them out of work for 6 to 8 months. Again, you will be making a lot more money if you agree to the movie, but hearing your employee concerns is almost too overwhelming.

Discussion Questions

What do you do? What are the pros and cons for each decision? Which decision will lead to more benefits for the facility? Can you afford to lose members? If not, how would you compensate the members if you choose to close the facility? Also, if you choose to close the facility, how are you going to compensate your staff? Or will you? Is the publicity from the movie worth the disappointment of your current members and staff? Are there any policies about freezing memberships? If so, what are they and how would they apply to this situation? What are the policies for the employees as well?

Female Clientele Demand Equity

Problem Situation

You are the director of the local fitness club. At a staff meeting, it is brought to your attention that there have been numerous complaints regarding the personal trainers at your facility. Actually, the complaints are in reference to the lack of female personal trainers within your club. The common complaint is that many women feel uncomfortable with a male trainer and would like to have a female trainer. The female members wish you would hire more female trainers, or they might rethink their membership with your club and go elsewhere. Curves, a major fitness chain for women, is about to open up a club in the town next to yours.

You feel very strongly that your current staff is very qualified and fits the image of the club. While hiring the personal trainers in the past, it was merely coincidental that they were all male. Your personal trainers have been bringing in a lot of business since the day the club opened. They are one of the reasons why the club took off as fast as it did. After looking at the records of the membership, you realize that more women make up the clientele of the club than do men. Being that the club is still relatively new, there is no way that you can afford to lose any clientele. The personal trainers on staff are now in fear of their jobs, and they are awaiting your response to the women's concerns.

Discussion Questions

What do you do? Can you afford to hire more female trainers? If not, what do you do? Could this become a legal issue regarding equity? Do you fire current staff and hire new staff just to please your members? How would you go about doing this? Do you hire the perfect fit over most qualified, or do you stick with perfect fit and most qualified? If you decide not to do anything, could this turn into a more serious issue? If so, what type of problems could arise? How else might you please your members?

F
I
N
A
N
C
I
A
L

M
A
N
A
G
E
M
E
N
T

The Soccer Association Monopoly

Problem Situation

For the past 8 years, the Waterville Soccer Association (WSA) has leased a soccer club complex that includes 12 soccer fields and a clubhouse with showers, snack bar, and lounge area from the city for $1 per year. The upkeep and maintenance are the responsibility of the city recreation and park department. In order to use these facilities, residents must pay a membership fee to the soccer association. These fees are retained by the association to employ personnel to supervise the area. The personnel employed are directly responsible to the board of directors of the association. The department of recreation and parks has no jurisdiction over the operation of WSA or its program. The president of WSA also serves as chairperson of the recreation and park advisory board and, because of his position, he has been able to influence other members of the recreation and park board not to "disturb the administration of the WSA."

Since you are the new director of recreation and parks, you have not had the opportunity to review all existing lease agreements. However, while you are attending the Central Civic Association meeting, a citizen was turned away because he would not purchase a membership. He indicated that this was unfair, since these are publicly owned facilities. He was told by the attendant on duty that he was required to fill out a membership application that would then need approval by the board of directors of the soccer association before he would be permitted to play. As a quick reply, you indicate that at this time you are unfamiliar with the details of the soccer association, but you will look into the matter.

You immediately contact the chair of the recreation and park advisory committee and request an opportunity to discuss this situation. Upon hearing your concern, he becomes quite defensive and tells you that the WSA has operated this way for years and he can see no reason to change it. He further informs you that he wants the matter dropped, and that he does not want you to discuss it with other board members. You tell him that the present operation of the soccer association is not in the best interest of all the citizens in the community and that you feel obligated to make your views known to the board at its next meeting. He informs you that, if you are wise, you will not bring this to the attention of the board and, if you do, there will be repercussions.

Discussion Questions

What should be the policy regarding the leasing of public facilities to private groups? Will you bring it up to the board? Is it acceptable to charge a membership fee for the use of the facilities? Under what conditions would it be acceptable? If you decide to bring this situation to the attention of the board, what strategy will you use? Would you discuss this situation with the mayor and council before you bring it to the attention of your board? Would you attempt to get public support for your position? If so, how would you do it?

When It Comes to Money, Safety Comes Second

Problem Situation

You are the financial director at a local parks and recreation department, and it is your job to make sure that the money from programs is used properly. You have been getting complaints from the men's and women's softball leagues that the fields need more dirt and the fences need to be fixed. In essence, the fields are in need of improvement.

There have been injuries because there are rocks on the field and the balls are taking bad hops. Also, legs are getting badly cut from sliding into bases, even with sliding pads or pants. The drainage of the fields is horrendous. There are three fields and only one is playable after rain and even that is only sometimes.

It is the policy of the town that all money coming in from programs must be put into a general fund where money is spread out to all of the different programs. However, players who use the fields feel that the money they spend to get into the league ($150 per team) should be spent making the conditions of the fields better. They feel as though they pay taxes for the town, as well as league and "out-of-town" fees, which should cover the cost of field maintenance.

Discussion Questions

If we take the money out of the general fund, then the money won't be there for other town-sponsored events, such as memorials and parades that do not bring in as much money. Should these town-sponsored events be cut from the budget since they don't make a profit or even pay for themselves? Also, some of the money goes for seasonal staff. Should you take money from the fund and hire a seasonal person that is trained and has a degree in field maintenance? This could be rather expensive if they have a degree in this field, and what if they are looking for a full-time job? Do you keep them on for the full year? And if so, what do you have them do? How would you handle this entire problem situation?

Non-Resident Fee Strikes Unharmonious Chord

Problem Situation

The village of Greenfield recently enacted a policy of charging 100% higher fees to persons outside the village for programs. This is causing misunderstanding and financial burdens to some people, according to opinions expressed at the recreation and park meeting last Tuesday.

John Stangle, director of Lots for Tots, a preschool day care program, said that the policy will drive out some long-term users of the program because they cannot afford the extra fee. Stangle said seven children from six families may be forced to drop out of the program. The enrollment in summer usually has a waiting list, but filling those vacancies in the fall and spring may be difficult.

The board agreed to consider a modified policy for the preschool program. One board member, Sue Petri, said that it might not be practical to make an exception for just one program. This issue has been before the board before, but not much has been done to enforce the policy. Since the news media are giving it more attention, community opinion has been both for and against the policy. Some taxpayers feel that it is unfair for them to carry the burden for the public recreation program: "If persons outside the village want to participate in the recreation program, let them pay their fair share." Opponents of the ordinance argue that the recreation program attracts people from other communities and that this helps theirs. As one citizen stated, "On weekends, over 2,000 persons from outside the city go to the zoo—they spend an entire day in our community—this sure helps our economy."

The commission has asked the recreation and park staff to prepare a report on this issue. They have requested that a recommendation for future action be included.

FINANCIAL MANAGEMENT

F
I
N
A
N
C
I
A
L

M
A
N
A
G
E
M
E
N
T

Discussion Questions

Is charging double fees to citizens outside the village legitimate? What kind of policy would you suggest to the recreation and park board? Should the citizens living in the village be responsible for paying the greater cost of the recreation program? If so, why? If not, why? Are there other solutions to this problem? Would you consider this a fair policy if the "100 percent" was reduced? What kind of modified policy could be recommended? Are there any legal problems in this policy?

Forest Preserve Board Wants Surplus

Problem Situation

You are the assistant director of the Franklin County Forest Preserve District. Due to property tax cuts, fewer lake permits, less boat rentals, and a drastic reduction in the use of the golf course, you are facing a huge budget deficit of over $60,000, with one month to go in the current fiscal year.

As the recreation director, the board has asked you to determine what should be done to keep the Franklin County Forest Preserve District financially sound. Several board members have ideas:

- Drop the environmental education coordinator position.
- Decrease the number of maintenance workers and simply perform routine mainte-nance less frequently.
- Reorganize the job hierarchy so that expensive middle management positions are eliminated.
- Freeze wages until further notice, even though wage reviews and pay raises have been promised.
- Develop a long-term plan.

The board believes that declining revenues are a fact of life, not a temporary set-back. Due to financial pressure, the board insists that you present a proposal to cut the budget losses and to provide a surplus in next year's budget.

Discussion Questions

Which of the board's ideas would you suggest be implemented? Is education an important part of the mission of a county forest preserve agency? Are there minimum maintenance standards that must be upheld? Is it ethical to freeze wages after wage reviews have been promised? Is a long-term plan an extra expense or a worthwhile in-vestment?

What other ideas can you suggest to help remedy the situation? Would hiring a marketing coordinator likely increase usage of the golf course and boats, thereby bringing in more revenue? Would leasing the boating facility to a private company be a viable option? Could bonds be sold to meet the debt?

Admission Charge Urged at City Parks

Problem Situation

Plagued by little money, inadequate maintenance, vandalism, overuse, and litter, park officials are considering instituting an admissions charge at the city's 238 parks. "It is certainly conceivable," said George Monti, president of Westchester's recreation council, "that people would be willing to pay a nominal charge to visit a park to simply sit or picnic, if that park were clean and well maintained, and if noise were controlled."

Mr. Monti made his proposal yesterday at the annual meeting of the recreation council. The council is a private organization that functions as a recreation, parks, and conservation advocate. The group has just finished a report on the problems facing the city's recreation and park department.

In a report entitled "The Prospect for Parks," Mr. Monti said that it was recognized that the "notion of fees for the use of public parks, popular in other countries, somehow bothers the citizens of Westchester." Immediately bothered was George Bolton, director of Westchester's recreation and parks department. "I am astonished," Mr. Bolton said when asked to comment, "that the council should propose such an idea. I am 100 percent against the proposal to have a general admission charge to any city park. This is entirely against the whole theory of city maintained parks."

Ron Buchanan, an assistant administrator for public information, said that the legal office of the park and recreation department asserted that the admission charge was "highly questionable from the legal point of view."

"There are admissions fees to skating rinks, wading and swimming pools, and boating facilities. A $15 tennis permit is required for an individual to play on city-owned courts, more for control than for revenue," Mr. Buchanan said. "But there is no cost for the use of the grass or for the use of a bench."

Mr. Monti's suggestion was one of four offered in the report. The others were (a) a decentralization of the park's day-to-day operation, (b) the use of streets and temporarily available space for park-related activities, and (c) the public pressure to protect parks from encroachment by "those who are looking for land for other purposes." Mr. Monti's premise was that "the prospect for the parks of our city is poor." He predicted that the city park system, "as it now generally operates and exists, cannot last until the end of this century. Lack of money is a major woe," he said. "It results in a loss of staff and makes all but impossible preventative maintenance and prompt repair of damaged or worn-out facilities."

Vandalism, overuse, and litter are, according to Mr. Monti, "euphemistically called signs of the times." He also stated that the park system needs three million dollars a year for the next 10 years "just to keep the present park facilities intact and in operable condition." Yet, he said, "they would be fortunate to have $1 million annually."

Discussion Questions

Should a fee be charged for the general use of the parks in Westchester? Under what conditions would you charge a fee? Is it fair to charge a fee for special facilities in the park and not for its general use?

Other than increasing taxes, what can the officials do to increase revenue for the recreation and park department? Should parks be limited to a "certain number of people at one time?" If so, how would you control this? Regarding Mr. Monti's other suggestions, what are the advantages and disadvantages of decentralizing the park's day-to-day operations? Is the use of streets for recreation purposes a good idea? If so, what is the city's liability? What laws and ordinances could be created to protect the city from encroachment on parklands?

FINANCIAL MANAGEMENT

Assume you are the director of recreation and parks, Mr. George Bolton. Draft a reply to the report presented by Mr. Monti that will respond to the issues and his suggestions.

Roadbed Causes Sleepless Nights

Problem Situation

You have been hired as a consultant by your state's Department of Conservation. The Department has proposed that the abandoned railroad line's roadbed be turned into a state park, a trail of natural prairie to be used by hikers and bikers. According to the plan, the railroad right-of-way would be converted into a crooked ribbon of oak trees and prairie plants.

Landowners, fearing increased liability, noise, and litter from the city crowds who would likely use the park, have protested against it. Most landowners could accept the railroad bisecting their property, but they oppose the presence of the trail. "When the railroad was here, it brought us a service. The trail, meanwhile, will do nothing for us," summarized one landowner.

Landowners are especially concerned about who would be liable if someone should wander from the trail onto their property. The Conservation Department has suggested fencing the land, but both sides nixed the proposal. Landowners don't want to incur the expenses and environmentalists don't want the wire to ruin the view.

"I don't see how the matter can be so complex," the Conservation director tells you. "Some farmers think only of themselves individually. Everyone should be able to see the miles of ancient plains and natural wildlife, the bubbling creeks, the tiny villages, and the green patchwork of farm country which line this trail. Everybody should have the opportunity to enjoy the prairie."

Discussion Questions

Should the state build a trail on the railroad's bed? What approaches could be used to convince the landowners of the value of the trail? Should rare prairie land be in the hands of farmers or in the hands of the state? Should farmers be required to share the expense of installing fences? Who should be held liable if someone does climb over a fence onto a farmer's property? Is there a difference between accidentally wandering off the trail and trespassing? If no fences were used, how could the trail boundaries be designated? How would the trail be patrolled for unauthorized hunters and beer parties?

Good Help Is Hard to Find

Problem Situation

You have been hired as the personal recruiter for the aquatics division of the department of recreation. Your job is to attract the best lifeguards possible. The job is not as easy as it sounds, however. Currently, there are three job applications on file and over 55 vacancies to fill. The reasons for the low number of applicants have been explained in four ways:

1. Private pools pay three times as much as the public pools.
2. The population of young people is smaller than in the past.
3. Other employment opportunities provide the same pay, but with better hours and fewer responsibilities.
4. Potential lifeguards fear getting AIDS during a rescue.

A consultant has offered some suggestions for increasing the pool of applicants. His suggestions include (a) seek to attract teachers and other adults who might seek seasonal summer employment, (b) restructure the pay scale and include it with all job announcements, and (c) offer lifeguard training programs free of charge to anyone in the hopes that class members will later apply for jobs.

Discussion Questions

Design a recruitment campaign for lifeguards. Overcome each of the objections to becoming a lifeguard. Evaluate the consultant's advice. Are his ideas good ones in view of reasons people give for not becoming lifeguards? Can you think of ideas to add to, or replace ideas on the consultant's list? How could you enrich the jobs of those lifeguards returning from last year?

Lifeguards are traditionally young people. What advantages and disadvantages are there in hiring young people? What are the advantages and disadvantages in hiring a middle-aged adult? Is it legal to discriminate based on age? How could you protect yourself from a lawsuit by a disgruntled adult who was not hired because you selected a young person for the position?

Public Golf Course Makes Money but not Friends

Problem Situation

You are a recreation supervisor in charge of the community golf course. Your golf course takes in over $300,000 annually, however, it only spends about $200,000. The difference is used to supplement the city's general recreation fund. Golfers, though, are not happy about the arrangement.

"I want the money I pay for my membership to be spent on the golf course," said Sam Soa, president of the local golfer's club. "I paid taxes to take care of the general recreation fund. I paid $330 to take care of this golf course."

The golf course made a net profit of more than $223,000 last year. The profit was 27% of operating costs. Not only do golfers believe this is too high; they believe that the money should have been reinvested into the grounds of the golf course.

"The golf course needs to be maintained," Soa said. "The city has the philosophy that they fix something only if it is broken; they don't believe in preventive maintenance. Sure, they are making a profit now and subsidizing many programs that cannot stand on their own merit; but before long they are going to have to pay huge repair bills here at the golf course. Such costly bills could be avoided by shelling out a few of those dollars for routine maintenance now."

Discussion Questions

Should money designated for one form of recreation be used for another form of recreation? Should high profit recreation centers be used to support recreation centers that lose money? What is a "reasonable" profit percentage for a golf course? What

F
I
N
A
N
C
I
A
L

M
A
N
A
G
E
M
E
N
T

percentage of money should be reinvested back into the golf course? What consideration must you make when setting a fee? Should you look at supply and demand, competition from the private sector, and/or something else?

Should public recreation agencies seek to make a profit? Should public recreation agencies contract golf course management to a private firm that specializes in golf course maintenance? Develop pro and con arguments.

Financing of Harbor Café Perceived as Fishy

Problem Situation

You are the chief executive officer of a large recreation and parks department. Your assistant director has recently proposed that a harbor café and fish cleaning station be built next to the lake in Flintsone Park. When asked how the department would pay for the $600,000 restaurant and fish cleaning station when only $500,000 was budgeted, she proposed that the remaining $100,000 be taken from the budget of Odie Park, a crumbling West Side park.

Her logic is that it is better to have only a few quality parks rather than several mediocre parks. "Our money is spread too thin," she contends. "If we want to provide quality recreational experiences, we are going to have to start spending our money on quality, not quantity." She also states that the boating facility will be a revenue producer for the recreation and parks department, netting over $25,000 per year in profit. Meanwhile, vandals are likely to destroy all work done to Odie Park within days of its completion, something that has happened many times before.

Your public relations advisor disagrees. "You can't take $100,000 approved for repairs of Odie Park, a recreation department that's already under-funded, and give it to boaters to make a convenience station for them. We are not in the business of creating a White Hen Convenience Store for boaters."

Discussion Questions

Do you recommend the harbor café to the parks board? Why would quality be preferred over quantity of parks? Why would quantity sometimes be better than quality? What standard(s) should be used to describe how many parks are maintained by a district?

Should parks be maintained if vandals constantly destroy them? Do park directors owe more attention to the poor, the middle class, or the rich? Should park directors treat all citizens equally, or should they try to please those groups most likely to vote?

Should park districts operate a venture that makes a considerable profit? If so, how should that profit be utilized? Can money be taken from one park and be used in another, if it is already promised to the former park?

Board Looks at Park User Fees

Problem Situation

You are a member of the Grant County Forest Preserve Board. Tonight, as part of the June meeting, the president of the board is expected to attempt to enact a one-month trial user fee. The special fee, which would be in effect Saturdays and Sundays in July and on the Fourth of July, would be $1 per car and be collected at all of the park's entrances.

"Our costs have just skyrocketed, and we are trying to put some of the cost on the user rather than on the general public," explained the president at the previous board meeting. "We already have golfers paying $7 a round, and swimmers and boaters pay a fee, too. What's wrong with a dollar a car anyway? Everyone else is paying for a service. This may be the only way to prevent a tax increase." The president emphasized that the user fee would only be collected on weekends and on the single July holiday. He said it might help to "spread out" the use of the park, which has been described as "very heavy" on recent weekends and "light" during the week.

The entrance user fee would be established in such a way so golfers, swimmers, and boaters do not have to pay an additional fee on top of the special facility charge they pay to use the golf course, beach, or rental boats. The fee will be collected from car and motorcycle riders but not from bicyclists.

Assuming typical July attendance patterns, the president projected that the district will be able to raise approximately $20,000 with the user fee.

Discussion Questions

Do you vote in favor of the proposed fee? Is it fair to charge the public if they have already paid for it with their taxes? Develop an argument for voting for the fee. Develop an argument for voting against the fee. Why does the board distinguish between "cars and motorcycles" and "bicyclists"? How will the board avoid charging the golfers, swimmers, and boaters twice? Is such a proposed fee workable? Discuss problems that must be overcome if such a fee is to be implemented. How should the board evaluate whether the fee is successful?

Dreaming of a Field of Dreams

Problem Situation

You are the director of parks and recreation for Donsville, a medium-sized city. One day you are approached by a turf sales agent who says that he wants to cover your Little League fields with Turface, a commercial dirt that is used on three-fourths of the baseball diamonds in the major leagues. He cites the following reasons:

- He wants to study the effects of the turf in a Little League setting.
- The field would be a model for prospective buyers of his product to examine.
- His supervisor's wife comes from Donsville and that his supervisor wanted to do the town a favor.
- Donsville could never afford to buy Turface.
- The players will have a lot of fun playing on the surface.
- A field that is a lot of fun to play on usually attracts more players than one that is not fun to play on.

Not only will the Turface Company waive the costs of the turf, it will work closely with local volunteers to install the turf. All that you have to do for this "dream field" is to give your okay.

F
I
N
A
N
C
I
A
L

M
A
N
A
G
E
M
E
N
T

Discussion Questions

Do you accept the gift? Who benefits the most from the deal if you agree to it? What, if anything, do you lose by accepting the deal? Is this a decision an administrator needs to make alone or should other people be consulted? If others should be consulted, who do you recommend and why do you recommend them?

What questions should you ask before accepting the gift? Why would you want to ask questions about upkeep cost, insurance cost, risk of getting hurt on the turf, and how often the turf has to be replaced?

What is the backbone of a successful Little League program? Is it the turf or something else? What role do the grounds and maintenance aspects of a parks department play in the program aspect of the department?

Are Arguments Against the Water Slide All Wet?

Problem Situation

You are the public relations director for Hampton Park, a small city serving 100,000 people. One day the recreation director calls you into his office. He reminds you that the recreation department has recently entered into a contract with a private corporation to build and operate a water slide. In recent weeks many citizens have protested the venture. The most vocal opponents have been Citizens against Needing the Slide (CANS). CANS has produced a brochure and mailed it to all local residents. Among the arguments against the slide outlined in the brochure are

- The slide is scarcely a substantial recreational opportunity. The only exercise it involves is walking up the steps to the top of the fiberglass troughs. The experience provided by the slide itself is not "recreational" but sheer razzle dazzle.
- The slide will transform recreational space into an amusement park. The park will be little more than a carnival, and it will attract people who are not in the best interests of the town.
- The slide is likely to be the first of many profit-making ventures in the park, all of which could be built on private capital. The recreation administration plans to meet its budget with revenue-producing contracts, rather than relying solely on free and tax-supported activities.

The brochure concludes by asking citizens to help finance the CANS goal to prevent the slide from being built. The brochure indicates that court challenges, recreation meeting protests, and newspaper ads will all be undertaken to promote the CANS cause.

Discussion Questions

After showing you the arguments, the director asks that you counter each of them. How could you show that the slide will not "crowd" the park? How do you explain the "recreation experience," and how does a water slide offer that experience? What could you use as evidence that the slide will not draw undesired rowdies from other towns? Is the slide likely to cause an increased need for police protection? Will property values go up or down when the slide opens? Should public property be used for private enterprises? Why or why not?

As public relations director, what kind of a campaign would you want to organize for the slide? Would you use the print media, mailings, radio, something else, or a combination of media outlets? What audience(s) should you target? Should your appeal be the same to all audiences, or should you gear your approach for each audience? Describe in detail the public relations campaign you would conduct.

THEME FIVE: FINANCIAL MANAGEMENT RELATED WEBSITES

Benefits to the Economy (Green County Parks)
http://www.co.greene.oh.us/parks/benefits.htm

Economic Benefits (New Britain Parks and Recreation)
http://www.new-britain.net/recnpark/benefits.htm#econ

Fiscal Affairs (2003 Horsham Township Park and Recreation Plan Update)
http://www.horsham.org/pdf/parks/appendixg.pdf

Financial Analysis and Financial Model (UB Campus Recreation Master Plan)
http://www.student-affairs.buffalo.edu/student-unions/report.pdf

Our Forests: Free or Fee? (author unknown)
http://www.sespewild.org/freeorfee.html

Public Parks and Recreation Trends by Ruth Russell
http://hubcap.clemson.edu/~trourke/prtrends.html

State Budget Shortfalls Impact Correctional Recreation by Gary Polson
http://www.strengthtech.com/correct/white/budgets/papers/ncra2002p.pdf

Would You Pay to Ride the Best Trails? (Dirtworld.com)
http://www.dirtworld.com/Trails/TrailStory.asp?id=229

F
I
N
A
N
C
I
A
L

M
A
N
A
G
E
M
E
N
T

Index